CONFRONTING DOGMATISM IN GIFTED EDUCATION

This title looks at the dogmatism that limits the perspectives of professionals, policymakers, and other stakeholders in gifted education. In a field where concepts and definitions surrounding high ability have been contested for many years, there is increasing interest in clarifying these notions today. This book offers such clarity, searching outside of the predominant conceptual frameworks that dominate thinking about giftedness and talent, and examining ways in which conceptual fog stunts and warps the development of gifted minds and limits the effectiveness of curriculum development and instruction. The book directly addresses the connection between dogmatism and high ability, exploring ways in which otherwise bright individuals can make unintelligent decisions.

Each contributor in this edited collection connects educational theory with teaching practice, examining the impact of policies such as No Child Left Behind. The chapters also explore the ways in which economic, cultural, and academic contexts affect both the gifted mind and education of the highly able in America and the rest of the world, while making recommendations for positive changes that can be enacted within gifted education in the future.

Don Ambrose is Professor of Graduate Education at Rider University, editor of the *Roeper Review*, and past chair of the Conceptual Foundations Division of the National Association for Gifted Children. He serves on the editorial boards of most of the major journals in the field of gifted education, and for several book series. His numerous publications address the conceptual frameworks that influence conceptions of creative intelligence.

Robert J. Sternberg is Provost and Senior Vice President of Oklahoma State University, past Dean of the School of Arts and Sciences and Professor of Psychology at Tufts University, and past Director of Graduate Studies at Yale University. He is also Honorary Professor of Psychology at the University of Heidelberg, Germany. He is a former president of the American Psychological Association and the Eastern Psychological Association. He has won the E. Paul Torrance and Distinguished Scholar Awards from the National Association for Gifted Children. His 1,000+ publications include over 70 books.

Bharath Sriraman is Professor of Mathematics in the Department of Mathematical Sciences and also on the Faculty and Advisory Board of Central/SW Asian Studies at The University of Montana, where he occasionally offers courses on Indo-Iranian and Turkic studies and languages. He has published over 240 journal articles, commentaries, book chapters, edited books, and reviews in his areas of interest, and presented over 110 papers at international conferences, symposia, and invited colloquia.

CONFRONTING DOGMATISM IN GIFTED EDUCATION

Edited by
Don Ambrose, Robert J. Sternberg,
and Bharath Sriraman

Routledge
Taylor & Francis Group

NEW YORK AND LONDON

First published 2012
by Routledge
711 Third Avenue, New York, NY 10017

Simultaneously published in the UK
by Routledge
2 Park Square, Milton Park, Abingdon, Oxon OX14 4RN

Routledge is an imprint of the Taylor & Francis Group, an informa business

Library of Congress Cataloging in Publication Data
Confronting dogmatism in gifted education / [edited by] Don Ambrose, Robert Sternberg, Bharath Sriraman.
    p. cm.
    1. Gifted children—Education—United States. I. Ambrose, Donald, 1950– II. Sternberg, Robert J. III. Sriraman, Bharath.
    LC3993.9.C665 2011
    371.950973—dc23
    2011021935

ISBN13: 978-0-415-89446-3 (hbk)
ISBN13: 978-0-203-80932-7 (ebk)

Typeset in Bembo and Stone Sans
by EvS Communication Networx, Inc.

Printed and bound in the United States of America on acid-free paper.

CONTENTS

SECTION 4
Concluding Thoughts: Patterns in the Analyses of Dogmatism and Giftedness — 205

ILLUSTRATIONS

Figures

Tables

CONTRIBUTORS

Don Ambrose is professor of graduate education at Rider University in Lawrenceville, NJ, editor of the *Roeper Review,* and past chair of the Conceptual Foundations Division of the National Association for Gifted Children. He serves on the editorial boards of most of the major journals in the field of gifted education. Most of his numerous publications are theoretical syntheses and philosophical analyses based on a wide-ranging, interdisciplinary search for theories, philosophical perspectives, and research findings that challenge, refine, and expand thinking about the development of creative intelligence. Honors include the Creative Scholarship award from the International Center for Innovation in Education, the Iorio research prize, and Administrator of the Year in a Western Canadian school system (in a prior career). Among other outlets, his work has been discussed in *Wired Magazine* and *Scholastic.* His other books include *How Dogmatic Beliefs Harm Creativity and Higher-level Thinking* (Routledge, with Robert J. Sternberg); *Expanding Visions of Creative Intelligence: An Interdisciplinary Exploration* (Hampton Press); *Morality, Ethics, and Gifted Minds* (Springer, with Tracy L. Cross); *Creative Intelligence: Toward Theoretic Integration* (Hampton Press, with LeoNora M. Cohen and Abraham J. Tannenbaum); *Imagitronics* (Zephyr press); and *The Roeper School: A Model for Holistic Development of High Ability* (Springer, with Bharath Sriraman and Tracy L. Cross), among others.

James H. Borland is a professor of Education in the Curriculum and Teaching Department at Teachers College, Columbia University and founder of Columbia University's Center for the Study and Education of the Gifted, now the Hollingworth Center. He received his BA from Johns Hopkins University (English Literature), MS and PhD from Clarion State College (Special Education with an emphasis in diagnostic–prescriptive intervention strategies for handicapped learners), and from Teachers College (Special Education with an emphasis on the education of gifted and research). Borland's scholarly interests deal with education of gifted students, economically disadvantaged gifted students, and conceptions of giftedness. His publications include *Rethinking Gifted Education* (Teachers College Press) and *Planning and Implementing Programs for the Gifted* (Teachers College Press). His areas of scholarly interest include the education of gifted students; economically disadvantaged gifted students; and conceptions of giftedness.

LeoNora M. Cohen is Associate Professor of Teacher Education at Oregon State University. LeoNora Cohen has been at OSU since 1994. Founder of the Conceptual Foundations Division of the National Association for Gifted Children, her research interests include teacher and administrator perspectives on the Oregon school budget crisis, gifted children, creativity, theory development, children's interests, coping strategies, teaching and learning, school–university partnerships, and work sample development. She has published extensively in the fields of gifted education and creative studies. Books include *Creative Intelligence: Toward Theoretic Integration* (Hampton Press, with Don Ambrose & Abraham J. Tannenbaum), and *Coping for Capable Kids* (Hawker Brownlow, with Erika Frydenberg).

Laurence J. Coleman is the Daso Herb Professor of Gifted Education and a member of the Department of Early Childhood, Physical and Special Education at the University of Toledo. He is a special education teacher who became a teacher educator and researcher. He is past editor of the *Journal for the Education of the Gifted* (1994–2005) and teaches courses in theoretical analysis, gifted education, and qualitative inquiry. Among his many professional activities, he is proud of creating an innovative model of teaching as a talent; building the Summer Institute for Gifted Children in 1980 which has been "taken over" by the original students and is still in operation, receiving the Distinguished Scholar award from the National Association for Gifted Children and the Outstanding Service Award from The Association for the Gifted of the Council for Exceptional Children and publishing *Being Gifted in Schools*, with Tracy Cross, and *Nurturing Talent in High School: Life in the Fast Lane*. Dr. Coleman's scholarly interests are the experience of being gifted, program evaluation, and teacher thinking. He is principal investigator of a 5-year longitudinal study funded by the U.S. Department of Education, "Accelerating Achievement in Math and Science in Urban Schools."

Tracy L. Cross is the Jody and Layton Smith Professor of Gifted Education at the College of William and Mary. For 9 years he served as the executive director of the Indiana Academy for Science, Mathematics and Humanities, a public residential school for academically gifted adolescents. Dr. Cross has published numerous articles and book chapters, and a coauthored textbook *Being Gifted in School: An Introduction to Development, Guidance and Teaching.* He is the editor of the *Journal for the Education of the Gifted* and editor emeritus of the *Roeper Review, Gifted Child Quarterly,* and the *Journal of Secondary Gifted Education.*

David Yun Dai is Associate Professor on the faculty of Educational Psychology and Methodology at the State University of New York, Albany. He received his doctoral degree from Purdue University, and worked as a post-doctoral fellow at the National Research Center on the Gifted and Talented, University of Connecticut. He also holds degrees from East China Normal University. In recent years, he has been engaged in classroom-based research on incorporating teaching cases and case methods in teacher education courses to facilitate teacher reflection and learning. His practical interest is to incorporate an inquiry-based mode of learning in a variety of domains and settings. Dr. Dai is the recipient of the Early Scholar Award in 2006 conferred by the National Association for Gifted Children. He currently serves on the advisory and editorial boards of the *Gifted Child Quarterly* and the *Journal for the Education of the Gifted.* His theoretical interests include developing a more integrative, functionalist perspective on intellectual functioning and development, involving text comprehension and conceptual understanding. He has published numerous journal articles and several books in the field of gifted education.

Donna Y. Ford is Professor of Education and Human Development in the Department of Special Education at Vanderbilt University. She has served as Professor of Special Education at the Ohio State University, an Associate Professor of Educational Psychology at the University of Virginia, and a researcher with the National Research Center on the Gifted and Talented. She also taught at the University of Kentucky. Dr. Ford is the author of several books, including *Reversing Underachievement Among Gifted Black Students* and *Multicultural Gifted Education,* and has published over 100 articles and book chapters. She has made more than 500 presentations at professional conferences and school districts. Dr. Ford conducts research primarily in gifted education and multicultural/ urban education. She also consults with school districts and educational organizations in the area of gifted education and multicultural/urban education. Dr. Ford is a board member of the National Association of Gifted Children, and has served on numerous editorial boards, including the *Gifted Child Quarterly, Exceptional Children,* the *Journal of Negro Education,* and the *Roeper Review.*

James J. Gallagher is currently William Rand Kenan Jr. Professor Emeritus at the University of North Carolina at Chapel Hill. He held faculty appointments at Michigan State University and the University of Illinois before becoming Associate Commissioner of Education in the U.S. Office of Education in 1967.

He served for three years as director of the Bureau of the Handicapped and Deputy Assistant Secretary for the department of HEW. He became director of the Frank Porter Graham Child Development Center in 1970 at the University of North Carolina where he served until 1987 and then continued as Kenan Professor of Education to the present time. He has been president of the Council for Exceptional Children, the National Association for Gifted Children, and the World Council for Gifted and Talented Children. He has received numerous awards including the CEC Wallin Award for contributions' to special education and the American Psychological Association award for Psychologists in the Public Interest.

Laurie R. Kash holds a PhD from Oregon State University and investigates the potential of creative dramatics, service learning, Socratic processes, and problem-based learning. As a school district administrator (special education and student services director) in Oregon she works with at-risk student populations and provides in-service training in the areas mentioned above as well as in curriculum development and design.

Diane Montgomery is Professor in the Oklahoma State University College of Education's School of Applied Health and Educational Psychology where she serves as program coordinator for educational psychology. She has received the President's Excellence in Teaching Award at OSU-Tulsa. She also served as the principal investigator for "Project CREATES," an arts integration research project conducted in north Tulsa schools. She is a member of the Board of Examiners for the National Council for Accreditation of Teacher Education and is Past President of the Association of the Gifted, a Division of the Council for Exceptional Children. Dr. Montgomery's research interest areas include creativity, transpersonal development, gifted education and American Indian education. She earned a Master of Arts in Teaching from Western New Mexico University and a PhD in Special Education from the University of New Mexico.

Jean Sunde Peterson is professor and director of school counseling at Purdue University. Extensive school-based small-group work related to the social and emotional development of gifted adolescents led to her research focus, and to eventual licensure as a mental health counselor. She has contributed over 80 publications to the school counseling and gifted education literature and has won several national awards for research, including the Mensa Education & Research Foundation: the Award for Excellence in Research; and the National Association for Gifted Children Early Scholar Award, as well as Purdue awards for teaching, scholarship, and service. She consults nationally, usually with gifted-education teachers and administrators and usually with a focus on the social and emotional development of gifted children.

Kathleen M. Pierce has a PhD from the University of Pennsylvania and serves as associate professor and chair of the Department of Graduate Education, Leadership, and Counseling in the School of Education at Rider University. Having worked as a high school English teacher for over 20 years, she includes among her current scholarly interests the nature of collegial teacher collaboration to promote inquiry-based learning and interdisciplinary understanding. She employs ethnographic inquiry methods to uncover the dynamics of professional acculturation and teacher development.

Jennifer Riedl Cross, PhD, is a research fellow at Center for Gifted Education at the College of William and Mary. She received her doctorate in educational psychology from Ball State University with a cognate in cognitive and social processes. Her research emphasizes the development of beliefs, particularly those that influence public policy and issues of equity. She has served as the assistant editor of the *Gifted Child Quarterly*, and managing editor of the *Roeper Review*.

Charles Rop is an Associate Professor of science education and curriculum in the Department of Curriculum and Instruction at the University of Toledo's College of Education. He holds a PhD in Curriculum, Teaching and Educational Policy with cognates in Science Education, Teacher Education, and Disciplinary Knowledge from Michigan State University. The overriding theme of Dr. Rop's professional work is exploring ways to construct learning experiences that engage the passions and perceptions of learners in ways that transform their views of the world and their relationships to it. In his research in science education he is working to discover ways that thoughtful engagement with the natural world can enable teachers and prospective teachers to catch a vision for authentic inquiry and discovery in science. Melding qualitative and quantitative methodologies, he is looking at how these new experiences might influence their presentation of science in their classrooms.

Margie Spino is a doctoral candidate in early childhood special education at the University of Toledo. She earned a MA from Boston College and taught visually and multiply impaired children for over 10 years. Currently, her research interests focus on effective instructional practices for young children with disabilities as well as their teachers. As such, she is interested in how early childhood special education teachers' theories influence their practices and how their collaborations with other adults impact child outcomes.

Bharath Sriraman is Professor of Mathematics in the Department of Mathematical Sciences and also on the Faculty and Advisory Board of Central/ SW Asian Studies at The University of Montana, where he occasionally offers courses on Indo-Iranian and Turkic studies and languages. He lives in Western

Montana by way of the merchant marine; Alaska (BS in mathematics, University of Alaska-Fairbanks) and Northern Illinois (MS & PhD in mathematics, minor in mathematics education). He comes from a background of one interested in linguistics and comparative philosophy accidentally turning to mathematics as an easy route to academic degrees, who later "found" himself in mathematics education as a result of teaching in U.S. public schools. He maintains an active interest in mathematics education, educational philosophy, history and philosophy of mathematics and science, creativity; innovation and talent development; gender studies; and political and social justice dimensions of education. He has published over 240+ journal articles, commentaries, book chapters, edited books, and reviews in his areas of interest, and presented over 110 papers at international conferences, symposia, and invited colloquiua.

Robert J. Sternberg, PhD is Provost and Senior Vice President as well as Professor of Psychology at Oklahoma State University. Prior to that, he was Dean of the School of Arts and Sciences and Professor of Psychology at Tufts University, and IBM Professor of Psychology and Education in the Department of Psychology at Yale University. Dr. Sternberg received his BA from Yale and his Ph.D. in Psychology from Stanford University. He also holds 11 honorary doctorates. He has received numerous awards, including the James McKeen Cattell Award from the American Psychological Society; the Early Career and McCandless Awards from the APA; and the Outstanding Book, Research Review, Sylvia Scribner, and Palmer O. Johnson Awards from the AERA. Dr. Sternberg has served as President of the American Psychological Association and of the Eastern Psychological Association and is currently President-elect of the Federation of Associations of Brain and Behavioral Sciences. In addition, he has been editor of the *Psychological Bulletin* and of the *APA Review of Books: Contemporary Psychology* and is a member of the Society of Experimental Psychologists. He was the director of the Center for the Psychology of Abilities, Competencies, and Expertise at Yale University and then Tufts University.

Taisir Subhi Yamin is a professor of gifted education. He has a BSc in Physics, an M.A. in Special Education, and a PhD in Gifted Education and Computer Assisted Learning from Lancaster University in England. He is the recipient of academic prizes and fellowships from Jordan, England, and the United States, including a Fulbright Award (1996) and the British Council scholarship. Prof. Yamin is active in the field of science popularization, and has written 16 books, a large number of articles, chapters in edited books, and research papers. In addition, he has developed a number of training packages to develop productive thinking skills. He is an active member of an impressive list of academic institutions including: the British Educational Research Association (BERA), the European Council for High Ability (ECHA), Bahrain Association for the Gifted and Talented; President, Jordanian Association of Physicists, the

National Committee for Gifted Education; Founder, the Qatari Centre for the Gifted and Talented. He is also the National Chancellor and Vice President of the International Association of Educators for World Peace (IAEWP). He was a delegate of the World Council for Gifted and Talented Children (WCGTC) for about 10 years. In 2002, he was elected as a member of the executive committee of the WCGTC. Professor Yamin was involved in developing UAE project for the gifted and talented in Ulm University. In addition, he has established, in cooperation with Todd Lubart and Sandra Linke, the International Centre for Innovation in Education (ICIE). The ICIE has five branches in: France, Germany, Sweden, Turkey, and Jordan. In 2005 he was named editor-in-chief of the journal *Gifted and Talented International*. More recently he joined the teaching staff at Université Paris Descartes. In 2009, he was elected as the President of the WCGTC.

Joyce VanTassel-Baska is the Smith Professor Emerita at The College of William and Mary in Virginia where she developed a graduate program and a research and development center in gifted education. Formerly, she initiated and directed the Center for Talent Development at Northwestern University. She has also served as the state director of gifted programs for Illinois, as a regional director of a gifted service center in the Chicago area, as coordinator of gifted programs for the Toledo, OH, public school system, and as a teacher of gifted high school students in English and Latin. Dr. VanTassel-Baska has published widely including 27 books and more than 500 refereed journal articles, book chapters, and scholarly reports. Her major research interests are on the talent development process and effective curricular interventions with the gifted.

FOREWORD

Dogmatism and Creativity

Howard Gardner

HARVARD UNIVERSITY

What's in a word? For most of us, the words *dogma* and *dogmatic* have pejorative connotations. On this reading, one should not be dogmatic and one should avoid preaching or adhering to dogma. But etymologically, *dogma* is determinedly neutral: "dogma" refers simply to a strongly held belief, quite possibly one that is part of a religious system. Moreover, at times and in places where an established religion held sway, to adhere to dogma was both expected and desirable. Indeed, during periods of religious strife, deviation from church dogma might result in excommunication, imprisonment, or even death.

Dogma is in the eye of the beholder and/or in the ear of the listener. If I state that I believe in the scientific method and that it is the optimal way in which to resolve disagreements, I may well communicate to many that I am a fair and temperate person. But if I make this statement to a man who is a creationist, or to a woman who believes that global warming is a hoax, I am not likely to gain approbation. Instead, I appear to be a dogmatic scientist or, worse, an apostle of scientistic thinkers—in the sway of a singular way of thinking, and a wrong-headed one at that. One person's flexibility is another person's wishi-washiness; one person's stubborn adherence is another person's brave steadfastness.

In the scholarly world, cogent answers are important, but the posing of good questions and intriguing puzzles is at least as prized. Indeed, once the right question has been raised—"What is it like to travel on a beam of light," à la Einstein, or "What is the structure of the genetic material DNA," à la Watson and Crick—the correct answer is likely to be forthcoming, in the measure of time. As soon as I learned that Don Ambrose and Bob Sternberg were proposing a volume—which has now morphed into two volumes (this book and a sister volume on creativity)—on the nature of dogmatic thinking, I muttered to myself "Hey, what a good idea." And when the possibility arose that I might compose a foreword, I responded with an enthusiastic (if not dogmatic) "yes."

The posing of good questions is vital but, once posed, interest shifts to plausibility of the answers offered. This volume does not disappoint—indeed, it exceeds expectations! Nineteen scholars have thought seriously about the nature and reasons for dogmatism; drawn on their own forms of expertise; and offered a panorama of responses with respect to the nature, causes, and consequences of dogmatic thinking—in its benign, malignant, and neutral forms.

In their surveys, the editors give an excellent summary of the various contributions. It is neither necessary nor wise for me to duplicate their efforts. Instead, I offer a brief reflection on how I perceive this issue, in light of the chapters in these volumes and in terms of my own conceptual framework.

As a starter, nowadays, almost no one declares proudly: "I am a dogmatic thinker, unwilling or unable to change my mind." (Who, for that matter, says that her sense of humor, or her driving skills, are below average?) Some years ago, I published a book on the art and science of mind changing called (not surprisingly) *Changing Minds*. For fun, when I spoke to various audiences, I asked how many people were willing to change their minds on issues of significance. Nearly everyone would raise his or her hand. I would then ask people to state issues of significance on which they had changed their mind and would wait, sometimes quite a while, before anyone would offer a convincing response.

I concluded that we ourselves are often not the best judges of how dogmatic we are—and that, indeed, we are more likely to think of ourselves as being flexible than we are able to offer compelling examples of our flexibility. As I analyzed the issue, I identified three factors that influence the likelihood that someone would change his or her mind: (a) How *long* one had held a certain belief; (b) how *strongly* one held that belief; (c) whether one had made a *public* (e.g., published or posted) commitment to that belief. Needless to say, individuals who had held a belief long and emotionally, and had issued speeches and writings on that topic, were far less likely to change their minds than those who were new to a belief, had little emotional stake in it, and had not publicly voiced that conviction.

As one who typically thinks in terms of the different domains or sectors of life (it's almost dogma for me!), I naturally wondered about the extent to which one's dogmatism, or non-dogmatism, was a general property of individuals. Those who endorse the concepts of the "authoritarian personality" or the "true believer" are likely to think of dogmatism as a pervasive feature of human beings. In contrast, those who accentuate the contextual nature of human behavior have no difficulty in conceiving of individuals who are dogmatic in one sphere, or under one circumstance, while proving quite flexible on another day, or another topic, or in front of a different audience. (As one amusing example, think of the strong positions presidential candidates take during the primary season, and the way these positions dissolve as election day approaches).

No doubt, one can accumulate evidence in favor of a domain-general dogmatism, as well as evidence in favor of a dogmatism that proves specific to topic and site. Here, I think, a cognitive lens—how we frame a particular issue—can prove helpful. As one example, say that a teacher has a commitment to punish plagiarism—and indeed that teacher has gone on record as favoring expulsion. So long as unattributed quotation is coded as plagiarism, the consequences attendant to this act are clear. But then suppose that one's own child commits plagiarism, or that plagiarism is carried out by a student from a faraway country in whose development one has taken a special interest. Here, one may well avoid employing the damning term "plagiarism" and instead reframe the situation as a "learning experience" or an "unfortunate blunder"—thereby preserving one's hostility to plagiarism while at the same time highlighting extenuating circumstances. Or, as another example, say Jack has long and vocally opposed same-sex marriage. When Jack's own child declares that he/she wants to marry an individual of the same sex, Jack may reframe the issue in terms of "love" rather than as the violation of natural law.

Pursuing these examples an additional step, one should observe these apparent "mind changers" at a later time. In some circumstances, the individual will have reverted to his earlier position, having seemingly forgotten his earlier reframing of that position. In other circumstances, either gradually or more rapidly, the individual will actually have scuttled his once entrenched belief—now, less judgmental about plagiarism, more open to same sex marriage. In the latter cases, one can clearly say that the dogmatism has dissolved—at least with respect to that particular issue. Experience tells me that true Damascene moments—a sudden and permanent change of mind—are very rare.

Indeed it is difficult for dogmatism to diminish or disappear in its entirety. If dogmatism dissolves, such a trend is likely to happen gradually: We may characterize it as *wisdom*. For every individual who becomes less dogmatic with the passage of years, there is likely to be an individual who actually becomes more judgmental, more dogmatic, less likely to change *any* idea. It would be instructive to determine which individuals lessen their profiles of dogmatism, and which dig in their dogmatic heels … and then, why they do so.

Such considerations have led me to postulate that one's degree and form of dogmatism may best be construed as a developmental issue. The notions of "remaining youthful" or "attaining maturity" have a range of connotations. With respect to very young people, one can imagine the child who flits from one notion to another as well as the child who is incredibly stubborn. With respect to adolescents, one can imagine the youth who is in the grip of a powerful ideology as well as the youth who embraces a new cause with each season. With respect to the young worker, one can envision the professional who completely buys the "company line" at the first place of employment, as well as the professional who second guesses the norms of his or her workplace and seeks out a different milieu. With respect to parents, one can imagine the father who does just what his father did, the mother who attempts the opposite of what her mother did, as well as the parent who attempts to think through issues on his or her own. Finally, there are the elders who exhibit admirable flexibility and tolerance as well as elders who adhere vociferously to the beliefs honed over the course of a lifetime.

As a developmentalist, I reject the idea that these stances, over the course of a lifetime, are formulaic or predictable. Rather, they are a joint product of early dispositions and models, powerful influences in one's community and in the media, and the accidents of life, both positive and negative, day in and day out. Far from individuals being dogmatic or not, or being dogmatic in some situations and not in others, I believe that one's stance toward dogma is a continuing life drama, with the final acts not necessarily yoked to those that came before. As I head into the last years of life, I am willing to believe that my own "dogma profile" may continue to change, even with respect to the ideas in this foreword.

Clearing Away Conceptual Fog in Thinking About Giftedness and Talent

1

CONSIDERING THE EFFECTS OF DOGMATISM ON GIFTEDNESS AND TALENT DEVELOPMENT

Don Ambrose

RIDER UNIVERSITY

Robert J. Sternberg

OKLAHOMA STATE UNIVERSITY

Bharath Sriraman

UNIVERSITY OF MONTANA

Conceptions of giftedness have been under dispute for decades. Giftedness has been viewed broadly by some as varying clusters of outstanding abilities, but also by others narrowly as a single score on a standardized test. Leading scholars in the field of gifted education have argued that lack of clarity about the essence of giftedness has hindered progress in the field (see Ambrose, 2009; Cohen, 1988; Coleman, Sanders, & Cross, 1997; Dai, 2005, 2010; Gagné, 1985; Grant & Piechowski, 1999; Piirto, 1999; Renzulli, 1999; Sternberg & Davidson, 2005; Winner, 1996). This book is an attempt to clarify the reasons why thinkers in the field have experienced such difficulty in elucidating the core phenomena of interest to theorists, researchers, and practitioners. Our purpose is to tease out and clarify the conceptual stumbling blocks—the barriers that often imprison our thinking.

Interest in big-picture conceptual frameworks and the entrenchment that plagues them has been growing considerably in gifted education; consequently, there have been numerous attempts to identify and redress confusions and conflicts in the field. For example, major journals have run special issues on topics that overlap significantly with our emphasis on conceptual entrenchment. The *Roeper Review* recently ran three special issues on "conceptual frameworks" and one on "global awareness"; The *Gifted Child Quarterly* recently ran a special issue on "demythologizing gifted education." The *Journal for the Education of the Gifted* recently featured a collection of articles attempting to clarify the

nettlesome, contested issue of identification. Many of the articles in these journal issues addressed various dimensions of theoretical, philosophical, ideological, or paradigmatic entrenchment. In addition, two special-interest networks
of the National Association for Gifted Children (Conceptual Foundations and
Global Awareness) offer many presentations and discussion forums on issues
related to conceptual entrenchment, dogmatism, and their influences on the
development of high ability. Overall, professionals in gifted education are
interested in these issues because these educators are frustrated by the conceptual calcification of the field.

Gifted Education as Fragmented, Porous, and Contested

The structure and dynamics of the field of gifted education could be causing
problems that lead to conceptual stagnation and dogmatism. In a recent macro-
analysis of the field of gifted education, Ambrose, VanTassel-Baska, Coleman,
and Cross (2010) argued that the field fits a pattern identified by a group of
social scientists and scholars of the humanities. In a collaborative attempt to
determine the structure and dynamics of four academic disciplines—economics, philosophy, English literature, and political science—scholars from these
disciplines eventually determined that two of the disciplines were unified,
insular, and firmly policed, while the other two were fragmented, porous, and
contested (see Bender & Schorske, 1997).

Classical economics and analytic philosophy fit the former pattern. They
tend to be unified because they are dominated by a favored theoretical perspective and any other theories have little influence. They are insular because they
are not open to influence from ideas originating in other disciplines. Consequently, their conceptual borders are closed. They are firmly policed because
the gatekeepers of these fields (e.g., journal editors) punish and marginalize
those who deviate from the orthodoxy.

In contrast, the disciplines of political science and English literature tend to be
fragmented because no single theory dominates. They are porous because ideas
from foreign disciplines easily wend their way through the conceptual borders of
these disciplines and exert influence on theories and practices. They are contested
because the lack of a dominant, central theory enables numerous subgroups to
form around various theories, which end up competing with each other.

Entrenched thinking can plague both kinds of academic disciplines. The
potential for dogmatism is more obvious in the unified, insular, firmly policed
disciplines because they are dominated by a single theoretical perspective or
conceptual framework. If the dominant theory is not an absolutely perfect
representation of human behavior, then the tendency for leading scholars and
practitioners in the field to align their work religiously with the tenets of that
theory reveals at least some dogmatism, which can seriously hinder progress.

Philosophers of science long have warned that theories are tentative representations of reality and should not become calcified (see Popper, 1959).

Coleman (2003) made similar arguments about theory in gifted education. Theories should be tentative placeholders for better explanations of phenomena, which will emerge as new evidence comes forth. Faith-based adherence to a theory arises when scholars tweak the theory here and patch it there to protect it from anomalous new evidence. Such tweaking and patching ultimately creates a cumbersome theory that does not represent reality very well (see Kuhn, 1962). The centuries-long dominance of the Ptolemaic, Earth-centered model of the structure of the universe, which persisted in spite of the increasing weight of anomalous evidence, provides a classic example of dogmatic protection of a theory in the natural sciences. A more recent example in the social sciences comes from neoclassical economic theory, which portrays the human as a logical actor making perfectly rational, emotionless decisions based on perfect sets of information for selfish purposes. Various critics of this model have revealed its weaknesses and ill effects, which include the tilting of the world economy toward hyper-materialistic, exploitative, environmentally destructive, selfish greed (see Chang, 2007; Madrick, 2008; Marglin, 2008; Sen, 2009; Stiglitz, 2004). Nevertheless, the theory has shown remarkable persistence.

The emergence of dogmatic theorizing might seem less obvious in fragmented, porous, contested disciplines because no single theory dominates. Such a situation should create more room for open dialogue about theoretical refinement. Nevertheless, entrenched thinking can arise in these disciplines as well because warring camps tend to form around multiple, competing theories and theoretical interchange becomes conflict-prone, when it occurs at all.

Gifted education seems to be a fragmented, porous, and contested field (Ambrose et al., 2010) so no single theory dominates conceptions of giftedness. Consequently, dogmatism in the field takes the form of insular or competing camps, each promoting a particular perspective and either ignoring or denigrating the others. The result has been an unsettled field with practical program development and curricular and instructional initiatives insufficiently grounded in theory and research.

The following is a non-comprehensive list of constructs and phenomena in gifted education that have been prone to misconception and contestation: giftedness as a stable trait over the long term; giftedness as high IQ; the use of high-stakes, standardized testing to identify and sort the gifted; the impact of social and emotional problems on the gifted; the extent to which specialists are needed in the education of gifted; the extent to which differing investigative paradigms (e.g., positivist versus post-positivist paradigms, holistic vs. reductive; quantitative versus qualitative research) can generate productive discoveries in the field; and creativity as important and measurable in programs for the gifted (for elaboration on these and other topics see Ambrose, 2009; Borland, 2003; Coleman et al., 1997; Dai, 2010; Heller, Mönks, Sternberg, & Subotnik, 2000; Shavinina, 2009; Treffinger, 2009; Winner, 1996). We cannot treat all of these issues effectively in this chapter, but fortunately our collaborators in later chapters engage in some interesting explorations of these and other important subjects.

Perspectives on Giftedness and Entrenchment of Ideas in this Volume

The book includes three major sections, each of which addresses a different dimension of dogmatism in the field. The first section considers ways in which dogmatism has plagued the fundamental, conceptual frameworks for the field. The second looks at ways in which dogmatism in large-scale sociopolitical, economic, ideological, and scholarly contexts can warp or stunt the aspiration discovery, talent development, and life trajectories of the gifted. The third section addresses dogmatic influences in the practical work pertaining to curriculum, instruction, and scholarly inquiry.

Clearing Away Conceptual Fog

After this brief introduction to the project, the chapters in the first section address various ways in which insular, habit-bound, dogmatic thinking has plagued the field of gifted education over the long term. Contributors to this section attempt to clear away the conceptual fog obscuring clear, big-picture perceptions of high ability. They question fundamental assumptions in the field, including notions about the wellsprings from which giftedness and talent arise, and the ways in which students are selected for gifted programs. They also analyze conceptual shifts in the field and some ways in which those shifts might be facilitated and made more productive.

James Borland analyzes some aspects of the closed, passive, dogmatic mind in Chapter 2, "You Can't Teach an Old Dogmatist New Tricks: Dogmatism and Gifted Education," and then applies these insights to the field of gifted education. He makes the case that the field is influenced by its own form of dogmatism, which shapes its basic conceptions and practices. After outlining the nature of these dogmatic influences, he argues for the establishment of a fundamentally different, contradiction-free system for the development of concepts and practical applications pertinent to high ability.

LeoNora Cohen investigates some historical dimensions of the field in Chapter 3, "Dogma and Definitions of Giftedness and Talent." Part of the analysis addresses the shifting of paradigms over time. She also delves deeply into the ways in which theorists define important phenomena such as giftedness and talent and then suggests some refinements to those definitions. Finally, she concludes by mapping some of these phenomena onto a map of ignorance and knowledge, which clarifies some of the thought processes that underpin dogmatism in the field.

David Yun Dai explores some of the dogmatism in the conceptual foundations of the gifted-education field in Chapter 4, "The Nature-Nurture Debate Regarding High Potential: Beyond Dichotomous Thinking." Arguing that researchers fall prey to conceptual entrenchment in their alignment with established ontological beliefs, epistemic positions, and investigative paradigms, Dai teases out some of the thinking behind scientific and social dogmatism and the ways in which it prevents us from seeing more dynamic, complex pluralistic visions of gifted potential.

Jean Sunde Peterson employs the analogy of an overcorrecting driver on icy roads to argue that the field of gifted education has navigated somewhat errati-cally between attention to academic concerns and emphases on the inner world of the gifted child. In Chapter 5, "Overcorrecting: Spinning Out and Missing Many," she assesses the dogmatism that can emerge when dynamic tensions between quantitative and qualitative inquiry, and between measurable versus somewhat less tangible abilities are not well understood.

In Chapter 6, "Dogmatism, Policy, and Gifted Students," James Gallagher explores some of the dogmatism that has saturated national policy pertaining to provisions for the gifted. As a scholar who has straddled the fields of gifted edu-cation and special education while contributing significantly to both, Gallagher provides specific examples of ways in which local and national trends and influ-ences often have worked against the best interests of bright young people. His recommendations provide some ways in which the gifted can be better served by corrections to national priorities.

In Chapter 7, "Equity Issues and Multiculturalism in the Under-Representation of Black Students in Gifted Education: Dogmatism at its Worst," Donna Ford reveals some of the dogmatism that has plagued the field of gifted education since its inception. The dogmatism of individual scholars contributes to the persistence of underrepresentation by limiting the flexibility needed for the assessment and revision of definitions and identification criteria.

Large-Scale Contexts Warping Gifted Minds

Section 2 explores ways in which contexts beyond the field of gifted educa-tion shape or warp the development of bright young minds. More specifically, authors in this section address the influences of entrenched thinking on mani-festations of high ability in large-scale socioeconomic systems, in the minds of individuals, and in the knowledge production of academic disciplines.

The recent worldwide economic collapse largely derived from the folly of powerful, greedy individuals who aligned themselves with the tenets of neo-classical economic theory. In Chapter 8, "The Not-So-Invisible Hand of Eco-nomics and Its Impact on Conceptions and Manifestations of High Ability," Don Ambrose employs an environmental-economics perspective to explore the narrow-minded, shortsighted selfishness that saturates the neoclassical paradigm in economics. While capitalism arose as a large-scale method for distributing prosperity throughout previously marginalized populations, the dogmatic neoclassical framework has done much to pervert the socioeconomic system. This perversion has warping effects on the development of aspirations in many gifted young people.

Scrutinizing another large-scale context influencing the development of high ability, Bharath Sriraman explores the dynamics of knowledge production in the academic world in Chapter 9, "Dogmatism and the Knowledge Industry: More Accurately Assessing the Work of Gifted Scholars." Based on his analysis of the ways in which citation indexes, impact factors, and other bibliometric tools are used to manage the knowledge industry, he concludes that knowledge production is plagued with subjectivity and fallibility. As a consequence, some of the most gifted thinkers might be marginalized in academicia while other highly productive but somewhat more pedestrian minds stand in the spotlight. Shortsighted, narrow-minded thinking might be obscuring some high-potential talent in academia.

Jennifer Riedl Cross and Tracy Cross look at some of the psychological dynamics behind dogmatism in Chapter 10, "Motivated Dogmatism and the High Ability Student." Premature cognitive closure tends to occur when an individual settles on a particular conclusion pertaining to an issue or problem. A number of psychological needs reinforce this tendency to seek closure and creatively intelligent individuals certainly are not immune to these needs. The implications of premature closure operating on bright minds can be serious.

Challenging predominant conceptions of reality appeals to some if not many creatively intelligent individuals. Diane Montgomery mounts such a challenge in Chapter 11, "Facing Dogmatic Influences with Consciousness Work." Drawing from the literature in depth psychology as well as other sources, she suggests ways in which researchers and educators can become trapped by stagnant ideas about giftedness and talent. Overall, she argues for expansions of our creative and critical consciousness.

Taisir Subhi Yamin and Don Ambrose employ an international, contextual perspective in Chapter 12, "Dogmatic Influences Suppressing Discovery and Development of Giftedness and Talent in the Arabian Gulf and Middle Eastern Region." They unravel some of the dogmatic thinking in the region that gave rise to narrowly confined identification practices instead of procedures that would be more dynamic, flexible, and likely to recognize diverse, hidden abilities. The chapter shows how education of the gifted in the Middle East and the Arabian Gulf tends to be weak, ill conceived, and dogmatically reserved for the privileged few. As a result, nations suffer because their strongest human potential isn't developed just when needed most in a complex 21st-century, globalized environment.

Dogmatism Hidden in Curriculum, Instruction, and Research

Section 3 includes chapters that explore the influences of entrenched thinking on curriculum development, instructional implementation, and scholarly inquiry in the field of gifted education, and to some extent general education. Joyce VanTassel-Baska turns to the curricular dimensions of gifted education in Chapter 13, "Curriculum and Dogmatism in Gifted Education." Operating simultaneously at several levels of analysis, she draws connections between practical applications and deeper conceptual frameworks, arguing that curriculum in American education as a whole is locked in modernist philosophy and misses some fruitful insights that could come from postmodern perspectives. Extending beyond currently dominant reductionist, discipline-bound notions, the more context-sensitive visions of education could enrich the structure and dynamics of curricula for the gifted.

Kathleen Pierce and Laurie Kash narrow the curricular scope by looking deeply into one academic subject area. They illustrate the dynamics of secondary English curriculum and instruction in Chapter 14, "Paralysis from Analysis: Arguing for a Break from Traditional High School English." The inertia of established, historical practice often prevails in this niche of the educational system, buttressing traditional literary analysis while marginalizing more creative instructional options that can enliven the minds of the brightest students. Pierce and Kash discuss some ways that educators can move beyond this predicament.

Laurence Coleman, Margie Spino, and Charles Rop conclude this section by taking us in another direction that reveals some potential dogmatism in research strategies and theory development. In Chapter 15, "Loosening Dogmatism by Using Disciplined Inquiry," they navigate through the procedures employed in a creative process of analytic theoretical inquiry, which reveals the logical and empirical nuances in the works of established scholars. The process enables novice investigators to discover these often hidden and taken-for-granted dimensions of inquiry.

Putting It All Together

In Section 4, Chapter 16, "Dogmatism and Giftedness: Major Themes," Robert Sternberg concludes the volume by highlighting some patterns that emerge from our collective exploration of the conceptual landscape in the field of gifted education. He generates some embryonic syntheses and tentative recommendations that can help theorists, researchers, and practitioners steer clear of entrenched thinking as they strive to improve the education of gifted students.

Of course, the ideas in this volume do not leave us with a complete, detailed roadmap for future work in the field. Some of our ideas can and should be challenged. If they are, that likely is a positive development because it will prevent us from establishing just another set of ideas that will calcify and limit future progress. Consistent with the advice about holding theory lightly and using it as a springboard to further development of better ideas (see Popper, 1959; Coleman, 2003), we hope that readers will hold our ideas lightly and use them to inspire their own thinking about theory development, new research trajectories, and stronger development of curriculum and instruction. If this occurs, we should make some progress toward clarifying panoramic views in the field of gifted education while also making it more likely that we will more effectively and efficiently develop more young minds of high ability.

References

Ambrose, D. (2009). *Expanding visions of creative intelligence: An interdisciplinary exploration.* Cresskill, NJ: Hampton Press.

Ambrose, D., VanTassel-Baska, J., Coleman, L. J., & Cross, T. L. (2010). Unified, insular, firmly policed or fractured, porous, contested, gifted education? *Journal for the Education of the Gifted, 33,* 453–478.

Bender, T., & Schorske, C. E. (Eds.). (1997). *American academic culture in transformation: Fifty years, four disciplines.* Princeton, NJ: Princeton University Press.

Borland, J. H. (Ed.). (2003). *Rethinking gifted education.* New York: Teachers College Press.

Chang, H. (2007). *Bad Samaritans: The myth of free trade and the secret history of capitalism.* New York: Random House.

Cohen, L. M. (1988). To get ahead, get a theory: Criteria for evaluating theories of giftedness and creativity applied to education. *Roeper Review, 11,* 95–100.

Coleman, L. J. (2003). An essay on rethinking theory as a tool for disciplined inquiry. In J. H. Borland (Ed.), *Rethinking gifted education* (pp. 61–71). New York: Teachers College Press.

Coleman, L. J., Sanders, M. D., & Cross, T. L. (1997). Perennial debates and tacit assumptions in the education of gifted children. *Gifted Child Quarterly, 41,* 103–111.

Dai, D. (2005). Reductionism versus emergentism: A framework for understanding conceptions of giftedness. *Roeper Review, 27,* 144–151.

Dai, D. (2010). *The nature and nurture of giftedness: A new framework for understanding gifted education.* New York: Teachers College Press.

Gagné, F. (1985). Giftedness and talent: Reexamining a reexamination of the definition. *Gifted Child Quarterly, 29,* 103–112.

Grant, B. A., & Piechowski, M. M. (1999). Theories and the good: Toward child-centered gifted education. *Gifted Child Quarterly, 43,* 4–12.

Heller, K. A., Mönks, F. J., Sternberg, R. J., & Subotnik, R. (Eds.). (2000). *International handbook of giftedness and talent* (2nd ed.). Oxford, UK: Pergamon.

Kuhn, T. (1962). *The structure of scientific revolutions.* Chicago, IL: University of Chicago Press.

Madrick, J. (2008). *The case for big government.* Princeton, NJ: Princeton University Press.

Marglin, S. A. (2008). *The dismal science: How thinking like an economist undermines community.* Cambridge, MA: Harvard University Press.

Piirto, J. (1999). Implications of postmodern curriculum theory for the education of the talented. *Journal for the Education of the Gifted, 22,* 324–353.

Popper, K. R. (1959). *The logic of scientific discovery.* New York: Basic Books.

Renzulli, J. S. (1999). What is this thing called giftedness, and how do we develop it? A twenty-five year perspective. *Journal for the Education of the Gifted, 23,* 3–54.

Sen, A. (2009). Capitalism beyond the crisis. *The New York Review of Books, 56*(5), 27–30.

Shavinina, L. V. (Ed.). (2009). *International handbook on giftedness.* New York: Springer.

Sternberg, R. J., & Davidson, J. E. (Eds.). (2005). *Conceptions of giftedness* (2nd ed.). New York: Cambridge University Press.

Stiglitz, J. E. (2004). *The roaring nineties: A new history of the world's most prosperous decade.* New York: W. W. Norton.

Treffinger, D. J. (2009). Guest editorial, special issue: Demythologizing gifted education. *Gifted Child Quarterly, 53,* 229–232.

Winner, E. (1996). *Gifted children; Myths and realities.* New York: Basic Books.

2

YOU CAN'T TEACH AN OLD DOGMATIST NEW TRICKS

Dogmatism and Gifted Education

James H. Borland

TEACHERS COLLEGE, COLUMBIA UNIVERSITY

Two Forms of Dogmatism

When I first contemplated writing a chapter on dogmatism and gifted education, it struck me as a good idea to try to pin down the actual meaning of dogmatism. I soon found that, as is the case with so many constructs, the definitions of this term are many and varied. However, it is possible to discern two distinct classes of meaning into which the various definitions can be grouped.

On the one hand, dogmatism refers to an epistemology, defined by the online Ism Book (n.d.) as "an approach to ideas that emphasizes rigid adherence to doctrine over rational and enlightened inquiry." In this sense, dogmatism is an approach to knowing in which truth claims are tested and either affirmed or rejected by reference to dogma, as opposed to, say, empiricism.

Despite one's (my, at least) tendency to view the phrase "rigid adherence to doctrine" in a pejorative light and such terms as "rational" and "enlightened" in a positive one, dogmatism, in this sense, should not be considered aberrational or pathological. This variety of dogmatism is a conscious epistemological stance, one that is incommensurable with logic or empiricism. To criticize this as "irrational" is meaningless because it involves imposing a criterion from one frame of reference onto another in which the criterion lacks validity.

Central to this form of dogmatism, unsurprisingly, is reliance on dogma. Wikipedia (n.d.) defines dogma as "the established belief or doctrine held by a religion, ideology or any kind of organization: it is authoritative and not to be disputed, doubted, or diverged from." If "ideology or any kind of organization" can be stretched to include the discipline of gifted education (a discipline in the Foucauldian sense of a group of "objects, methods, their corpus of propositions considered to be true, the interplay of rules and definitions, of techniques and tools," Foucault, 1982, p. 37), then this variety of epistemological dogmatism may be found in this field, or at least in one segment of it, a position I will attempt to develop below.

The other class of meanings of dogmatism prompted a visit to a book I read long ago during my doctoral studies, Milton Rokeach's *The Open and Closed Mind* (1960), perhaps the classic psychological treatment of dogmatism. Rokeach characterized dogmatism, or "the closed mind," as "resistance to change of a total system of beliefs" (p. 22). According to Rokeach, even when confronted with patent "inherent contradictions" (p. 24) in his or her belief system, the dogmatist of this stripe is unable to alter or abandon the belief system and instead clings to an illogical conviction that the contradictions can somehow be resolved within the confines of the belief system. Because of its inability to reject and replace demonstrably dysfunctional systems of axioms and practices, the closed mind, Rokeach argues, is "a passive mind" (p. 23).

Unlike the previous form of dogmatism, which, irrespective of one's feelings about dogma, rationalism, and empiricism, is more appropriately regarded as a coherent epistemological stance, dogmatism as Rokeach (1960) defines it is properly thought of as pathological, or at least maladaptive, as the very phrase "the closed mind" suggests. Dogmatism here is conceived of as a stubborn refusal to acknowledge the truth, as willful irrationality within a context in which rationality is a valid criterion for assessing the soundness of one's thinking.

So, we have two forms of dogmatism. In one form, dogma is the basis for knowledge and belief, and it trumps all other bases for judging truth claims, such as empiricism or logic, which are irrelevant in this context. Whatever one thinks of this epistemological stance, it is internally consistent; dogma determines truth, period. Dogmatism of the second type consists of a closed-minded refusal to abandon a belief or system of beliefs despite overwhelming evidence that the belief or belief system is flawed. This form of dogmatism is characterized by a lack of internal consistency. An example would be an individual who purports to base his or her beliefs on hard empirical facts yet clings to the belief that the war in Iraq is justified on the basis of Saddam Hussein's involvement in the September 11th attacks.[1]

The Two Fields of Gifted Education

The question as to the extent to which dogmatism characterizes the field of gifted education depends on how one defines "the field of gifted education." In this regard, it is useful to distinguish between those of us who write, conduct research, educate teachers—the chattering classes of the field—and the much larger segment of the field engaged in the day-to-day practice of gifted education—teachers, administrators, policy makers—those who actually make this form of education happen. Although I would not claim that the former group is devoid of dogmatic thinking, one could be forgiven for believing that it tends to view the latter as perpetually mired in it.

This is illustrated by a recent issue of the *Gifted Child Quarterly* (October 2009), a reprise of an issue of the same journal that appeared over a quarter of a century earlier (January 1982). Both were entitled *Demythologizing Gifted Education*, and both were devoted to debunking what were thought to be wide-spread "myths"[2] about gifted education. For example, the misconception I was asked to write about was "The Gifted Constitute 3% to 5% of the Population. Moreover, Giftedness Equals High IQ, Which Is a Stable Measure of Aptitude" (Borland, 2009a), which suggests the kind of wrong thinking the editor and authors of the special issue were trying to correct.

Clearly, there is a perception on the part of those in the field who write for publications such as the *Gifted Child Quarterly* that the larger group that teaches in and administers gifted programs were, in the late 20th century, and continue to be, in the early 21st century, given over to benighted ways of conceptualiz-ing and practicing gifted education. This illustrates both the dichotomy within the field between the preachers and the preached to and, admittedly, the persis-tence and extent of beliefs that *are* misguided; that lead to the miseducation, of students who participate in many gifted programs; and that Donald Treffinger, the editor of both the *Gifted Child Quarterly* "Demythologizing" issues, was right to try to disabuse people of.

Implicit in all of this is a belief among us ivory-tower types that the practice of gifted education is, to an alarming extent, characterized by dogmatism. If we are convinced that the 15 misconceptions laid out in the 1982 issue of the *Gifted Child Quarterly* are still alive and kicking 27 years later (and, alas, have been joined by 4 additional fallacies) despite their patent speciousness and our best efforts to eradicate them or attenuate their influence, what does this sug-gest about how we regard the thinking of those who make decisions that shape gifted programs? To me, it suggests that we think the field of practice is full of closed minds, "resistan[t] to change of a total system of beliefs" (Rokeach, 1960, p. 22). I will return to this theme below.

Dogmatism as Adherence to Dogma: Defenders of the Faith

I want to make a connection between the first type of dogmatism—dogmatism as epistemological stance—and that segment of the gifted-education field that conducts research, educates teachers and scholars, publishes, and, some would argue, pontificates. What is the dogma to which this group clings, even as it chastises the rank and file for wallowing in "myths," in other words, for being dogmatic?

I would argue that this dogma consists of what could be called the "cre-ation myth"[3] of gifted education. This runs roughly as follows: Gifted children have always existed. For years they were unrecognized and suffered educational neglect in the U.S. public schools until their discovery—and the creation, *ex nihilo*, of the field of gifted education—by Lewis M. Terman and others early in the 20th century. From this creation myth sprang numerous beliefs and practices:

- Since this population exists, it must have certain defining traits and characteristics.
- Delineating these traits leads to definitions of giftedness in school children, some of which are closer approximations of the "true" nature of giftedness than others.
- This population has certain specific needs, none of which is more important than the need for differentiated curriculum.
- Accurate identification of this population is necessary in order to allocate differentiated curriculum appropriately.
- Differentiated curriculum requires the creation of at least semi-segregated gifted programs labeled, if only implicitly, as such.
- Gifted education is a variety of educational reform and an attempt to make American education more equitable.

I have taken issue with this view of both the field's creation and the axioms and practices that have arisen in the field over the years (e.g., Borland 2003, 2005, 2009b). In response to the above, I have argued that:

- Although there have always been precocious students whose academic excellence has been noteworthy, the notion that these individuals constituted a distinct, discrete population is a creation—or social construction— prompted by specific historical forces (e.g., the advent of widespread mental testing) operating in the second and third decades of the 20th century. Confronting the educational issues created by these historical forces did not require the social construct of "the gifted student."
- The history of defining giftedness has not constituted an inexorable march toward enlightenment and consensus driven by systematic inquiry but instead a process whereby this construct has been defined in wildly and increasingly divergent ways reflecting values and beliefs and the influence of subsequent historical forces (e.g., the Cold War and the launching of *Sputnik I*).
- Differentiated curriculum is necessary for all students in our highly diverse school population, not just those labeled gifted.
- Differentiated curriculum in most gifted programs is something provided on an enrichment basis to a group of students, implicitly labeled "generically gifted," all of whom are given the same, and therefore undifferentiated, curriculum.

Failure to come around to my way of thinking about the use of the construct of the *gifted child* is hardly evidence of dogmatism of the second, aberrant, sort, as much as I might like to think it is, but I think it *is* evidence of dogmatism as epistemology. The set of assertions found in our field's creation myth so deeply inform the thinking of many in the field that beliefs inconsistent with the myth are not met with attempts at logical refutation but rather with dismissal because they are inconsistent with the truths found in the field's orthodox dogma.

For example, I think—and I acknowledge that others may in good faith disagree—that, despite our field's sincere commitment to ethical educational practice, gifted programs have exacerbated racial and socioeconomic inequities in American education while providing questionable benefits to those placed in the programs (Borland, 2003). This could be argued with, which would be fair, but that rarely happens. Rather, such opinions are typically seen as annoying and heterodox or simply fail to register because they are at variance with established dogma.

Adherence to orthodox dogma has, in my opinion, a number of serious negative consequences for the field of gifted education, but the most important one has to do with the effectiveness of our practice, which, I think, has yet to be established. Put simply, if paradoxically, I believe that the greatest impediment to effective gifted education has been the construct of the gifted child.

We have, over the last nine decades, spent a considerable amount of time and effort trying to arrive at the "true" definition of giftedness, only to arrive at the current state of affairs in which numerous, varied definitions abound.[4] This leads to such things as the phenomenon I semi-facetiously refer to as "geographical giftedness," a situation in which a student, by virtue of a school's identification process, "becomes gifted" and then, as a result of moving to another school district, "becomes ungifted" because the new district uses a different definition of giftedness from the one used in the old district.

This is, in many respects, ludicrous, and it illustrates the extent to which worrying over the "true" definition of giftedness and identifying the "truly gifted" have distracted us from what really matters: ensuring that students of high ability receive an appropriate education, something that should be the right of every student in our schools.

To simplify, there are two ways to try to achieve this outcome. One is to promulgate definitions of giftedness and see them adopted willy-nilly, one definition here, one definition there. The result is that certain children, should there be a fortuitous match between their (often unreliably) measured traits and abilities and those found in their school's definition of giftedness, are identified as gifted and placed in a program where, more often than not, they all receive the same hodge-podge of enrichment activities, activities that typically lack a scope and sequence, usually lack any connection to the core curriculum, fairly can be considered to be what Julian Stanley (see Benbow, 1986) called "irrelevant academic enrichment," and too often lack sufficient academic rigor (Sawyer, 1988).

The alternative is to go back to the locus of the problem, the regular classroom,[5] where gifted students' needs become apparent in the first place. What we should be focusing on is not "giftedness," on whose very nature we cannot agree, but educational need, which is less abstract and easier to demonstrate and recognize. Educators with varying opinions as to what constitutes giftedness may argue over whether a particular child is or is not gifted. It is easier to agree on whether a particular child has a need for a more demanding, in-depth curriculum in a given school subject. Moreover, once this is determined, the path ahead is clear. Instead of placing all "gifted" students in the same one-size-fits-all-gifted-students enrichment program, we can accelerate mathematically precocious students, provide students who are advanced readers with books on an appropriate reading level, encourage students who are highly capable in science to engage in individual or small-group projects, broaden and deepen the social studies curriculum for students with interest and ability in that subject area. In short, we can engage in instructional differentiation, as advocated by Tomlinson (e.g., 1999, 2001, 2003) and others.

There are three salient facts about instructional and curricular differentiation that should be noted here. The first is that it is more than a desideratum in American education; it is, or ought to be, a necessity. At its core, differentiation consists of instruction that takes into account the obvious diversity of educational needs found in our student population. It is difficult to imagine how instruction could be effective without it, since undifferentiated instruction is based on the obviously spurious notion that students are a monolithic group for whom one-size-fits-all instruction is effectual. Borrowing the language of PL 94-142 and IDEA, a free and appropriate education, which ought to be every child's birthright, requires differentiation, without which education cannot be appropriate for any child (i.e., almost every child) who deviates from an imaginary average.

The second fact about differentiation is that, despite the logical and ethical mandate for its use in public education, it is rarely practiced. This was documented in a review of the literature by Tomlinson et al. (2003), and there is little reason to believe that much has changed in the years since the research reviewed in that paper was conducted. Looking specifically at gifted students, Westberg, Archambault, Dobyns, and Salvin (1993) found that such students rarely received differentiated instruction appropriate to their needs in heterogeneous settings.

The third fact, which, I believe, explains the logical disconnect between the first two, is that it is easier for people like me to preach about the necessity of differentiation than it is for teachers and administrators to make it happen. Differentiation is much more difficult than whole-class, teaching-to-the-middle instruction. It requires skill, support in the form of professional development and resources, patience, and time, only the first of which is plentiful in American schools. This is why, although differentiation is the policy in a number schools and school districts, it is actual practice in many fewer.

Nonetheless, as we envision a future for gifted education, I believe that it is imperative for us to envision one in which the current norm of part-time pull-out enrichment programs is replaced by universal differentiation. We should do this although we know that this goal will be extremely difficult, to achieve. However, the same could be said for the goal of providing a special program for every gifted student, a professed goal of the field of gifted education. We have to acknowledge that realizing the goal of universal differentiation will be slow, incremental, and imperfect. But it is a goal well worth pursuing.

The benefits of conceiving of gifted education as universal differentiation are manifold and include the following:

- Effective gifted education—As I stated above, I am not convinced that the typical part-time pull-out enrichment gifted education program is effective because we do not have the evidence that it is (see Borland, 2003). In my experience observing and evaluating gifted programs, I have seen few that have anything resembling a considered scope and sequence, a logical connection to the core curriculum, or sufficient academic rigor.
- Full-time differentiated education for gifted students—Even if, unlike me, one concedes that many pull-out programs are effective, they typically account for a small percentage of the time gifted students spend in school classrooms. Why would we be willing to write off 90% of a gifted student's schooling because 10% might be appropriate?
- More efficient gifted education—Differentiation does not require the various trappings of gifted education. For example, the time and anguish spent identifying students for admission to gifted programs would be eliminated were differentiation to replace typical gifted programs
- More equitable education—Inequities in gifted education along socioeconomic, racial, ethnic, and linguistic lines have been a sad part of gifted education for decades (Borland, 2004; Borland & Wright, 1994, 2001; Ford & Harmon, 2001; Ford & Harris, 1999; U.S. Department of Education, 1991). Such inequities occur when certain groups of students are identified for admission to gifted programs at levels disproportionate to their representation in the general school population. Were differentiation to replace traditional gifted education programs, inequities in identification would disappear simply because formal identification would disappear.[6]

I am convinced that gifted education in the form of universal differentiation would be immeasurably preferable to gifted education as it now exists. However, there are at least two major impediments to its realization. The first is the sheer difficulty of implementing differentiation on a scale that would make an appreciable difference in American education, for reasons I mentioned earlier. The second is the dogmatism of the epistemological variety that characterizes mainstream thinking in gifted education. For those who cling to the dogma, gifted education means gifted programs, with students identified as gifted students who meet in homogeneous groups with gifted education teachers in a gifted education classroom. For these folks, differentiation in heterogeneous settings is not gifted education.

This approaches the realm of fanaticism and recalls Santayana's famous definition: "Fanaticism consists in redoubling your effort when you have forgotten your aim" (1905, p. 284). We need to think again about what our aim really is. Is it the proliferation of gifted programs? Or is it making education more effective for gifted students? If it is the latter, as I believe, then we need to recognize the former as a means, not an end, and critically examine whether there might be a better approach. That, however, would require freeing ourselves from our dogmatism.

Dogma as the Closed Mind

Let me consider what I identified as the second form of dogmatism, which Rokeach (1960) associated with *the closed mind*. To recapitulate, this is characterized by a stubborn refusal to change one's beliefs in the face of overwhelming evidence that those beliefs are contradicted according to criteria that one deems valid. This is what the contributors to the *Gifted Child Quarterly* "Demythologizing" issues railed against, and it is true that a good amount of this sort of dogmatism can be found in gifted programs across the country.

I will not repeat the arguments developed by the writers of the *Gifted Child Quarterly* articles; the articles speak for themselves.[7] Instead, I will discuss two examples of what I see as dogmatism in the practice of gifted education that, I believe, contribute to the practice of gifted education being less than it should be.

Programs Without a Raison d'être

When I conduct an evaluation of a gifted program, one of the first questions I ask administrators is why the program exists. This usually elicits hemming and hawing, references to nebulous goals in the program handbook, or blank looks. When pressed, educators typically reveal that the reason they have a gifted program is so they can have a gifted program.

This, obviously, is unsupportable. Like any other educational enterprise, a program should exist only if there is an educational reason for it. A gifted program is justified if, without it, the regular curriculum does not adequately serve certain able students, students with clear educational needs. The program should be a systematic attempt to meet these needs, and the goals of the program should relate to these needs.

This requires asking some important questions:

1. In what ways is the regular core curriculum insufficient for high-ability students?
2. What specific educational needs result from this?
3. How can these needs best be addressed?

The answer(s) to question #2 should be the basis for the goals of the gifted program. The answer(s) to question #3 should guide the design or restructuring of the program, especially its curriculum. The program ought to be the best practical, systematic response to students' identified needs.

This may seem obvious, but far too many educators cling dogmatically to the idea that a gifted program is its own raison d'être. This is reflected in the paucity of pull-out enrichment programs that have a scope and sequence that provides a systemic, well-thought-out plan for differentiating the curriculum to address identified educational needs (instead of providing a hodge-podge of enrichment activities). In every other aspect of education, educators have developed a carefully planned sequence of knowledge, understandings, and skills that serves as the backbone of a subject area or program (although it may not be strictly adhered to in every classroom). Gifted programs seem to be sadly unique with respect to the laissez faire attitude administrators have toward what is taught and learned in such programs.

Does this constitute dogmatism? Yes, because it is a practice widely tolerated by educators who profess to do things for a reason. Although their belief systems revolve around meeting student needs, they tolerate the existence of programs whose purpose is a mystery to all involved, probably because there is no purpose beyond the tautological "we-need-a-program-so-we-can-have-a-program assumption."

The Fetish for Objective Measures for Identification (and Evaluation)

There is a widespread belief among educators in the absolute value of objective measures for the identification of gifted students and the evaluation of gifted programs, and this belief, dogmatically adhered to, can compromise the effectiveness of both processes. I focus on identification here because it is a critical function in gifted programs and because it actually takes place in most programs.

If one were to propose to administrators, as I have on many occasions, that subjective measures be used for identification, one is likely to meet with considerable resistance because it is believed that only objective measures are appropriate for such an important undertaking. This betrays a lack of understanding as to what an objective measure is. According to Dictionary.com (n.d.), an objective test is "a test consisting of factual questions requiring extremely short answers that can be quickly and unambiguously scored by anyone with an answer key, thus minimizing subjective judgments by both the person taking the test and the person scoring it." In Thorndike's classic *Educational Measurement,* Wesman (1977) wrote that an objective measure is "one that can be scored by mechanical devices or clerks who have no special competence in the field" (p. 81).

Neither of these definitions defines *objective* in a manner that makes it a desirable aspect of an identification method. In fact, whether a measure is objective or subjective is irrelevant in identifying gifted students. What *is* relevant is whether the measure is valid.

As we all learned years ago, a test is valid if it truly measures what it is designed to measure. A slightly more technical definition that, in essence, says the same thing is found in the authoritative *Standards for Psychological and Educational Testing*: "validity refers to the degree to which evidence and theory support the interpretations of test scores entailed by proposed uses of tests" (American Educational Research Association, American Psychological Association, & National Council on Measurement in Education, 1999, p. 9). Validity is the most important property of assessment measures, both from a psychometric (Popham, 2008) and ethical (Messick, 1980) perspective. To be consistent with best assessment practices, a test need not be objective, but it must be valid. The mistake educators often make, and to which they dogmatically cling, is either to posit objectivity as a good in and of itself, ignoring the true good of validity, or believing that objectivity insures validity.

The best measures are not always objective ones. The measurement of creativity provides a good example. This construct is central to many definitions of giftedness (e.g., Renzulli, 1978), but it is difficult to assess. Objective measures are plagued by psychometric problems (e.g., Hocevar, 1981; Hocevar & Bachelor, 1989; Cooper, 1991), concerns over construct validity (e.g., Almeida, Prieto, Oliveira, & Ferrándiz, 2008), and, despite some favorable assessments (e.g., Cramond, Matthews-Morgan, Bandalos, & Zuo, 2005; Plucker, 1999; Torrance, 1972), skepticism over whether paper-and-pencil measures have validity as assessments of creativity.

One method that has strong empirical support is Amabile's *consensual assessment* (e.g., Amabile, 1982, 1996; Hennessey & Amabile, 1999; Hickey, 2001). According to Baer and McKool (2009),

"The basic technique is quite simple:

1. Subjects are asked to create something (e.g., a poem, a short story, a collage, a composition, an experimental design).
2. Experts in the domain in question are then asked to evaluate the creativity of the things they have made. (p. 4)"

This approach is clearly subjective, relying as it does on expert judgment. Moreover, Amabile's research provides strong evidence supporting the validity of consensual assessment.[8,9]

Given a choice between objective measures of questionable validity and a subjective approach with empirical support, the choice should be simple. Only dogmatic thinking that values objectivity over validity would lead educators to prefer "creativity tests" over informed professional judgment. I would make a similar argument in favor of narrative teacher recommendations over teacher checklists (whose scores are of dubious validity and reliability and are easily manipulated) and in favor of committee decisions for program placement over identification matrices (which combine non-additive, arbitrarily scaled scores into an uninterpretable hodgepodge that is judged against an arbitrary cut-off).

Of course, there is another explanation as to why educators prefer objective measures to subjective ones, even when the latter are superior, and this is grounded less in dogmatism than in expedience. The more identification relies on objective measures and procedures, the easier it is to explain identification decisions to parents and others. The typical matrix approach to identification has so much error variance built into it that many placements are the result of chance. I am convinced that placement by a committee of educational professionals who reach consensus with respect to identification decisions is a much superior method with much greater validity. However, the matrix approach yields a score, however psychometrically meaningless, and a cut-off, however arbitrary, and an administrator can explain to disappointed parents that, in the case of their son or daughter, the numbers simply fell the way they did, that there was no human judgment involved. What I see as a psychometric and educational liability thus becomes a political asset.

Recognizing that validity is the only criterion that should matter should lead to greater acceptance of subjective assessment in the identification of gifted students. Dogmatic thinking, however, which valorizes objectivity in the identification of gifted students, makes this difficult and, thus, lowers the standard of our practice.

Conclusion

Kuhn's (1962) notion of a *paradigm shift,* in which an entire system of scientific thought is replaced when the accretion of empirical findings inconsistent with the reigning paradigm proves to be more than it can accommodate, is a well-known example of a defense against dogmatism. In an earlier paper (Borland, 2003), I suggested the need for a paradigm shift in gifted education. Should that not happen, it would be presumptuous of me to cite dogmatism as the reason. I could simply be misguided in my thinking, and it would be dogmatic of me to gainsay that possibility. However, should we as a field, after all this time, refuse to rethink our practices and even (especially) our core beliefs, I would feel quite comfortable in implicating dogmatism. Questioning our beliefs is not a threat. Dogmatism is.

Notes

1. What makes this an example of dogmatism is not the belief that the war was justified, which is at least open to argument, but the basis for the justification, which is not only empirically unsupported but empirically contradicted.
2. Actually, these are not myths in the way Campbell (1949/1968) and others use that term. They are more accurately thought of as misconceptions.
3. Here I am using the term *myth* in the sense of a sacred story from the past with explanatory power for understanding our world, not as a synonym for *misconception.*

4. As one example, Sternberg and Davidson's (2005) anthology, *Conceptions of Giftedness*, contains 24 chapters, 23 of which set forth definitions of giftedness, which are remarkable for their variety and divergence. These 23 conceptions do not begin to exhaust the explicit definitions of giftedness, let alone the implicit ones and the operational definitions used by schools.

5. I am locating the problem of gifted education primarily in elementary schools rather than in secondary schools. Although it would be an exaggeration to say that the educational needs of highly capable secondary students are universally met in American schools, the secondary curriculum in most schools is sufficiently differentiated, through honors and Advanced Placement courses and the like, that students do not have to endure a one-size-fits-all curriculum or approach to instruction.

6. Inequities in American education as a whole would, of course, not disappear.

7. Honesty compels me to note that one of the beliefs treated as a fallacy in the 2009 *Gifted Child Quarterly* "Demythologizing" issue was "Differentiation in the Regular Classroom Is Equivalent to Gifted Programs and Is Sufficient: Classroom Teachers Have the Time, the Skill, and the Will to Differentiate Adequately" (Hertzberg-Davis, 2009). If one changes the word *programs* to *education*, the first part of the title of this article would essentially state what I argue above.

8. That this approach is supported empirically should be unsurprising in light of the extent to which it mirrors how important decisions, many regarding the presence or absence of creativity, are made in the real world. Were I to wish to occupy a seat in the New York Philharmonic or have a role in a Broadway play or to show a painting in a juried exhibition, I would not sit for the Torrance Tests of Creative Thinking (Torrance, 1974). I would produce one or more examples of my creativity, which would be judged, subjectively, by experts—professionals in the world of music or theater or painting. Moreover, no one has won a Nobel Prize for Literature as a result of scoring high on an objective test of creativity.

9. One of the editors of this volume made a good point in reviewing an earlier version of this chapter, namely that, in order to be accorded an expert in a field, and thus a likely participant in a consensual-assessment activity, one would probably be influenced by the prevailing paradigm in his or her field and thus strongly affected by a form of groupthink akin to dogmatism. The extent to which consensus and dogmatism are at least partially isomorphic illustrates the near ubiquity of the latter.

References

Almeida, L. S., Prieto, L. P., Oliveira, E., & Ferrándiz, C. (2008). Torrance Test of Creative Thinking: The question of its construct validity. *Thinking skills and creativity, 3,* 53–58.

Amabile, T. M. (1982). Social psychology of creativity: A consensual assessment technique. *Journal of Personality and Social Psychology, 43,* 997–1013.

Amabile, T. M. (1996). *Creativity in context: Update to the social psychology of creativity.* Boulder, CO: Westview.

American Educational Research Association, American Psychological Association, & National Council on Measurement in Education. (1999). *Standards for educational and psychological testing.* Washington, D.C.: American Educational Research Association.

Baer, J., & McKool, S. (2009). Assessing creativity using the consensual assessment. In C. Schreiner (Ed.), *Handbook of assessment technologies, methods, and applications in higher education* (pp. 65–77). Hershey, PA: IGI Global.

Benbow, C. P. (1986). SMPY's model for teaching mathematically precocious students. In J. S. Renzulli (Ed.), *Systems and models for developing programs for the gifted and talented* (pp. 1–26). Mansfield Center, CT: Creative Learning Press.

Borland, J. H. (2003). The death of giftedness. In J. H. Borland (Ed.), *Rethinking gifted education* (pp. 105–124). New York: Teachers College Press.

Borland, J. H. (2004). *Issues and practices in the identification and education of gifted students from under-represented groups.* Storrs, CT: National Research Center on the Gifted and Talented.

Borland, J. H. (2005). Gifted education without gifted children: The case for no conception of giftedness. In R. J. Sternberg & J. Davidson (Eds.), *Conceptions of giftedness* (2nd ed., pp. 1–19). New York: Cambridge University Press.

Borland, J. H. (2009a). The gifted constitute 3% to 5% of the population. Moreover, giftedness equals high IQ, which is a stable measure of aptitude: *Spinal Tap* psychometrics in gifted education. *Gifted Child Quarterly, 53,* 236–238.

Borland, J. H. (2009b). Gifted education without gifted programs or gifted students: Differentiation of curriculum and instruction as an instructional model for gifted students. In J. S. Renzulli, E. J. Gubbins, K. S. McMillen, R. D. Eckert, & C. A. Little (Eds.), *Systems and models for the education of gifted and talented students* (2nd ed., pp. 105–118). Mansfield Center, CT: Creative Learning Press.

Borland, J. H., & Wright, L. (1994). Identifying young, potentially gifted, economically disadvantaged students. *Gifted Child Quarterly, 38,* 164–171.

Borland, J. H., & Wright, L. (2001). Identifying and educating poor and under-represented gifted students. In K. A. Heller, F. J. Mönks, R. J. Sternberg, & R.F. Subotnik (Eds.), *International handbook of research and development of giftedness and talent* (pp. 587–594). London, England: Pergamon Press.

Campbell, J. (1968). *The hero with a thousand faces.* Princeton, NJ: Princeton University Press. (Original work published 1949)

Cooper. E. (1991) A critique of six measures for assessing creativity. *Journal of Creative Behavior, 25,* 194–204.

Cramond, B, Matthews-Morgan, J. Bandalos, D., & Zuo, L. (2005). A Report on the 40-year follow-up of the Torrance Tests of Creative Thinking: Alive and well in the new millennium. *Gifted Child Quarterly, 49,* 283–291.

Dictionary.com. (n.d.). Retrieved from http://dictionary.reference.com/browse/objective+test

Ford, D. Y., & Harris J. J. III. (1999). *Multicultural gifted education.* New York: Teachers College Press.

Ford, D. Y., & Harmon, D. A. (2001). Equity and excellence: Providing access to gifted education for culturally diverse students. *Journal of Secondary Gifted Education, 12,* 141–147.

Foucault, M. (1982). *The archaeology of knowledge and the discourse on language.* New York: Pantheon.

Hennessey, B. A., & Amabile, T. M. (1999). Consensual assessment. In M. A. Runco & S. R. Pritzker (Eds.), *Encyclopedia of creativity* (Vol. 1, pp. 346–349). San Diego, CA: Academic Press.

Hertzberg-Davis, H. (2009). Differentiation in the regular classroom is equivalent to gifted programs and is sufficient: Classroom teachers have the time, the skill, and the will to differentiate adequately. *Gifted Child Quarterly, 53,* 251–253.

Hickey, M. (2001). An application of Amabile's consensual assessment technique for rating the creativity of children's musical compositions. *Journal of Research in Music Education, 49,* 234–244.

Hocevar, D. (1981). Measurement of creativity: Review and critique. *Journal of Personality Assessment, 45,* 450–464.

Hocevar, D., & Bachelor, P. (1989) A taxonomy and critique of measurements used in the study of creativity. In J. A. Glover, R. R. Ronning, & C. R. Reynolds (Eds.), *Handbook of creativity* (pp. 53–76) New York: Plenum.

The Ism Book. (n.d.). Retrieved from http://www.ismbook.com/dogmatism.html

Kuhn, T. S. (1962). *The structure of scientific revolutions.* Chicago: University of Chicago Press.

Messick, S. (1980). Test validity and the ethics of assessment. *American Psychologist, 35,* 1025–1037.

Plucker, J. A. (1999) Is the proof in the pudding? Reanalysis of Torrance's (1958 to present) longitudinal data. *Creativity Research Journal, 12,* 103–114.

Popham, W. J. (2008). All about assessment: A misunderstood grail. *Educational Leadership, 66*(1), 82–83.

Renzulli, J. S. (1978). What makes giftedness? *Phi Delta Kappan, 60,* 180–184, 261.

Rokeach, M. (1960). *The open and closed mind*. New York: Basic Books.

Santayana, G. (1905). *Life of reason: Reason in common sense*. New York: Charles Scribner's Sons.

Sawyer, R. N. (1988). In defense of academic rigor. *Journal for the Education of the Gifted, 11*, 5–19.

Sternberg, R. J., & Davidson, J. (Eds.). (2005). *Conceptions of giftedness* (2nd ed.) New York: Cambridge University Press.

Tomlinson, C. A. (1999). *The differentiated classroom: Responding to the needs of all learners*. Alexandria, VA: Association for Supervision and Curriculum Development.

Tomlinson, C. A. (2001). *How to differentiate instruction in mixed-ability classrooms*. Alexandria, VA: Association for Supervision and Curriculum Development.

Tomlinson, C. A. (2003). *Fulfilling the promise of the differentiated classroom: Strategies and tools for responsive teaching*. Alexandria, VA: Association for Supervision and Curriculum Development.

Tomlinson, C. A., Brighton, C., Hertberg, H., Callahan, C. M., Moon, T. R., Brimijoin, K., et al. (2003). Differentiating instruction in response to student readiness, interest, and learning profile in academically diverse classrooms: A review of literature. *Journal for the Education of the Gifted, 24*, 119–145.

Torrance, E. P. (1972). Predictive validity of the Torrance Tests of Creative Thinking. *Journal of Creative Behavior, 6*, 236–252.

Torrance, E. P. (1974). *Torrance Tests of Creative Thinking Norms-technical manual*. Lexington, MA: Ginn & Co.

Treffinger, D. J. (1982), Demythologizing gifted education [Special issue]. *Gifted Child Quarterly, 26*(1).

Treffinger, D. J. (2009). *Demythologizing gifted education* [Special issue). *Gifted Child Quarterly, 53*(4).

United States Department of Education. (1991). *National educational longitudinal study 88. Final report: Gifted and talented education programs for eighth grade public school students*. Washington, DC: United States Department of Education, Office of Planning, Budget, and Evaluation.

Wesman, A. G. (1977). Writing the test item. In R. L. Thorndike (Ed.), *Educational measurement* (2nd ed., pp. 81–129). Washington, DC: American Council on Education.

Westberg, K., Archambault, F., Dobyns, S., & Salvin, T. (1993). *An observational study of instructional and curricular practices used with gifted and talented students in regular classrooms*. (Research Monograph 93104). Storrs, CT: University of Connecticut, National Research Center on the Gifted and Talented.

Wikipedia. (n.d.). Retrieved from http://en.wikipedia.org/wiki/Dogma

3

DOGMA AND DEFINITIONS OF GIFTEDNESS AND TALENT

LeoNora M. Cohen

OREGON STATE UNIVERSITY

This chapter opens with criteria for definitions, the connection of dogma to definitions, and some general issues related to defining these terms. It then focuses on specific issues related to definitions of giftedness and talent, concluding with a few suggestions for overcoming the conceptual blocks and a map of knowledge and ignorance to help consider future and less dogmatic approaches.

Over 30 years ago, Gallagher (1979) emphasized that delineating definitions of giftedness would be one of the most substantial contributions researchers could make to the field. Renzulli (1979) stated that an operational definition for giftedness, "as an explicit written statement" (p. 16) is needed to give direction to educational practices. Such a definition would be used in policies and regulations. For Renzulli, an operational definition of giftedness must meet the following three criteria:

1. Be based on the best available research on characteristics of the gifted.
2. Provide guidance in selection and/or development of instruments or procedures for defensible identification systems.
3. Give direction and relate logically to program practices.

Later, Renzulli (1986) added that it must be able to generate research studies that verify (or not) the validity of the definition. Broadening Renzulli's criteria for definitions and including talent, I believe any definition should:

1. Be generalizable across cultures yet recognize socio-cultural specificity.
2. Avoid jumbling the terms gifted, talented, creative, genius, and clarify distinctions among them.
3. Span the gap between childhood and adulthood.

4. Be based on philosophical frameworks and theory as well as research and practice.

It is rare that definitions address all or most of these criteria, leading to greater probability of dogmatic assumptions and interpretations.

The noun dogma means belief system, ideology, or credo. The adjective dogmatic, means unquestioned, biased, or convinced. These meanings relate to definitions of giftedness and talent in that we have a plethora of interpretations of these terms, each with its attending belief system and each used with certainty and unquestioned assumptions. Freeman (2005) suggested that there are perhaps 100 definitions just for the term "gifted," which, she said, generally focus on children's precocity or high grades in school. The definition of talent likewise has multiple versions.

There is also dogmatic insularity in hanging on to one's own interpretation of the term. Each definition is "gospel according to St. Guru," perpetuated by proponents who each stay in their own silo, claiming theirs is the correct one. Their definition is learned and touted by new learners (their students), who defend their teachers' definitions or create their own, perpetuating the lack of coherence in defining these terms. Discussing the 1986 version of Sternberg and Davidson's Conceptions of Giftedness, Gagne (2004) noted:

> Within that book, no one ever adopts another scholar's definition; each of them prefers to create his/her own. All these conceptions develop in parallel, without ever confronting their respective contradictions and divergences. It seems that anyone can propose his/her own definition of giftedness and/or talent; no special expertise appears needed to introduce a personal conception. It says a lot about the level of respect for the knowledge base specific to our field! The present situation reminds me of Humpty Dumpty's well-known egocentric saying: 'When I use a word, it means just what I choose it to mean, neither more nor less.'
>
> *(p. 12)*

Defining giftedness and related terms is critical to some scholars, for example, "clear definitions reflect clear thinking, and clear thinking is THE prerequisite for scientific progress" (Gagne, 2004, p. 13; see also Coleman, 2004). Others (e.g., Cramond, 2004) stated that we do not need such definitional clarity. In addition to multiple definitions, lack of coherence, resistance to considering alternative definitions by various scholars, and even whether definitions are important. Another issue is that of world views, their prevailing paradigms, and the definitions these generate.

World Views

Following Pepper's (1942) work, Overton (1984) defined a world view as a conceptual lens, a general, abstract model of unlimited scope, characterized by "certain metaphysical and methodological commitments which provide a set of guidelines for the construction of specific theories and the employment of specific methods of procedure" (p. 7). A world view is a "set of ontological and methodological 'do's' and 'don't's'" (p. 7). The world is always perceived through the 'lenses' of some conceptual network ... which ... provide an inelimable 'tint' to what we perceive" (p. 10). A world view goes beyond a research program or paradigm and its application to scientific theories because it is broad and encompasses belief systems, values, biases and general attitudes as well as the way research is carried out. For Overton, only two such world views exist that are integrative: the mechanistic and the organismic (although Ambrose, 1998, argued that both contextualism and formism are also integrative). Both world views have certain indisputable aspects that Lakatos (1978) called the hard core, characterized by a root metaphor, and the positive heuristic, the source for research and derivation of theories. Theories that share these central notions have a natural relationship to each other and can be considered members of the same family of theories (Overton & Reese, 1973).

The mechanistic world view has a machine as its central metaphor and regularity and fixedness as its hard core, a positivist perspective (scientific method focused on hard empirical evidence to uncover physical and human events). The research heuristic is reductive: find the antecedent cause. Therefore, mechanistic paradigms and related definitions of giftedness and talent focus on the measurable, fixed traits, factors, or qualities in the individual, entity aspects.

The organismic world view has a living thing as its metaphor and a hard core that views the world as changing and dynamic. The research heuristic is holistic structure-function analysis to understand the pattern, organization, and direction of change. Paradigms and definitions derived from this conceptual lens focus on the development of giftedness and talent, contextual aspects, mutability, and transition points (Cohen, 2003).

While this organismic world view represents a major shift towards more post-positivist thinking (which values qualitative research, recognizes that observation is value-laden, questions the possibility of objectivity, does not separate knower and known, and considers human knowledge as mutable)—a becoming rather than being view, there are still problems, such as institutional and individual barriers to this paradigm (Cohen, 1998). One institutional barrier is that stated definitions of giftedness or talent often rest heavily on measures of intelligence or academic aptitude, related to the old measurement paradigm. Another is mixing and matching approaches from all four paradigms, detailed in the next section. Most problematic is the difficulty of changing beliefs in a field, which has been heavily positivistic. World views and the paradigms they induce act as conceptual blocks and create dogmatic insularity, researchers in one camp simply excluding those in another, based on their beliefs and assumptions (Ambrose, 1998, 2000, 2009).

Paradigms

A paradigm is the prevailing way of doing things and looking at things, a set of rules that must be followed (Kuhn, 1970). It is an established way of thinking within a discipline or field. A paradigm defines the orthodoxy, the accepted views and practices of a field. Therefore, a paradigm can also be a set of blinders that excludes possibilities (Cohen, 2000). Ambrose (2003b) described the connection between the zeitgeist, or spirit of the times, and prevailing paradigms, wherein beliefs and values of the time dominate ways of thinking and researching. Definitions, likewise, reflect the paradigm of the day. Ambrose noted that "the zeitgeist of an era, and the paradigms it spawns, are stubbornly resilient. Those whose ideas are too far beyond the mainstream often are ignored or rejected, regardless of their ultimate worthiness or brilliance" (p. 13). He added that an investigative paradigm locks in minds as vested interests prevail, engendering dogmatism. When a paradigm no longer adequately explains a range of phenomena, it loses power, requiring catalytic thinkers to overturn it.

Measurement Paradigm

Cohen (1998) described three paradigms in gifted education. The earliest focused on specific measurable traits and abilities, identifying those students who met the criteria, and providing a hodge-podge of programs or special classes after school or Saturday that separated the gifted from their less able peers. Giftedness was defined as quantifiable traits or aptitudes, as determined by IQ or achievement test cut-offs.

Needs-based Paradigm

A second approach began in the mid-1970s, perhaps as a result of PL 94-142 Education of the Handicapped Act, with a shift focusing on identified learning needs. A gifted child was defined as an apt learner having specific educational needs to be addressed. Programs and services were provided and students assigned to classes or services based on learning needs. However, this perspective largely remained connected to the measurement paradigm, as students were still measured for abilities and needs.

Talent Development Paradigm

Cohen (1998; Cohen, Ambrose, & Powell, 2000) noted that a third shift happened in the early 1990s called talent development. Treffinger and Sortore (1994) suggested that this new paradigm was linked to changes in general educational policy, changes in workforce requirements, new technologies, and new approaches to teaching and learning. They described three areas where the gifted/talented paradigm was shifting: (a) the nature of giftedness from fixed to modifiable; (b) identification from finding and labeling a fixed group of students to diagnosing needs and opportunities among many students; and (c) programming based on differentiating instruction through many and varied services that respond to needs, talents, strengths, or interests of students. Treffinger and Feldhusen (1996) described the talent-development movement as the successor to gifted education.

Particularly in the 1990s, this shift included definitional emphases on multidimensional talents and potential for excellence (Callahan, 1997; Feldman, 1992; Piirto, 1999b; Renzulli, 1995), multidimensional and context-sensitive conceptions of intelligence (Gardner, 1999; Perkins, 1995; Sternberg, 1997), and awareness of diversity and societal context (Ford, 1996, Ford & Harris, 1999; Frasier & Passow, 1994; Maker, 1996; Peterson, 1999; Piirto, 1999a). More recently the focus includes development of expertise, lack of predictability, and giftedness as malleable (Horowitz, 2009; Matthews, 2009; Subotnik, 2009). The most recent federal definition (1994) dropped the term "gifted" and focused solely on talent development (Stephens & Karnes, 2000).

Asynchrony Paradigm

Almost simultaneously with the talent development paradigm, the Columbus group[1] proposed asynchrony as a definition in 1991, with differences in the inner experiences of the self as central to the gifted child, particularly discrepancies, or being out-of-synch, between emotional and cognitive development, but also including other aspects such as the physical or perceptual (Lovecky, 1999; Morelock, 1992; Roeper, 1998; Silverman, 1997; Tolan, 1998). Morelock (1996) suggested that the self-as-gifted movement (giftedness as asynchronous development) or the Dabrowski group[2] (overexcitabilities and greater potential) competes with the talent-development movement. She offered a rapprochement (both giftedness and talent are distinct social constructs and both are educationally and psychologically useful), but self-as-gifted is not currently front and center as a paradigm in the field.

Fixed or Developmental Mindsets

In her popular book summarizing her many years of research, Dweck (2006) described two different mindsets, beliefs people hold about whether giftedness or talent are fixed traits or entities that need to be proven or they are potentials, changeable abilities developed through effort and hard work, a mastery orientation. These beliefs are much like the world views and paradigms described above, wherein the mechanistic and measurement approaches are more akin to the fixed entity beliefs, while the organismic and developmental approaches are more related to the growth or changeable perspectives. These mindsets influence how we define giftedness, talent, and creativity.

30 LeoNora M. Cohen

Potential or Actualized Gifts and Talents?

The recent paradigm movement towards talent development suggests a shift towards considering potential, rather than actualized gifts and talents reflected in the measurement paradigm. At the same time, the asynchrony (self-as-gifted) movement recognizes the uniqueness of children with considerable divergence in their levels of development and their overexcitablities, focusing more on the actualization or being of gifted. The most recent federal definition recognized that talent can be developed across socioeconomic and cultural groups, given appropriate experiences that support development of potential (Stephens & Karnes, 2000).

Paradigm Pulls

The two more current paradigms, talent development and asynchrony, as well as considerable vestiges of older measurement-and needs-based paradigms continue to compete with each other and are reflected in varied definitions that abound. Whether we have arrived at a final destination regarding paradigms is debatable, as is our ability to resist political pressures in considering what is good and right for gifted children, however they are defined. Advancing or receding with the prevailing winds, these competing paradigms are related to current national ideologies and world views, subject to dogmatic interpretations (Cohen, 2006).

Giftedness and Talent

Varied definitions include some aspects and exclude others. For example, some definitions focus on potential for exceptional ability, while others view giftedness or talent as innate and either present or absent. Measurement definitions exclude a developmental focus, while developmental definitions might exclude the notion of inborn talents.

How we define giftedness and talent determines who is selected and who is not, as well as the types of programs, services, and curricula, with dogmatic approaches prevailing. A student may no longer be identified as gifted if she or he leaves a state; for example, moving from Connecticut (top 5% cut-off) to Oklahoma (top 3%). States vary considerably in their definitions, ages of students considered, use of terms gifted and/or talented, types of abilities, and which version of the federal definition form the base for the states' definition (the majority of states still use the 1978 version and three use the 1972 version), leading to lack of consistency, affecting children's lives, and perpetuating old paradigms, with the 1994 federal definition largely ignored (Stephens & Karnes, 2000). Chosen definitions reflect powerful political, social, and economic forces rarely considered in dogmatic assumptions made.

Renzulli (1979, 1986) discussed four issues related to defining giftedness. The first is whether giftedness is based on a unitary concept of intelligence, or whether there are many kinds of intelligence. At issue here is the predictive power of tests, which are based on a unitary general notion (g). How to predict creative-productive giftedness in childhood is the issue. A second issue is the purpose for gifted education. Two purposes are commonly stated: to provide opportunities for self-fulfillment, and to increase the supply of individuals who can contribute to society by solving the world's problems. A third issue is a distinction between gifted and potentially gifted. The notion of potentially gifted implies that certain conditions are conducive to the development or emergence of giftedness. The fourth issue is whether individuals are "gifted" all the time, discussed below, as well as some additional issues.

Are Gifted Always Gifted?

Renzulli (1995, 2002) questioned whether individuals are "gifted" all the time or whether they display "gifted behaviors," which indicate a need for special support and services at specified times. Horowitz (2009) noted that a paradigm shift from defining giftedness based on IQ "involves relinquishing a reliance on categorical definitions—one individual is labeled permanently gifted; another, without any label, is assumed permanently not gifted" (p. 9). She described the need to adopt a developmental understanding, as giftedness is not innate or permanent, calling for a shift to a mastery lens.

> From a mastery model perspective, the identification of individuals having gifts and talents is determined by the presence of high-end, exceptional behavior in a specific domain with an initial emergence of those behaviors possible at different points in development and, once in evidence, not necessarily a stable characteristic of the individual's behavioral repertoire.
>
> *(p. 9)*

Similarly, Borland (2005) described giftedness as a dichotomous social construct (they are or are not gifted) that focuses on individuals situated in a particular place and time, arraying students on the basis of standardized test scores. It reflects "specific forces that served sociopolitical interests as they played out in the educational system ... a historical, not empirical, necessity" (p. 3). He noted that the giftedness construct serves interests of those controlling schools as well as perpetuating inequalities, particularly among diverse populations, and promoting elitism. Borland suggested that we should have instead a "gifted education without gifted children" (p. 12), differentiating instruction and curriculum for all students.

Whose Cultural Lens?

Whose cultural lens to use is an issue in defining giftedness. In Anglo Western cultures, many can agree on the gifts or talents to be developed. However, we have not done enough work (with certain notable exceptions, i.e., Ford & Harris, 1999; Frasier & Passow, 1994; Graham, 2009; Peterson, 1999) to know which should be developed, particularly in cultures that may share different values, nor have we acknowledged the different definitions of giftedness and talent from cultural perspectives both within the United States and outside.

Prism of Giftedness: Short Shopping Lists

We look for a short shopping list of abilities in our gifted children. Cohen (1991/1992) described this as looking through a prism for a small spectrum of light, while strengths that might be of great value to our world, such as peace-making, humor, altruism, honesty, or engendering are simply not visible. For example, Valdes (2003) found that bilingual children who serve as interpreters for their families are often exceptionally able and capable of high levels of accomplishment, but frequently are overlooked. Although there may be funds attached to any definition thereby rationing which children are served and limiting the categories of giftedness, a broader perspective could net a wider array of abilities that could truly benefit self and society.

Metaphors for Giftedness

In the United States, the metaphor for giftedness is often a gift, bestowed on an individual. Such a metaphor suggests that it might be unearned, students with gifts do not need any additional support because they have been given more than others, or that giftedness is given only to a worthy recipient, rather than any child. The term has different connotations in different nations. In Portuguese, the term for gifted is *superdotado,* meaning super-endowed. Again, endowed has a connotation of being given something that may be unearned. Giftedness or high achievement in Australia has been synonymous with *cutting down tall poppies* wherein those that stand out through their strengths need to be taken down a peg (Gross, 1999). In Spanish, the term is *adelantado,* meaning advanced, suggesting a metaphor of accelerated development. Any metaphor not only provides a rich possibility for term understandings but also can limit such understandings and exclude possibilities.

Talent Paradigm

As noted earlier, the talent development paradigm has taken center stage in our field but lacks specific links to social and emotional development. Two groups strongly disagree with the focus on success and achievement in this paradigm: the Dabrowski overexciteabilities group and the Columbus school asynchrony group (Roeper, 1998). Talent development may also be imposed from the outside. Roeper suggested that such development must come from the self, the inside. She questioned if it is imposed from the outside, does it lead to compliant, linear thinking? Below are other areas where dogmatism and talent development intersect.

The "I Want To" Factor

Talent development may not recognize the *I want to factor*. At the fourth world conference on the gifted in 1981, Alvin Nikolai, world-famous dancer and choreographer and winner of the presidential medal for his work in dance, described how he would not have been identified as having talent in dance as a young person because he did not have the right confirmation or form. "But I wanted to be a dancer, and so, a dancer I became!" Who determines what a talent is in the young and whether the *I want to factor* is more powerful or at least as powerful in talent development? As Feldman (1986) noted, an incredible set of coincidences have to come together to support extraordinary development. Allowing the child's interests and passions to guide us, their "I want to" factors, rather than the other way around may be the key (Cohen, in press).

Talent Development—for What End?

Roeper (1996) suggested that there is too much emphasis on becoming some-thing or developing one's talent for the benefit of society. This notion had certainly been part of earlier federal definitions of the gifted. She stated that the focus should be on the self-actualization of the gifted child and interdepen-dence. Grant and Piechowski (1999) suggested that the focus in education be about the inner agenda of the child. Cohen's (2009, in press) study of two cre-ative Brazilian brothers who had very different trajectories but who passionately pursued their own interests through their own internal fire to learn and excel led to rapid development in their domains of endeavor. Largely self-directed, each boy invested himself purposefully to master his art, predicting future adult accomplishment and eminence (see Subotnik & Olszewski-Kubilius, 1997; Winner, 1996). Defining talent needs to consider the purpose for talent devel-opment, lest presumptions be made.

Talent Development and Eminent Creative Development

Cohen (2009, in press) noted that there appears to be two major routes for developing eminence. One is the identification of and careful honing of a talent (or what Feldman, 1980, called a nonuniversal area of development) resulting in extraordinary performances or production, typical in such fields as playing a musical instrument, mathematics, chess playing, or a sport (see Bloom, 1985). The second considers development of creative eminence in the great renaissance types of thinkers, such as Darwin, Piaget, or da Vinci. This type of creativity Gruber (1989) described in his evolving systems approach as involving multiple talents, with creative borrowing from one field to another. In a talent-development paradigm the first trajectory is emphasized more, but talent development does not necessarily imply high levels of creative development. To reach creative eminence, Subotnik (2009) noted psychosocial variables are required to transition through three levels: from ability evidenced in talents to competency, from competency to expertise, and from expertise to artistry, each requiring investment of much effort. Assuming that identifying and developing talents in children leads to adult eminence is dogmatic.

Exposure and Social Class

Children living in poverty have little exposure to possibilities for talent development; thus chances of discovering their abilities and honing them through hard work and effort are very limited. Unfortunately, greater current focus in schools on core academic subjects and psychometrics have resulted in reducing diversity. These aspects function against developing talents in underrepresented groups, along with poverty, racial discrimination, family dysfunction, drug abuse, and so forth (Horowitz, 2009). Multiple barriers to aspiration development impede fulfillment and reaching of dreams (Ambrose, 2003a), and we do not address the underlying beliefs that create obstructions for these children.

Assessment and Measurement

Rather than tests of mental abilities, talent assessment often focuses on academic achievement tests. The obsession with measurement may ignore the child whose passion ignites a fire to learn and master or whose interests reside outside of school subjects (Cohen, in press). Whether such tests truly can predict talent development to very high levels is questionable, as there is coincidence of many other factors (Feldman, 1999). Definitions that have assessment or measurement of talents as central may not be linked later to eminence, which is often assumed.

Channeling and Honing Too Soon

If we are to be developers of talents, then our job as parents and educators is to find out what kids are good at and begin to hone their abilities. While there is nothing inherently wrong with this approach, we may limit children in their possibilities. If prodigious development is desired, talent development is certainly the right approach. Chess players, athletes, musicians all must have their talents developed rigorously to reach extraordinary levels when young. But if we want to develop renaissance thinkers, individuals who can make highly creative connections among fields, children probably need to be given the freedom to explore a variety of interests rather than being channeled too soon. As they request support, certainly it should be given, but perhaps talent development is not the route for all (Cohen, 1998, in press). How to define talent development without suggesting intensive training regimens for all is the danger.

Too Much Instruction: Taking Away Childhood

A parent of an extremely bright child came to talk with me about her son. She told me that when the child asked, "Mommy, what is Persian?" she was struggling to find a person to provide Persian lessons for him. She also told me that he was already taking Spanish, Hebrew, and French lessons, music classes, and receiving tutoring in other areas as well. This was an exceptionally bright child, but he was only 3½ years old! In her zeal to develop his talents, I fear too much was being imposed from the outside. At such a young age, the little boy was losing the opportunity to explore his own world and be in charge of his own learning. In the eagerness to ensure that children's talents are developed, too much instruction may be offered and joys of childhood taken away. The pressure on parents to have talented and gifted children needs examination, as this is a type of dogmatic societal demand that should be questioned.

Map of Knowledge and Ignorance

I have proposed mapping the domains of ignorance and knowledge in gifted education, a tool that might also serve to figure out where our field has become dogmatic and where it has not, relative to definitions as well as other issues. Kerwin's (1992) Map of Ignorance, with five key zones to consider about what is not known, along with the recognition that finding answers to each question zone moves us into the Domains of Knowledge (Cohen, 1996) could be a useful strategy for looking at the flow between knowledge and ignorance. Each time we learn something new, we also open doors for new questions, puzzles, disequilibrium, which moves us into the transition zone and down to the Map of Ignorance. When we recognize what we don't know and learn about it through research, practice, theory, intuition, or cross-cultural perspectives, we transition to the Domains of Knowledge. There is constant movement between these zones if we are open to learning and examining our assumptions. This map can help us consider what is dogmatic, particularly zones within the Domains of Ignorance, what we think we know we don't, what we think we don't know we do, and at what we deny or refuse to look at. Acknowledging our partial knowledge in the Domains of Knowledge likewise can help pinpoint areas of dogmatism in definitions, as well as other aspects of our field.

A MAP OF THE DOMAINS OF KNOWLEDGE AND IGNORANCE and DEFINITIONS © 2010 based on Cohen (1996) and Kerwin's Map of Ignorance (1992)			
The Domains of Knowledge What we think we know through:			
Practice	Theory	Intuition	Cross-cultural or Perspectives from other fields
State definitions of giftedness determine who is identified for gifted programs in a given state.	Giftedness is potential for verbal creativity; talent is potential for non-verbal creativity, actualized through stage escalation in Gowan's (1979) Periodic Theory of Creativity.	Different definitions of giftedness and talent make communication complex and difficult.	Giftedness is a culturally determined construct, based on values, practices, and perspectives of a given culture.
What we think we know through research:			
What we think we know well	What we think we know some	What we think we know a little	What we get mixed signals about
Gagne's (2005) research on his DMGT model suggests no single component stands alone, but the chance factor has the highest causal impact.	Giftedness is a dynamic construct that develops over time (Subotnik, 2009).	If the context changes, does the definition of giftedness change? I.e., with new technology, math calculations in the head vs. via computer.	Defining giftedness and talent as an entity or potential.
⬍ TRANSITION ZONE ⬍			
Map of Ignorance			
What we know we don't know		What we don't know we don't know	
How to make the gifted child become creatively eminent		(We cannot answer this except in retrospect)	
What we think we know that we don't		What we think we don't know that we do	
The connection between schoolhouse giftedness and creative productive giftedness.		World views and one's perspectives on definitions are entrenched	
What we deny or refuse to look at			
• Changing beliefs is difficult and complex. • Trying to define giftedness and/or talent with a person who has a different world view leads to frustration, misunderstanding, and blame.			

FIGURE 3.1 Mapping the domains of knowledge and ignorance with definitions of high ability. Adapted from Cohen (1996) and Kerwin's map of ignorance (1992)

However, Kuhn (1970) noted that a shift in the cycle of knowing and not knowing can be broken. If the bounds of what we know and don't know become crystallized, we cannot know outside these limitations, so paradigm change is needed. For example, if we are only able to consider definitions through a measurement or trait perspective, we may be so crystallized in our thinking that we cannot consider other possible definitions. This may be useful to explore what is known from research, practice, theory and intuition, while at the same time considering criteria for any definitions. Alternatively, starting with what we don't know about defining these terms could lead to breakthroughs and less dogmatic definitional perspectives. In Figure 3.1, the map is explicated with examples related to definitions.

Conclusions

To address several of these conceptual blocks in definitions of giftedness and talent, more work is needed to overcome these dogmatic barriers and to be able to "mean what we mean," come to greater agreement, and provide a quality education for able learners. Criteria for definitions proposed in this chapter as well as the Map of Knowledge and Ignorance may help. Here are a few additional possibilities.

1. Consider a focus on *optimizing development:* use information about how the brain grows and develops to enhance learning for all children, rather than identifying and labeling gifted or talented (see Clark, 1986; Haier & Jung, 2008; Kalbfleisch, 2008).
2. *Make education the gift.* Focus on the contextual aspects by investing a great deal more in *all* our children, so that every child receives an education so wonderful that he or she aspires to the highest levels, again avoiding identifying and labeling gifted or talented.
3. Focus more on the *gifted self* (psyche) (the current asynchrony paradigm).
4. *Creative intelligence*—Link the gifted/talented/creative individual with creative production/performance, using the mechanism of equilibration. This involves balancing of growth of self on the inside—more in the self model (Piaget's accommodation function) with adaptation to the outside—more the success or talent-development model (Piaget's assimilation function) (Cohen & Kim, 1999).
5. Recognize the interaction of several internal systems: the universal cognitive (Piaget's development in all children without instruction), the nonuniversal cognitive (specific aptitudes/talents that require special training and differ from one individual to another), the affective (emotional, motivational, personality characteristics, attributions, ethics, values), the physical (one's body and how it works), the perceptual, the system of purpose (deals with effort, task commitment, motivation, interest), and the intuitive and perhaps the spiritual systems with several external systems: the physical environment, social (the world of intimate others: home, school, peers), the cultural (world of the social group), the geopolitical system (geography, economics, politics, history, and time), as well as chance factors (Cohen & Frydenberg, 1996).

Notes

1. The Columbus Group was a group of international experts, theorists, parents, and practitioners who met in Columbus, OH in July, 1991
2. The Dabrowski group is a collection of psychologists, theorists, and researchers who have studied in depth Dabrowski's work on the overexciteabilities and on positive disintegration and apply it in the field of gifted education.

References

Ambrose, D. (1998). Comprehensiveness of conceptual foundations for gifted education: A world-view analysis. *Journal for the Education of the Gifted, 21,* 452–470.

Ambrose, D. (2000). World-view entrapment: Moral-ethical implications for gifted education. *Journal for the Education of the Gifted, 23,* 159–186.

Ambrose, D. (2003a). Barriers to aspiration development and self-fulfillment: Interdisciplinary insights for talent discovery. *Gifted Child Quarterly, 47,* 282–294.

Ambrose, D. (2003b). Paradigms, mind shifts, and the 21st century zeitgeist: New contexts for creative intelligence. In D. Ambrose, L. M. Cohen, & A. J. Tannenbaum (Eds.), *Creative intelligence: Toward theoretic integration* (pp. 11–31). Cresskill, NJ: Hampton Press.

Ambrose, D. (2009). World views. In B. Kerr (Ed.), *Encyclopedia of giftedness, creativity, and talent* (pp. 950–952). Thousand Oaks, CA: Sage.

Bloom, B. (1985). *Developing talent in young people.* New York, NY: Ballentine.

Borland, J. H. (2005). Gifted education without gifted children: The case for no conception of giftedness. In R. J. Sternberg & J. E. Davidson's (Eds.), *Conceptions of giftedness* (2nd ed., pp. 1–19). New York, NY: Cambridge University Press.

Callahan, C. M. (1997). Conceptions of talent. The construct of talent. *Peabody Journal of Education, 72,* 21–35.

Clark, B. (1986). *Optimizing learning: The integrative education model in the classroom.* Columbus, OH: Charles Merrill

Cohen, L. M. (1991/1992). A gifted education for all children. *Our Gifted Children, 6,* 22–30.

Cohen, L. M. (1996). Mapping the domains of ignorance and knowledge in gifted education. *Roeper Review, 18,* 183–189.

Cohen, L. M. (1998). Paradigm change in gifted education: Developing talent—is this the optimal set of possibilities? *Conceptual Foundations Newsletter, 6,* 3–5.

Cohen, L. M. (2000, November). *Talent development paradigm: A conceptual block? Conceptual blocks in gifted education.* Presentation at the National Association for Gifted Children Convention, Atlanta, GA.

Cohen, L. M. (2003). A conceptual lens for looking at theories of creativity. In D. Ambrose, L. M. Cohen, & A. J. Tannenbaum (Eds.), *Creative intelligence: Toward theoretic integration* (pp. 33–77). Cresskill, NJ: Hampton Press.

Cohen, L. M. (2006). Conceptual foundations in gifted education: Stock-taking. *Roeper Review, 28,* 91–110.

Cohen, L. M. (2009). Linear and network trajectories of creative lives: A case study of Walter and Roberto Burle Marx. *Psychology of Aesthetics, Creativity, and the Arts, 3,* 238–248.

Cohen, L. M. (in press). Natural acceleration: Supporting creative trajectories. *Roeper Review.*

Cohen, L. M., Ambrose, D., & Powell, W. (2000). Conceptual foundations and theoretical lenses for the diversity of giftedness. In K. Heller, F. Monks, R. Sternberg, & R. Subotnik (Eds.), *International handbook of giftedness and talent* (2nd ed., pp. 331–344). New York, NY: Elsevier Science.

Cohen, L. M., & Frydenberg, E. (1996). *Coping for capable kids* (revised American ed.). Waco, TX: Prufrock Press.

Cohen, L. M., & Kim, Y. (1999). Piaget's equilibration theory and the young gifted child: A balancing act. *Roeper Review, 21,* 201–206.

Coleman, L. (2004). Is consensus on a definition in the field possible, desirable, necessary? *Roeper Review, 27,* 10–11.

Cramond, B. (2004). Can we, should we, need we agree on a definition of giftedness? *Roeper Review, 27,* 15–16.

Dweck, C. S. (2006). *Mindset: The new psychology of success.* New York, NY: Random House.

Feldman, D. H. (1980). *Beyond universals in cognitive development.* Norwood, NJ: Ablex.

Feldman, D. H. (1986). *Nature's gambit.* New York, NY: Basic Books.

Feldman, D. H. (1992). Has there been a paradigm shift in gifted education? In N. Colangelo, S. G. Assouline, & D. L. Ambroson (Eds.), *Talent development: Proceedings from the 1991 Henry B. and Jocelyn Wallace National Research Symposium on Talent Development* (pp. 89–94). Unionville, NY: Trillium Press.

Feldman, D. H. (1999). A developmental evolutionary perspective on gifts and talents. *Journal for the Education of the Gifted, 22,* 159–167.

Ford, D. Y. (1996). *Reversing underachievement among gifted black students: Promising practices and programs.* New York, NY: Teachers College Press.

Ford, D. Y., & Harris, J. J. III (1999). *Multicultural gifted education.* New York, NY: Teachers College Press.

Frasier, M. M., & Passow, A. H. (1994). *Toward a paradigm for identifying talent potential.* Storrs, CT: University of Connecticut, The National Research Center on the Gifted and Talented.

Freeman, J. (2005). Permission to be gifted: How conceptions of giftedness can change lives. In R. J. Sternberg & J. E. Davidson's (Eds.), *Conceptions of giftedness* (2nd ed., pp. 80–97). New York, NY: Cambridge University Press.

Gagne, F. (2004). An imperative, but, alas, improbable consensus. *Roeper Review, 27,* 12–14.

Gagne, F. (2005). From gifts to talents: The DMGT as a developmental model. In R. J. Sternberg & J. E. Davidson (Eds.). *Conceptions of giftedness* (2nd ed., pp. 98-119). New York, NY. Cambridge University Press.

Gallagher, J. J. (1979). Issues in education for the gifted. In A. H. Passow (Ed.), *The gifted and the talented: Their education and development* (pp. 28–44). Chicago, IL: University of Chicago Press.

Gardner, H. (1999). A multiplicity of intelligences. *Scientific American, 9*(4), 19–23.

Gowan, J. C. (1979). The use of developmental stage theory in helping gifted children become creative. In J. J. Gallagher, J. C. Gowan, A. H. Passow, & E. P. Torrance (Eds.). *Issues in gifted education.* N/S-LTI-G/T Brief Number 6 (pp. 47–77). Ventura, CA: Ventura County Superintendent of Schools Office.

Graham, S. (2009). Giftedness in adolescence: African American gifted youth and their challenges from a motivational perspective. In F. D. Horowitz, R. F. Subotnik, & D. J. Matthews (Eds.), *The development of giftedness and talent across the lifespan* (pp. 109–129). Washington, DC: American Psychological Association.

Grant, B. A., & Piechowski, M. M. (1999). Theories and the good: Toward child-centered gifted education. *Gifted Child Quarterly, 43,* 4–12.

Gross, U. M. (1999). Small poppies: Highly gifted children in early years. *Roeper Review, 21,* 207–214.

Gruber, H. E. (1989). The evolving systems approach to creative work. In D. B. Wallace & H. E. Gruber (Eds.), *Creative people at work* (pp. 3–24). New York, NY: Oxford University Press.

Haier, R. J., & Jung, R. E. (2008). Brain imaging studies of intelligence and creativity. What is the picture for education? *Roeper Review, 30,* 171–179.

Horowitz, F. D. (2009). Introduction: A developmental understanding of giftedness and talent. In F. D. Horowitz, R. F. Subotnik, & D. J. Matthews (Eds.), *The development of giftedness and talent across the lifespan* (pp. 3–19). Washington, DC: American Psychological Association.

Kalbfleisch, M. L. (2008). Getting to the heart of the brain: Using cognitive neuroscience to explore the nature of human ability and performance. *Roeper Review, 30,* 162–170.

Kerwin, A. (1992, July). *Pilgrim's paradox: Learning through ignorance.* Featured presentation at Exploring Human Potential: Fifth International Conference on Thinking. Townsville, Australia.

Kuhn, T. S. (1970). *The structure of scientific revolutions* (2nd ed.). Chicago, IL: University of Chicago Press.

Lakatos, I. (1978). *The methodology of scientific research programmes: Philosophical papers* (Vol. 1, J. Worrall & G. Currie, Eds.). Cambridge, England: Cambridge University Press.

Lovecky, D. L. (1999). Identity development in gifted children: Moral sensitivity. *Roeper Review, 20,* 90–94.

Maker, C. J. (1996). Identification of gifted minority students: A national problem, needed changes and a promising solution. *Gifted Child Quarterly, 40,* 41–50.

Matthews, D. J. (2009). Developmental transitions in giftedness and talent: Childhood into adolescence. In F. D. Horowitz, R. F. Subotnik, & D. J. Matthews (Eds.), *The development of giftedness and talent across the lifespan* (pp. 89–107). Washington, DC: American Psychological Association.

Morelock, M. J. (1992). Giftedness: The view from within. *Understanding Our Gifted, 4*(3), 1, 11–15.

Morelock, M. J. (1996). On the nature of giftedness and talent: Imposing order on chaos. *Roeper Review, 19*, 4–12.

Overton, W. F. (1984). World views and their influence on psychological thoughts and research: Kuhn-Lakatos-Laudan. In H. W. Reese (Ed.), *Advances in child development and behavior, 18* (pp. 191–226). New York, NY: Academic Press.

Overton, W. F., & Reese, H. W. (1973). Models of development: Methodological implications. In J. R. Nesselroade & H. W. Reese (Eds.), *Life-span developmental psychology: Methodological issues* (pp. 65–86). New York, NY: Academic Press.

Pepper, S. C. (1942). *World hypotheses.* Berkeley: University of California Press.

Perkins, D. (1995). *Outsmarting IQ: The emerging science of learnable intelligence.* Old Tappan, NJ: The Free Press.

Peterson, J. S. (1999). "Gifted"—Through whose cultural lens? *Journal for the Education of the Gifted, 22*, 354–383.

Piirto, J. (1999a). Implications of postmodern curriculum theory for the education of the talented. *Journal for the Education of the Gifted, 22*, 324–353.

Piirto, J. (1999b). *Talented children and adults: Their development and education* (2nd ed.). Columbus, OH: Prentice Hall/Merrill.

Renzulli, J. S. (1979). *What makes giftedness: A reexamination of the definition of the gifted and talented.* Ventura, CA: Ventura County Superintendent of Schools Office.

Renzulli, J. S. (1986). The three-ring conception of giftedness: A developmental model for creative productivity. In R. J. Sternberg & J. E. Davidson (Eds.), *Conceptions of giftedness* (pp. 53–92). New York, NY: Cambridge University Press.

Renzulli, J. S. (1995). *Building the bridge between gifted education and total school improvement: Talent development research-based decision making series 9502.* Storrs, CT: National Research Center on the Gifted and Talented. (ERIC Document Reproduction Service No.388013)

Renzulli, J. S. (2002). Emerging conceptions of giftedness: Building a bridge to the new century. *Exceptionality, 10*, 67–75.

Roeper, A. (1996). A personal statement of philosophy of George and Annemarie Roeper. *Roeper Review, 19*, 18–19.

Roeper, A. (1998). The I of the beholder: An essay on the self, its existence, and its power. *Roeper Review, 20*, 144–149.

Silverman, L. K. (1997). The construct of asynchronous development. *Peabody Journal of Education, 72*, 36–58.

Stephens, K. R., & Karnes, F. A. (2000). State definitions for the gifted and talented revisited. *Exceptional Children, 66*, 219–238.

Sternberg, R. J. (1997). *Successful intelligence: How practical and creative intelligence determine success in life.* New York, NY: Plume.

Subotnik, R. F. (2009). Developmental transitions in giftedness and talent: Adolescence into adulthood. In F. D. Horowitz, R. F. Subotnik, & D. J. Matthews (Eds.), *The development of giftedness and talent across the lifespan* (pp. 155–170). Washington, DC: American Psychological Association.

Subotnik, R. F., & Olszewski-Kubilius, P. (1997). Restructuring special programs to reflect the distinctions between childrens' and adults' experiences with giftedness. *Peabody Journal of Education, 73*, 101–116.

Tolan, S. S. (1998). The lemming condition: Moral asynchrony and the isolated self. *Roeper Review, 20*, 211–214.

Treffinger, D. F., & Feldhusen, J. F. (1996). Talent recognition and development: Successor to gifted education. *Journal for the Education of the Gifted, 19*, 181–193.

Treffinger, D. J., & Sortore, M. R. (1994). *Programming for giftedness-A contemporary view* (Volume 1). Melbourne, Australia: Hawker-Brownlow.

Valdes, G. (2003). *Expanding definitions of giftedness: The case of young interpreters from immigrant communities.* Malwah, NJ: Erlbaum.

Winner, E. (1996). *Gifted children: Myths and realities.* New York, NY: Basic Books.

4

THE NATURE-NURTURE DEBATE REGARDING HIGH POTENTIAL

Beyond Dichotomous Thinking

David Yun Dai

UNIVERSITY AT ALBANY, STATE UNIVERSITY OF NEW YORK

The Nature-Nurture Debate Regarding High Potential: Ontological Commitments, Research Paradigms, and Policy Implications

In gifted education as well as in general psychological research, the issue of the extent to which high intelligence and specific talents reflect natural endowment versus enriched environmental experiences and dedicated efforts is vehemently debated (see Ericsson, Nandagopal, & Roring, 2007; Gagné, 2009; Howe, Davidson, & Sloboda, 1998). Although the answers may well depend on specific phenomena involved and no single theory can encompass the complexity and multitude of phenomena under investigation, researchers tend to adhere to their own entrenched ontological beliefs, epistemic stances, and research paradigms, resulting in polarized views regarding the nature and origins of high intelligence, extraordinary talent, and creative, eminent contributions.

Dogmatism is quite common in our social life because, for both cognitive and motivational reasons (e.g., self-serving beliefs for ego or some ulterior interests, the human tendency to seek certainty and simplicity), we are prone to seeking cognitive closure, often prematurely (Kruglanski & Webster, 1996), and succumbing to confirmation bias that perpetuates our existing beliefs by selectively attending to and memorizing confirming evidence while ignoring or filtering out disconfirming material (Baron, 2000). Dewey (1910/1997) pointed out this mental inertia and how it impedes progress:

> Facts and events presenting novelty and variety are slighted or are sheared down till they fit into the Procrustean bed of habitual belief. Inquiry and doubt are silenced by citation of ancient laws or a multitude of

miscellaneous and unsifted cases. This attitude of mind generates dislike
of change, and the resulting aversion to novelty is fatal to progress.

(p. 149)

Just as everyday memory is characterized by various forms of commission
and omission (Schacter, 2001), serious scholarship is not immune to premature
cognitive closure and confirmation bias. Discrediting others' criticism as ille-
gitimate or irrelevant is quite common in scholarly debates in psychology or
elsewhere (see Kahneman, 2003). Therefore, it is important that we understand
why is it that researchers, despite their claimed objectivity and open-mindedness, develop strong adherence to certain ideas and beliefs despite evidence to
the contrary. It is very likely that in "soft" sciences and ill-structured domains,
such as psychology, in which particular knowledge claims cannot be completely falsified and multiple theoretical perspectives and related methodologies
regularly co-exist, once a theoretical or ontological commitment is made, or a
research paradigm is adopted, it is hard to have a change of mind even though
alternative perspectives or models are apparently plausible and viable. Dogmatism is likely to happen when conditionality and complementarity of different theoretical perspectives give way to absolutism. Even in "hard sciences,"
paradigm wars are not unusual (Holton, 1981). It is likely that our enemy is
from within rather than from without; that is, our theoretical lens and methodological canons are by nature exclusive, if not looked upon from a higher-level
meta-perspective.

In this chapter, I attempt to uncover the inherent logic behind various forms
of dogmatism in the context of the nature-nurture debate on human potential.
I use two research paradigms to illustrate how our thinking and research, while
seeking logically coherent explanations and methodological rigor, tend to
exclude other possibilities. For the sake of this discussion, I distinguish between
the two forms of dogmatism based on their origins. Simply put, scientific dogmatism is derived from rigid adherence to a particular methodology or research
paradigm to the point of discrediting other methods or paradigms as fundamentally flawed or "unscientific," and findings as invalid. Social dogmatism, in
contrast, is derived from deeply entrenched belief systems regarding the human
nature and social conditions that resist changes despite evidence to the contrary.

In the sections to follow, I first delineate the recent nature-nurture debate
regarding the sources of high potential and achievement, and explain different underlying logics (conceptualization, methodologies) behind two research
traditions about the nature-nurture of high potential. I argue that a scientific
paradigm itself can lead to exclusivism in favor of nature or nurture accounts of
high potential in adhering to theoretical coherence and methodological consistency, potentially leading to scientific dogmatism and polarized views of the
role of nature and nurture. I then present social dogmatism as motivated, not
by paradigmatic thinking and inherent logic driving research, as is the case of

scientific dogmatism, but by an implicit belief system regarding the nature of human intelligence and the role of mental effort and motivation (e.g., persistence). I argue that one can get trapped with social dogmatism, either sticking to the notion of genetically based, fixed intelligence and an IQ-stratified society (what may be called a right-wing bias), or adopting a radical ideology of social equality that denies any biologically constitutional (including genetic) differences that contribute to variations in human development and accomplishments (a left-wing bias). Finally, I argue that both scientific dogmatism and social dogmatism lead to insulated, narrow views of the role of nature and nurture, and potentially have negative consequences on social practice and public policy. A more contextual, dynamic, developmental view of gifted potential would not only prevent dichotomous thinking, but also avoid either denying important individual differences in cognitive and affective functions, resulting in an educational policy that serves neither equity nor excellence, or holding a narrow, static, monolithic view of human potential, resulting in an educational policy that can deny many qualified individuals the opportunity to pursue excellence, and hinder the cultivation and utilization of diverse talents and potentialities.

The Nature-Nurture Debate and a "Paradigm War"

There is little disagreement among researchers and scholars regarding the role of nurture; even Einstein needed many years of dedicated efforts and necessary resources to develop the conceptual and analytic instruments for him to articulate his vision of the physical universe. Controversy starts with the role of nature, namely, is there evidence that natural talent or "raw" intelligence plays a major role in the development of high-level expertise and creative accomplishments. Gagné (2009) labeled the camp that supports a distinct role of natural endowment "Pronat" (pro-nature) and the camp that downplays the importance of natural ability or talent "Antinat" (anti-nature). In short, is giftedness a matter of "being" or "doing?"

The preponderance of evidence supports the claim that natural endowment matters. There is evidence that genetic makeup contributes to the variations in human abilities (e.g., Bouchard, 1997), that there are measurable individual differences in the rate of learning (e.g., Ackerman, 1988; Borkowski & Peck, 1986) and that differences in the ease of learning can be verified and explained as neural efficiency (e.g., Haier, 2001; see Dai, 2010, for a review). If we look at extreme cases at the high end of distributions, it is not difficult to conclude that there are cases of extremely high functioning individuals, or the gifted, domain-general or domain-specific. The question, however, is: Is high ability a necessary condition for development of exceptional competence? The logic of the Pronat is that if we can identify consistent individual differences in rate of learning and ultimate accomplishments beyond chance, and if these differences

can be linked to some ability differences that have a distinct genetic component, then the natural endowment argument is supported. The logic of the
Antinat is based on the demonstration there are proximal mediating mechanisms (various forms of "doing" accounts) leading to high-level expertise,
which are powerful enough to render any baseline differences insignificant and
baseline capacity explanations (various forms of "being" accounts) superfluous
(Ericsson, 1998, 2006).

Both arguments have supporting evidence, yet the respective evidence is
not so certain as to leave no room for alternative interpretations. In essence, the
Pronat fails to convince the Antinat that a certain form of "natural abilities" is
a necessary condition for developing high-level talent or expertise (given that
predictive relationships in behavioral sciences are merely stating a probabilistic
co-occurrence, not a necessity). Some Antinats even go as far as to claim that
many alleged "natural talents" amount to hearsay (e.g., Howe et al., 1998).
Conversely, the Antinat fails to convince the Pronat that rigorous training and
practice, strong commitment and effort, as well as the technical and social support of teachers, mentors, or coaches, are all it takes (i.e., constituting a sufficient condition) to become top-notch performers and major contributors to
a field, whether in academic, artistic, technical, or social-practical domains.

The nature-nurture tension not only reflects different ontological convictions and commitments (Lakatos, 1978), but also reveals inherent epistemological and methodological differences that "bias" researchers in favor of a
particular way of generating and interpreting data, and consequently making
particular claims. In the following section, I discuss two conceptual and methodological issues: prediction versus backtracking, and trait-level description
versus process-level explanation.

Prediction versus Backtracking

The placement/prediction approach is a prospective mode of inquiry used frequently in giftedness research: identifying a set of characteristics (IQ, SAT-
Math, etc.) as important predictors and verifying in the future whether they
indeed are associated with certain desirable outcomes. In this mode of inquiry,
giftedness is defined as aptitude or potential. Terman (1925) started this research
paradigm. More broadly, any studies that first determine predictor variables
that define a subgroup or subpopulation, and then use a set of criterion measures to validate the predictors (i.e., affirming predictive validity) belong to this
type of research (see the recent "Study of Mathematically Precocious Youth,"
Lubinski & Benbow, 2006). Most of the gifted-"nongifted" comparative studies also share this family resemblance.

In contrast to this prospective, predictive mode of inquiry, the looking-
backward approach used by the expertise researchers is a three-step "backtracking" mode of inquiry: (a) Superior expert performance is captured and reliably

documented in the laboratory using tasks representative of core activities in the domain; (b) process-tracing method and measures are used to identify mechanisms that mediate the reproducibly superior performance; and (c) the factors responsible for development of the mediating mechanisms are studied by retrospective analysis of training activities, such as deliberate practice (Ericsson & Williams, 2007). In short, the backtracking logic is that given an authenticated, reproducible high-level competence, what mechanisms best explain such a feat? In this research paradigm, "giftedness" is defined as high-level achievement or expertise.

Note that these two modes of inquiry do not necessarily contradict each other, but they do use very different criteria as "condition of satisfaction" for supporting their respective theoretical conjectures and arguments. For predictive studies in behavioral sciences, any prediction made is by nature probabilistic, not deterministic. Therefore, the threshold for a "proof" is low: As long as researchers establish some respectful predictive efficacy of certain predictor measures, they can declare success. Besides, longitudinal, predictive studies cannot be too specific about what outcomes will be and what intermediate processes are involved. In contrast, studies that use the backtracking mode of inquiry are more targeted and stringent, attempting to discover specific mediating mechanisms for a specific type of performance and level of attainment. They look at processes and contexts closely tied to performance conditions and therefore are biased toward identifying proximal rather than distal determinants, in favor of explaining the gifted accomplishment as a result of "doing" (nurture) rather than "being" (nature). Conceptually, these two paradigms use differing definitions of "giftedness," one as "aptitude," and the other as high-level achievement and expertise, leading to drastically different conclusions.

A thought experiment may help make it clear why the claims based on the predictive and backtracking modes of inquiry are not contradictory and both carry important practical implications: Suppose we have two teams of researchers, one on giftedness as potential (i.e., Pronat) and the other on giftedness as eminent achievement (i.e., Antinat). Both teams are equipped with the best research tools, measurement instruments, and material resources possible. The "giftedness as potential" team conducts an exhaustive talent search, aimed at identifying a group of children highly promising for a specific line of talent development and following them for 30 years. The "eminence" team starts a research project 30 years later, identifying a group of adults from the same population who have already achieved eminence in the same domain. The research question is: What is the likelihood that a child included in the first study also ends up in the second study? In other words, how well does high aptitude predict eminent achievement, and how large an overlap would we expect between the two groups of participants? Suppose that the early identification has a 50% success rate in predicting eminence in adulthood (i.e., there is a 50% overlap for the two groups of participants). The giftedness as potential team would declare a huge success, as the prediction rate is beyond the population base rate by enormous measure (of course, in actuality, the prediction rate would be much lower than 50%, as the identification instruments are not perfect, and life circumstances can vary and produce lots of "noises").

However, for the giftedness as eminence team, the 50% prediction rate is far less satisfactory, as the other 50% of eminence cases remain unaccounted for by the predictive measures. What is problematic is not the 50% "false positives" in the predictive study, those selected as gifted but failing to achieve eminence, as there were many life circumstances that might have derailed half of these children from achieving the level of competence of which they were capable. Rather, the issue is how to explain the accomplishments of those 50% of eminent individuals who were apparently not "gifted" in their childhood but managed to become top-notch performers and contributors and "unexpectedly" made their marks. There are two explanations: One is that the identification tools are fallible, leading to many "false negatives." This is a technical explanation, plausible but not pertinent here. The other explanation is that favorable social, educational, and developmental conditions, along with the right personality characteristics of the child, make some children grow to become more productive adults (Ericsson et al., 1993), even though they may not be as "gifted" as some of their identified "gifted" peers. The latter explanation lends support to the Antinat argument that nurture prevails over nature (Ericsson, 1998, 2006).

Thus, from the perspective of the eminence team, the best answers to the question of why some individuals end up in the "eminence" study is to study those individuals who have made eminent contributions, not the group of children who are identified and alleged as "gifted" and considered as most likely to make eminent contributions. One question here is: Were the half of gifted children in the predictive study who did not achieve eminence "gifted" in the first place? Because of the different definitions and criteria used, the two teams would have different answers. The gifted as potential team would say "yes" based on evidence of "aptitude," and the eminence team would say no (or at least remain agnostic) because they did not deliver what they promised. Thus, differing definitions and methodologies are responsible for the drastically different conclusions. However, their conclusions are not incompatible, in that findings of neither side invalidate findings from the other side. In addition to predictive versus backtracking mode of inquiry, different theoretical interests, trait description versus process explication, also lead to different conclusions.

Trait-Level Description versus Process-Level Explication

The Darwinian population thinking hinges on relative or comparative advantages through natural selection. Population thinking by nature characterizes "natural endowment" as a relative, rather than absolute, advantage. For that purpose, defining human traits and their norms and deviations is essential. Talent development, on a large social scale, can be seen as a cultural selection process whereby certain traits gain cultural distinction whereas others are marginalized or even die out. The social-cultural selection process is probabilistic rather than deterministic. Also, the well-known Matthew Effect makes the cumulative advantage argument more compelling than any strong nativist arguments that propose innate structural underpinnings of intelligence or talent (see Jensen, 2001; Ceci & Papierno, 2005; Papierno, Ceci, Makel, & Williams, 2005).

It is not accidental that a strong objection to giftedness as natural endowment came from experimental cognitive psychology, which characteristically favors process accounts of human behavior and performance rather than person accounts (Cronbach, 1957; Lohman, 2001). Trait-level description is often seen as lacking in scientific rigor when used to explain complex gifted and talented behaviors (Siegler & Kotovsky, 1986). More refined scientific procedures are advocated by expertise researchers, such as more objectively defined metrics for assessing excellence or superior performance, reproducible evidence of superior performance in controlled settings, and more controlled research on mechanisms and processes that explicate how one gains specific levels of competence over time (Ericsson, 1996, 2006; Ericsson & Williams, 2007).

It should be noted that process accounts do not always provide satisfactory answers to questions regarding trait differences. In the intelligence-component approach, for example, underlying components and processes identified by researchers often fail to account for a satisfactory proportion of variation in intelligence measures (see Lohman, 1994). One reason may be that molar-level trait measures and descriptions in the mode of population thinking on the one hand, and molecular-level cognitive processes in the mode of controlled experimentation on the other, simply represent different timescales and levels of human behavior and action (Newell, 1990). Without a clear solution to the problem of levels of analysis, they help create what might be called alpha and beta biases in respective research designs and data interpretation scheme. Alpha biases (or biases toward personal attributions) refer to a tendency to make dispositional attributions given a pattern of data (between–person variations). Thus, the correlation between intelligence tests and academic achievement is interpreted to mean a causal relationship when the two measures might just have a large overlap in construct representation or item similarities and redundancies. Beta biases (or biases toward process attributions) refer to a tendency to make more situational attributions. Thus, if the amounts of deliberate practice are correlated with high-level expertise in a monotonic fashion, then the two must be causally related, when there might well be a third variable accounting for both deliberate practice and achievement, such as aptitudes. The reason why biases can be built into our theorizing is that all these theoretical accounts, whether in favor of nature or nurture, are constructed, albeit empirically constrained, models of the realities, not realities themselves.

Summary

Thus far, I have been trying to make the point that researchers have their own biases and preferences in terms of ontological convictions and research paradigms. Specifically, they (a) use different criteria for giftedness or excellence and focus on different stages of development (aptitude versus eminent achievement); (b) tap into different levels of analysis (trait versus process); and (c) privilege a particular methodology and source of data.

These differences in research paradigms can be a source of scientific dogmatism in that they tend to grant some theoretical propositions and knowledge claims the status of "truth" to the exclusion of alternative, plausible explanations. In essence, a paradigm-based theory is by nature exclusive, lending itself easily to dogmatism when some theories gain more social-persuasive power and political clout than others in a Foucaultian fashion. As I argue later, multiple etiologies and pathways are the norm, rather than exceptions, in development of exceptional competence. Therefore, giftedness as potential may or may not convert to eminent achievement; and environmental and social advantages can also help some individuals not as "gifted" achieve eminence provided they are highly committed to do so. A key question here is whether biological constraints, if any, can be transcended by cultural tools and dedicated efforts; to what extent intelligence is malleable and culturally acquired, and one may further ask to what extent the brain is plastic, adaptive to experiences and challenges. On the flip side, the question is whether and to what extent high-level achievement is fundamentally constrained by the biological makeup. There is no way that research can answer these questions unequivocally. As I illustrated in the previous discussion of the two research paradigms, personal beliefs are naturally coming into play, including those deeply held assumptions about the nature of ability and effort.

Entrenched Beliefs about Ability and Effort, and Rhetoric of Social Justice

In his *Democracy in America*, de Tocqueville (1834/2004) made the following observation: "I recognize the general and systematic idea upon which a great people direct all their concerns. Aristocratic nations are naturally too liable to narrow the scope of human perfectibility; democratic nations, expand it beyond reason" (p. 62). There is a conservative view of human potential that predicts the inevitable emergence of a cognitive elite in a democracy over generations, based on genetic differences in intelligence (Herrnstein & Murray, 1994). There is also a liberal view that sees intelligence as pluralistic rather than monolithic, and diverse talents as widely and evenly distributed across the population so that "everyone is gifted in some way." An even more radical liberal view sees "men are created equal" as true not only in a political sense but also biologically. Thus, social dogmatism can take the form of conservatism as well as liberalism. As suggested by the above quote by de Tocqueville, a monolithic, nativist view of individual differences in intelligence would support a hierarchical, meritocratic society, whereas a pluralistic, malleable view of human intelligence would support an egalitarian, democratic society. To be sure, people can improve their abilities and develop their competencies if they are motivated to do so through proper education and training. But can people become gifted (e.g., making eminent contributions) through education and effort? Recent psychological research indicates the malleable and developing nature of human abilities (Lohman, 2006; Sternberg, 1999). However, it is likely that there are some threshold requirements, depending on the kind of work involved, the stages of development, and the level of attainment targeted (Lohman, 2005; Simonton, 2008). Research evidence does not support strong claims of either fixedness or infinite malleability of human traits, including those important for skill and talent development. This understanding has a direct bearing on the issue of equitable access and opportunity for excellence.

The Convictions of Efforts and Ability

The most simple and obvious form of the nature-nurture controversy is the respective role of ability and effort, reflected in Edison's famous dictum about the role of inspiration and perspiration. Dweck's (1999) research suggests that some people view intelligence or basic ability as fixed and others view it as incremental, improvable with efforts. However, folk belief systems tend to pit ability against effort rather than seeing them as reciprocal (Weiner, 1979). Like what is conveyed in the movie *Kung Fu Panda*, the secret ingredients for success turned out to be the audacity of self-beliefs, which have transformational power. However, the paradox is that while we can surely hone our skills and develop metacognitive insights, at least part of cognitive and intellectual functioning is opaque to our conscious awareness and control. In that sense, effectiveness of effort is constrained by ability. From a capacity point of view, intentional states such as desires and strivings are indeed constrained by ability; for example, not everyone can develop "the right feel" for a particular piece of music despite hard work; some children are more "musical" than others, and differences in the ease of learning can be quite striking at every phase of talent development. By the same token, only very few can achieve the kind of mathematical intuitions that John Nash had. Even motivational states, such as desires and interests (e.g., intellectual curiosity), are partly constrained by cognitive abilities.

However, it is also obvious that mental exertion (i.e., efforts) and reflective control of one's learning and performance significantly contributes to skill and knowledge development, even one's intelligence (Perkins & Grotzer, 1997). Unless one argues, along with Galton (1869), that level of effort a person is willing to exert, like ability, is also highly heritable and thus is merely nature's trick to make someone work harder than others, intentional states are a critical source of power to be reckoned with in their own right, rather than epiphenomenal or trivial, only to be explained away by some deeper "natural" forces.

A case in point is deliberate practice, which is strongly advocated by Ericsson (2006) as a main mechanism for skill development beyond the ordinary range. Deliberate practice by definition is a form of mental exertion involving intentionality (goals, beliefs, deployment of attention and efforts, etc.). Although Ericsson et al. (1993, 2007) acknowledged that deliberate practice can be constrained by both internal and external factors, including temperament, which is considered an enduring aspect of personality, there is a distinct situational aspect, as deliberate practice is a purposeful act to achieve desired goals (e.g., to win a music competition); it is not a "natural" part of human behavior as it is not intrinsically enjoyable and can easily break down without social support and determination (Ericsson et al., 1993).

A telling example is music training. Many Asian Americans in my local community (including myself) send their children for piano lessons. In most cases, playing piano was not a choice these children made. So, one would be hard pressed to argue that these children were born with musical inclinations. Suppose that this were a distinct pattern of upbringing not shared by other cultures; then, the overrepresentation of Asian students at the Julliard cannot be explained by arguing that children of the Asian descent are more musically talented, but could be explained by resorting to parental values and expectations, related childrearing practices, and consequently the children's dedicated efforts. The irony of a fixed ability mindset is that, in the face of setbacks, one's self-beliefs will dwindle, one's performance will be debilitated, leading to a self-fulfilling prophecy that the ability cannot be improved (Dweck, 1999, 2006).

Beyond Ability and Effort

The ability and effort accounts can easily miss the role of subjective, mental states as responsible for internalizing and transforming cultural knowledge in a personal way that makes creative contributions more likely (Gruber, 1986). An account of personal agency similar to what Gruber called organization of purpose or what Shavinina (2009) called unique kind of representation is needed to fully explain talent development. Are these subjective states nature or nurture, ability or effort? Maybe it is both, connecting both culture and biology. Maybe it is a form of agency in its own right, a force which, once formed, has its own momentum (Searle, 2004). What we still don't know is how much these intentional states are constrained by biology (e.g., natural ability) and to what extent they are empowered by culture (through its symbolic and technical tools) to the point of transcending the limits of whatever genes permit for human development. However, one thing is certain: if we refuse to get into this subjective realm for the fear of losing scientific objectivity, we will lose substantial explanatory power as far as exceptional human development is concerned, especially its culminating form: excellence and eminent contributions in arts and sciences, in technology and social enterprises.

Human Nature and Social Justice

Beliefs about the malleability (and the degree thereof) of human abilities have direct consequences for educational policy. If human potential is monolithic and fixed at birth (or even before birth), then it would support a social efficiency model of education, which categorizes and classifies children in early years as average, gifted, mentally retarded, and so forth, and educates them accordingly. A hierarchically structured society would be supported, with the cognitive elite ruling the cognitively inferior. If, on the other hand, human potential is extremely pluralistic and infinitely malleable, or, as some believe, humans are born equal biologically as well as politically, then everyone is or can be gifted in his or her way. Therefore, there should not be gifted education for only a very few. The former is a Hamiltonian elitist vision of human nature and social justice, and the latter a Jacksonian populist one, with power equally distributed among all. The truth, however, seems to lie between these two extremes, which supports a Jeffersonian model that provides equal opportunity for all but rewards people based on merits and excellence (Sternberg, 2000).

Beyond Dichotomous Thinking

Among other things, part of the problem we have an the nature–nurture debate, and its practical consequences of whether we should have gifted education at all, derives from polarized thinking; it serves neither the purpose of equity nor that of excellence. Neither excellence nor equity are served if a rigid definition of giftedness denies many otherwise qualified individuals the opportunity to pursue excellence, or if precocious and advanced students are educationally neglected in the name of equality. To maximally realize human potential for all, it is important to reconceptualize giftedness as contextually and dynamically shaped through learning and development in a complex, reciprocal interaction of nature and nurture (Dai, 2010; Dai & Renzulli, 2008). In the main, three principles need to be observed in gifted education provisions:

> *The Principle of Equifinality*
> Gifted children are not a homogeneous category. Etiologies as well as ontogenies of gifted development can be diverse. This principle stipulates that we should look at the current performance and proximal behavior of a child in deciding what kinds of educational provisions are appropriate for the child instead of seeking the Holy Grail of giftedness and using the abstract notion of aptitude such as general intelligence as practical guidance.

The Principle of Probabilistic Epigenesis

High potential or giftedness is not fixed at birth. Someone can become and demonstrate "giftedness" with the right kind of developmental interactions between genetic makeup and neural, behavioral, and environmental organizations. This principle stipulates that we should not just treat giftedness as a static quality sitting there to be identified once and for all, but rather as a dynamic quality that needs to be nurtured through rich environmental experiences and then identified in the active person-environment interaction. Competence we touted as "gifted" is itself an evolving quality in context.

The Principle of Emergence and Increasing Differentiation

Gifted development follows a trajectory of increasing differentiation in terms of competencies, self-concepts, interests, and values. There are emergent properties of the developing person that cannot be predicted from general traits manifested in early years. For example, doing extremely well in early years does not guarantee success later on with more challenging materials. Traits important in one domain may not be as important in another; traits important early on may not be as important in later stages of talent development. This principle stipulates that identification and curriculum differentiation should be based not on generic categories and criteria, but on increasingly differentiated and domain-specific, developmentally appropriate and responsive criteria and goals.

When these principles are followed, we will break loose the categorical approach to gifted education (with its homogeneity assumption), and consequently maximize the participation of education for excellence by the willing. We will be able to correct the traditional tendency to think of gifted children as born, not made, while in fact proper education and interventions play a major role for developing advanced competence in any domain, academic or otherwise. Equity will be achieved by attending and responding to all advancing needs of students, including the precocious and advanced students through continual assessment of what they are capable and what they are currently receiving. Ultimately, as I argue elsewhere (Dai, 2010), gifted education should change its focus from educating the gifted to educating for high-level excellence. In this sense, gifted education is not an isolated island, separate from the continent of general education, but an integral part of education with a distinct niche. Gifted education so conceived of will better serve the purposes of equity and excellence, not because it will appease the elitist criticism but because it is more in accordance with our understanding of the multifaceted and evolving nature of giftedness and the dynamic interaction of nature and nurture in talent development.

References

Ackerman, P. L. (1988). Determinants of individual differences during skill acquisition: Cognitive abilities and information processing. *Journal of Experimental Psychology: General, 117,* 288–318.

Baron, J. (2000). *Thinking and deciding* (3rd ed.). New York, NY: Cambridge University Press.

Borkowski, J. G., & Peck, V. A. (1986). Causes and consequences of metamemory in gifted children. In R. J. Sternberg & J. E. Davidson (Eds.), *Conceptions of giftedness* (pp. 182–200). Cambridge, England: Cambridge University Press.

Bouchard Jr., T. J. (1997). IQ similarity in twins reared apart: Findings and responses to critics. In R. J. Sternberg & E. L. Grigorenko (Eds.), *Intelligence, heredity, and environment* (pp. 126–160). Cambridge, England: Cambridge University Press.

Ceci, S. J., & Papierno, P. B. (2005). The rhetoric and reality of gap closing: When the "have-nots" gain but the "haves" gain even more. *American Psychologist, 60,* 149–160.

Cronbach, L. J. (1957). The two disciplines of scientific psychology. *American Psychologist, 12,* 671–684.

Dai, D. Y. (2010). *The nature and nurture of giftedness: A new framework for understanding gifted education.* New York, NY: Teachers College Press.

Dai, D. Y., & Renzulli, J. S. (2008). Snowflakes, living systems, and the mystery of giftedness. *Gifted Child Quarterly, 52,* 114–130.

Dewey, J. (1997). *How we think.* Mineola, NY: Dover Publications. (Original work published 1910)

Dweck, C. S. (1999). *Self-theories: Their role in motivation, personality, and development.* Philadelphia, PA: Psychology Press.

Dweck, C. S. (2006). *Mindset: The new psychology of success.* New York, NY: Random House.

Ericsson, K. A. (1996). The acquisition of expert performance: An introduction to some of the issues. In K. A. Ericsson (Ed.), *The road to excellence: The acquisition of expert performance in the arts and sciences, sports, and games* (pp. 1 50). Mahwah, NJ: Erlbaum.

Ericsson, K. A. (1998). Basic capacities can be modified or circumvented by deliberate practice: A rejection of talent accounts of expert performance. *Behavioral and Brain Sciences, 21,* 413–414.

Ericsson, K. A. (2006). The influence of experience and deliberate practice on the development of superior expert performance. In K. A. Ericsson, N. Charness, P. J. Feltovich, & R. R. Hoffman (Eds.), *The Cambridge handbook of expertise and expert performance* (pp. 683–703). New York, NY: Cambridge University Press.

Ericsson, K. A., Krampe, R. T., & Tesch-Romer, C. (1993). The role of deliberate practice in the acquisition of expert performance. *Psychological Review, 100,* 363–406.

Ericsson, K. A., Nandagopal, K., & Roring, R. W. (2007). Giftedness and evidence for reproducibly superior performance: An account based on the expert-performance framework. *High Ability Studies, 18,* 3–55.

Ericsson, K. A., & Williams, A. M. (2007). Capturing naturally occurring superior performance in the laboratory: Translational research on expert performance. *Journal of Experimental Psychology: Applied, 13,* 115–123.

Gagné, F. (2009). Debating giftedness: Pronat vs. antinat. In L. Shavinina (Ed.), *International handbook on giftedness* (pp. 155–198). New York, NY: Springer Science.

Galton, F. (1869). *Hereditary genius: An inquiry into its laws and consequences.* London, England: Macmillan.

Gruber, H. E. (1986). The self-construction of the extraordinary. In R. J. Sternberg & J. E. Davidson (Eds.), *Conceptions of giftedness* (pp. 247–263). Cambridge, England: Cambridge University Press.

Haier, R. J. (2001). PET studies of learning and individual differences. In J. L. McClelland & R. S. Siegler (Eds.), *Mechanisms of cognitive development: Behavioral and neural perspectives* (pp. 123–145). Mahwah, NJ: Erlbaum.

Herrnstein, R. J., & Murray, C. (1994). *The bell curve: Intelligence and class structure in American life.* New York, NY: Free Press.

Holton, G. (1981). Thematic presuppositions and the direction of scientific advance. In A. F. Heath (Ed.), *Scientific explanation* (pp. 1–27). Oxford, England: Clarendon Press.

Howe, M. J. A., Davidson, J. W., & Sloboda, J. A. (1998). Innate talents: Reality or myth? *Behavioral and Brain Sciences, 21,* 399–442.

Jensen, A. R. (2001). Spearman's hypothesis. In J. M. Collis & S. Messick (Eds.), *Intelligence and personality: Bridging the gap between theory and measurement* (pp. 3–24). Mahwah, NJ: Erlbaum.

Kahneman, D. (2003). A perspective on judgment and choice: Mapping bounded rationality. *American Psychologist, 58,* 697–720.

Kruglanski, A. W., & Webster, D. M. (1996). Motivated closing of the mind: "Seizing" and "freezing". *Psychological Review, 103,* 263–283.

Lakatos, I. (1978). *The methodology of scientific research programs.* Cambridge, England: Cambridge University Press.

Lohman, D. F. (1994). Component scores as residual variation or why the intercept correlates best. *Intelligence, 19,* 1–11.

Lohman, D. F. (2001). Issues in the definition and measurement of abilities. In J. M. Collis & S. Messick (Eds.), *Intelligence and personality: Bridging the gap between theory and measurement* (pp. 79–98). Mahwah, NJ: Erlbaum.

Lohman, D. F. (2005). An aptitude perspective on talent identification: Implications for identification of academically gifted minority students. *Journal for the Education of the Gifted, 28,* 333–360.

Lohman, D. F. (2006). Beliefs about differences between ability and accomplishment: From folk theories to cognitive science. *Roeper Review, 29,* 32–40.

Lubinski, D., & Benbow, C. P. (2006). Study of mathematically precious youth after 35 years. *Perspectives on Psychological Science, 1,* 316–345.

Newell, A. (1990). *Unified theories of cognition.* Cambridge, MA: Harvard University Press.

Papierno, P. B., Ceci, S. J., Makel, M. C., & Williams, W. W. (2005). The nature and nurture of talent: A bioecological perspective on the ontogeny of exceptional abilities. *Journal for the Education of the Gifted, 28,* 312–331.

Perkins, D. N., & Grotzer, T. A. (1997). Teaching intelligence. *American Psychologist, 52,* 1125–1133.

Schacter, D. L. (2001). *The seven sins of memory: How the mind forgets and remembers.* Boston, MA: Houghton Mifflin.

Searle, J. R. (2004). *Mind: A brief introduction.* New York, NY: Oxford University Press.

Shavinina, L. (2009). A unique type of representation is the essence of giftedness: Toward a cognitive-developmental theory. In L. Shavinina (Ed.), *International handbook on giftedness* (pp. 231–257). New York, NY: Springer.

Siegler, R. S., & Kotovsky, K. (1986). Two levels of giftedness: Shall even the twain meet. In R. J. Sternberg & J. E. Davidson (Eds.), *Conceptions of giftedness* (pp. 417–435). Cambridge, England: Cambridge University Press.

Simonton, D. K. (2008). Scientific talent, training, and performance: Intellect, personality, and genetic endowment. *Review of General Psychology, 12,* 28–46.

Sternberg, R. J. (1999). Intelligence as developing expertise. *Contemporary Educational Psychology, 24,* 359–375.

Sternberg, R. J. (2000). The concept of intelligence. In R. J. Sternberg (Ed.), *Handbook of intelligence* (pp. 3–15). Cambridge, England: Cambridge University Press.

Terman, L. M. (1925). Genetic studies of genius: Vol. 1, *Mental and physical traits of a thousand gifted children.* Stanford, CA: Stanford University Press.

Tocqueville, A. de (2004). *Democracy in America.* Washington, DC: Library of Congress. (Original work published 1834)

Weiner, B. (1979). A theory of motivation for some classroom experiences. *Journal of Educational Psychology, 71,* 3–25.

5

OVERCORRECTING

Spinning Out and Missing Many

Jean Sunde Peterson

PURDUE UNIVERSITY

My father gave me two admonitions when I was growing up on a midwestern farm. At that time, they were related just to driving: Watch the center line, and don't overcorrect on ice. The first was especially important. I did not "sit tall" and could not easily gauge how much space the car occupied. The second made great sense on ice-covered rural roads—for many months each year. There was always the threat of "spinning out"—even without overcorrection. I applied both guidelines often. Gradually, they became useful metaphors for many contexts—especially the second one.

Overcorrection in the Field

Education for highly able children and adolescents has been affected by dogma that has evolved over several decades, continues to be reinforced in the field, and is resistant to change. There have been significant repercussions. One is that educators and scholars have, perhaps not intentionally, avoided exploring and responding to aspects of high ability that are not advantageous, not assets. That neglect actually may have contributed to negative public perceptions and to significant gaps in services and in students served; it may also have been both cause and effect of dogma that persists.

The prevailing mindset is focused on demonstrated motivation (in ways that are familiar to teachers) to achieve academically and on measureable academic success (Peterson & Margolin, 1997). This mindset ignores the complex variation in tempo of various aspects of childhood and adolescent development, especially for gifted children (Silverman, 1993). As a result, countless highly able kids are not served or are not served appropriately (Peterson, 2006). Thus, they are not supported and affirmed for their abilities during a time when they cannot or will not, for reasons related to development or life circumstances, perform in the classroom at expected levels. In addition, untidy, complex, and even negative aspects of giftedness are not acknowledged, addressed, or examined.

An Applied Perspective

I came into the field referred to as "gifted education" through practice. I continue to look through teacher and counselor lenses. From the outset, I sensed an overcorrection in the field: an unacknowledged narrow, positive spin that invites charges of elitism, renders advocacy for addressing real and urgent concerns ineffective, and is presented, dogmatically, as "the way it is." I recognized the needs of highly able kids in my English classes and, later, during six years of development-focused small-group work (approximately 1,400 meetings) with approximately 500 secondary-level gifted students. However, I was uncomfortable with how needs were framed in the field, especially the implicit and explicit emphasis on motivation and achievement.

A more-and-faster emphasis in programming seemed not to attend to the affective dimensions of giftedness; to the reality that highly able students are highly idiosyncratic; that social and emotional development has impact on academic performance and is important to life satisfaction; that even the most poised achievers can struggle with developmental tasks; and that many hide dark struggles. Many of the best writers in my classes were academic underachievers. Yet some of them seemed more comfortable with themselves than were some high achievers. I sensed that some were farther along in identity development, perhaps because they had struggled to define themselves apart from their parents and had thought more independently than some compliant high achievers had. My later follow-up studies of achievers and underachievers (Peterson, 2000a, 2001, 2002) confirmed that it is difficult to predict educational trajectories. Some stellar graduates did not complete their first year of college, although some did later. Some underachievers remained content with Bs instead of As in college, but ultimately had satisfying careers and family situations. Some did better in college than in high school—41%, actually, in the 2000a study.

The field of gifted education often seems to be dismissive of highly able underachievers. Gifted-education teachers and coordinators drop them from special services, instead of moving into a different delivery mode or compassionately affirming them when aware of horrendous life circumstances. Researchers may study them, but deny that they are "gifted," reflecting a type of hypocrisy. Dogma rules. High academic achievement is often the only currency. If a child with impressive intelligence does not demonstrate it in ways educators view as "gifted," it may not be validated. Having no accommodation may have lifelong negative repercussions. The overcorrection is represented in dogmatic assumptions about who is worthy of attention.

Values, Agendas, Judgments, and Impact

To apply the idea of overcorrection to the focus of this chapter, I first refer to some experiences that underscore several points: the role of dominant-culture values in problems related to identification for services and how services are conceptualized; the role of research methods and foci in helping dogma to prevail; and the impact of assumptions about what gifted children need when in difficult circumstances. The last experience suggests that serious ramifications are possible when bright children are "left out."

A Study of Cultural Values

After a qualitative study of the language of dominant-culture middle-school teachers as they nominated children for a hypothetical program for gifted youth (Peterson & Margolin, 1997), I conducted a parallel study (Peterson, 1999) in five minority-culture communities (African American, American Indian, Latino, recent-immigrant Asian, and low-income White). The themes that emerged in both studies were essentially definitions of *gifted*. Each minority group's major themes differed from other groups' themes, and, collectively, those themes differed dramatically from the teachers' themes, whose five main themes were behavior, verbal ability and assertiveness, work ethic, family status, and social skills. Teacher sub-themes (e.g., performance, leadership, awards) reflected a major dominant-culture value: individual, conspicuous, competitive achievement (Spindler & Spindler, 1990). Contrasting themes in the non-mainstream groups' language were, for example, contribution to community, arts as expression (not as performance), adaptation, handiwork, wisdom, and non-bookish knowledge. A common theme in the non-mainstream groups' language was discomfort with "showing what you know" (particularly in the Latino and American Indian communities), a particularly important finding, since several teachers would not nominate anyone who did not "contribute."

Once, after I had presented the findings of that study at a conference, the audience noted that the teacher themes, if reflected in selection criteria, might leave out children who misbehaved, were hyperactive, were recent immigrants, showed a great work ethic only at home, had abrasive personalities, were from low-income families, or were inclined to be quiet out of respect to teachers. Someone also noted that intelligence of any kind (cf. Gardner, 2004), with the exception of verbal, was not a major theme. While they believed that dominant-culture values made sense in the interest of acculturation, they also noted that programs would need to change if non-mainstream gifted children were to be embraced. Someone mentioned that advanced classes might not engage bright students from cultures that do not value competitive performance, students whose learning preferences do not fit with teaching styles, students unable to concentrate because of difficult life situations, students for whom English is a new language, and students who are uncomfortable when sitting for extended periods of time.

Just before the conference session concluded, someone raised a hand and said, angrily, "The people in those other cultures—they just don't get it." Without meaning to, she had just represented the troubling perspectives the study had illuminated. Prevailing dogma reflects narrow, dominant-culture values.

What cultural groups value and respect has important implications for identification, for how programs engage and validate children from non-mainstream groups, and for formulating and following inclusive program philosophies. Decades-long discussion about underrepresented populations, multiple criteria for selection and inclusive philosophies have not generated significant breakthroughs. Cultural value differences may be a key.

Other Populations Not Fitting Common Stereotypes

As a researcher, I am interested in how gifted youth *experience* development, and how various phenomena intersect with giftedness and development. I often use qualitative methods.

Qualitative studies do not purport to offer "truths." The goal is deep *exploration*, not confirmation or broad generalizability. The emphasis is on the phenomenological lived experience, when giftedness is an overlay, of particular phenomena, such as underachievement, bullying, homosexuality, abuse and other trauma, severe conflict with parents, depression, resilience, and developmental impasse.

When I serve on committees outside of my area for dissertations involving qualitative methods, I often observe that students are guided firmly by a theory of interest, hoping to confirm assumptions. The committee chair might actually be uncomfortable with thoroughly open-ended exploration. In such work I am reminded that venturing outside of familiar territory can be unsettling, perhaps especially for veteran scholars. I think about the need for open-ended exploration in the face of entrenched dogma. I understand the need for students to be strong in quantitative methods, but I think about the role of dissertation work and doctoral students' later research in potentially contributing to conceptual narrowness related to giftedness and services.

I have also perceived discomfort in the field with complex dark (i.e., sobering) areas, which often are best explored initially with qualitative methods. Young researchers may not want to risk loss of affection and respect within their chosen field by venturing into areas that do not reflect mainstream thought about giftedness. Journal editors and reviewers may also vary regarding support of studies and findings that do not reflect prevailing dogma.

Parenting the Dark Side

After a presentation about social and emotional development, a parent told me that her pre-teen had experienced the death of a close relative, had gone downhill academically, had lost interest in activities, and had withdrawn from peers and even from family. The parent wanted to tell me that the problem had been resolved; the child was scheduled to enter a residential school for gifted children, where there would be greater challenge. The parent then abruptly left. Perhaps the comments were meant to underscore that giftedness is not as complicated as I had just made it.

I assume the child was grieving. The process and duration of active grief differs from person to person; grief can affect cognitive ability for a time; grief often looks different in children than in adults; a sensitive child might be reluctant to add extra sad layers to parents' own bereavement by communicating distress directly; and grief can certainly affect the ability to concentrate. I hope the new school had a nurturing environment. I hope the school paid attention to the whole child, not just to academic challenge. Children do not always need more-and-faster academic work, certainly in response to troubling life events, but that can indeed be the default response for anxious parents who want to control the future. Problematic dogma may have contributed to this outcome, encouraging a narrow, non-holistic, achievement-focused "solution."

Dogmatic Warping

I once observed a very bright seventh-grader when supervising an intern in a middle school. I could easily imagine him as a young radical doing high-profile damage to "the government," a school, or recent immigrants. Parental modeling had instilled an ugly, thorough bias toward non-White populations. I recognized his need to make sense of the rape of a relative and a poor economy. He articulated his world view matter-of-factly, apparently not meaning to upset anyone. He appeared to want to explain what he had figured out.

He represented asynchronous development: advanced cognitive ability, albeit with dichotomous thinking and limited access to print material beyond a grade-level social-studies textbook; social skills lagging to the extent that peer relationships were difficult and expulsion was imminent; and emotional rigidity. He reflected what I have often seen in gifted youth as a counselor: a low tolerance for ambiguity and a need to have a firm, prematurely foreclosed sense of how life works. His socioeconomic status and violent behavior may have precluded any school-based attention to his gifted mind. It is possible that no one had engaged him enough to recognize it.

He could have benefited from being able to interact with culturally and socioeconomically diverse students in a multi-faceted program for gifted kids. His social and emotional development might be affected positively, depending on program content and teacher. He might acquire a complex knowledge base over the next several years if encouraged toward highly capable, broad-based teachers. Being recognized for abilities and having positive interaction with teachers might prevent social withdrawal and redirect intelligence. But dogma, a parent's and perhaps educators' as well, is likely to preclude participation in, and exposure to, other kinds of thinking. He might be attracted to demagogues later in order not to have to sort through complex, competing messages and to avoid mental fatigue from not knowing anything for sure.

Programs for gifted kids should reach out to students like this boy, who has carefully, methodically, and purposefully constructed a world view. Much less methodical students also need an enriched, multidimensional curriculum to help them develop broad awareness. In the current educational climate focused intensely on reading and math, it is important for gifted-student programs to think "horizontally," instead of (or in addition to) an exclusively narrow, dogma-prodded, more-and-faster curriculum. Including solid emphasis on social studies can help bright minds embrace complexity and tolerate ambiguity. Encouraging service can connect students to a world they may not be familiar with (Peterson, Duncan, & Canady, 2009; Renzulli, 2009; Webster & Worrell, 2008). In a study of the impact of life events and experiences on high-achieving gifted students (Peterson et al., 2009), service projects were positively life-altering.

Factors Contributing to Overcorrection

Undoubtedly, several factors have contributed to overcorrection in the field. Some possibilities are particularly noteworthy: perceived threat, coupled with discomfort with associating negative life experiences or outcomes with giftedness, concern about image, invested adults' preoccupation with what affirms them, and an emphasis on measurement.

Dogma in Response to Threat

When a car begins to slide, the threat of a spin-out into a ditch or another vehicle can generate overcorrection. Perceived threat to the field of interest here may have resulted in an overcorrection in the form of emerging dogma, reflected in a narrow, exclusionary focus on giftedness as being synonymous with motivation for high achievement and high academic achievement itself. This focus is often evident in selection processes for programs and in program curriculum.

Perhaps early stereotypes (e.g., physically weak, emotionally fragile, "early-ripe, early-rot" gifted children and teens) precipitated a perceived need to offer images of gifted individuals who were healthy, strong, handsome, and socially smooth individuals. Terman and Oden's (1951) early findings served as one correction. As the field of education for gifted youth became established and sought scholarly respect, "truth" in the form of quantitative findings attesting to strengths and focusing on measureable characteristics was probably a useful currency.

Protection of Image

Protection of image might also have played a role—image related to giftedness, the field, individual teachers, coaches and directors, families, and students. When proud, invested adults considered what was at stake, it makes sense that the emphasis was on giftedness as asset, strength, and insurance for the future. Families experiencing dark aspects of giftedness may have believed that no one would be sympathetic. Denial might also have played a role—as if giftedness precludes difficult or horrendous life circumstances.

When the public wrapped its collective head around positive abstract and concrete images representing the construct of giftedness, images of dereliction and destitution, burden and pain, addiction and delinquency, and neglect and trauma were likely not what came to mind. Positive stereotypes, based on the type of high-ability students who were identified, served, studied, and written about, became entrenched. When nonstereotypical, "deviant" gifted individuals received media attention for creative achievements or for dysfunction, perhaps they were not viewed as "normal gifted" (cf. Piirto, 1998; Wells, Donnell, Thomas, Mills, & Miller, 2006).

The Role of Invested Adults

It makes sense that invested adults felt affirmed by bright, eager students who demonstrated their impressive talents. In arguments for financial support for program resources, the emphasis was probably on high-powered students who needed "more," and this thrust made sense because ability and achievement could be competitively measured. Advocacy implied that such services were "deserved," rather than "urgently needed" for well-being. The positive image became established (Margolin, 1996). Supporters felt validated for their investment or their genes. Underachievers did not reward invested parents or teachers with impressive performance.

An Emphasis on Measurement

Last, the measurement emphasis in the field may have both contributed to high-impact dogma and simultaneously been an outcome of it. The non-asset side of giftedness is not easily measured. The dearth of counselors, clinical psychologists, and family therapists active in the field, especially those involved in research, likely has also limited attention to non-stereotypical complexities. If qualitative methods are not used to explore the subjective experience of giftedness as connected with normal developmental tasks, life events, difficult circumstances, lack of motivation for academic work, competition, doubts, substance abuse, eating disorders, and depression, for instance, it is possible that teachers, counselors, and parents will lack pertinent information to apply in their work with gifted kids. In addition, surveys used to study giftedness will not capture a representative range of complex attitudes, beliefs, concerns or experiences. Theory confirmation may trump theory generation. Without qualitative exploration, scholarly activity may in fact become ever narrower regarding what is deemed worthy of study. Wanting "truth," researchers who are uncomfortable with ambiguity and who need to be productive are unlikely to venture into unfamiliar savannah without a secure vehicle. Accepting a measurement sense of giftedness, gifted students themselves may feel defined almost entirely by scores and grades. Teachers and even parents may not see much beyond these.

The Effects of Overcorrection

What has resulted is pervasive dogma. Characterizing it are high achievement as defining *giftedness*; narrow identification criteria, conceptualizations, and programming; a narrow research range; impaired advocacy; and little attention to social and emotional development.

Narrow Identification, Conceptualizations, and Programming

Educators, including specialists in gifted education, may not view low-achieving gifted youth as "gifted." Program philosophy might mention employing multiple criteria. However, reflecting narrow dogma, using standardized group-testing scores for efficient screening and not seriously considering error ranges make cutoffs clean. Certainty means that decisions are less likely to be challenged. The default curriculum is acceleration, heavier reading assignments, more writing, and possibly uncreative teaching approaches. Motivated students are likely to perform well, regardless, if co-existing disabilities do not interfere.

Missing or "Failing" a Program Unfortunately, highly intelligent students who are in difficult circumstances at home, unmotivated, unable to learn in mainstream ways, or otherwise not on solid footing in school might not be affirmed for their abilities if they are neither identified nor comfortable in programs for gifted students. When low-performing gifted students' abilities are not recognized and their intellectual needs not addressed, they may view themselves as "not who programs are for." Even when a broad net is cast, if the ultimate goal is excellent academic achievement (i.e., "making them gifted"), the emphasis stays narrow. Programs geared only to high achievers are probably not a good fit for gifted low-performers, who must fit the program, not vice versa. Even when a high achiever is brought into such a program, but later, for complex reasons, does not perform well, the gifted label and eligibility for services may be withdrawn. Maybe even more crucial than acceleration for high achievers is creative programming for gifted students who either cannot or will not achieve academically during a particular developmental stage. Such programming may be not only the sole support for what they are capable of, but also essential for their making sense of self and for general well-being.

A Narrow Research Range

The overcorrection has precluded systematic attention to factors associated with poor emotional health. Scholars may not perceive that how giftedness affects responses to negative life events, especially those leaving deep scars, is worthy of study. When unusual areas in the field are indeed studied, a measurement mindset might preclude open-ended exploration and, as Worrell (2009) noted, appropriately multivariate explanations. The relative rarity of qualitative research methods to study giftedness has limited exploration of complex psychological phenomena, social experiences, and troubling emotions. Pertinent stones then remain unturned, test scores reign, single scores are used to define students and predict their futures (Worrell, 2009), and narrow stereotypes continue. Gifted individuals who struggle may be viewed as anomalies—uncomfortably.

The prevailing dogma does not encourage exploration of the lived experience of gifted youth who, for example, perform poorly academically, demonstrate remarkable talent or productivity in a non-academic interest area, or are remarkable *former* underachievers. Other populations that have had only scant attention are homosexual or bisexual gifted youth; gifted individuals who have overcome great adversity, abuse or neglect, or natural disasters; and high achievers in chaotic lives for whom achievement is or was the only controllable aspect of life. Not much is known about how gifted youth experience depression, obsessive-compulsive disorder, oppositional defiant disorder, attention-deficit disorder, Asperger syndrome, post-traumatic stress disorder, eating disorders, specific negative life events, grief and loss, and substance abuse, for instance. Moving away from narrow measurement- or measureable-achievement-oriented research might yield information that could change lives of those who struggle, including those whose high achievement and tidy exteriors belie extreme emotions related to normal developmental hurdles. Such psychoeducational information might help them make sense of themselves and help their counselors and psychologists differentiate approaches.

Gifted students who are uncomfortable in programs or courses geared to highly motivated students and who do not fit common stereotypes are not likely to be in the research samples most convenient to study—at least in numbers representing their presence in school populations (Peterson & Moon, 2008).

Therefore, statements beginning with "Gifted children are …" are problematic when based on studies organized around narrow assumptions and samples. If *gifted* means "highly motivated high achievers," that needs to be clear, and scholars need to mention that high-ability students who do not fit that definition should be involved in similar or comparative studies.

Broad samples are not easy to access, of course, and finding unidentified gifted underachievers or gifted students with learning disabilities, for instance, usually requires laborious perusal of school files, difficult for outsiders to access. Fundamentally, even informal statements about giftedness need to describe what they are based on, need to be tenuous, and need to be framed according to how giftedness is being conceptualized.

In addition, voices from outside of the field are not overtly invited in—from anthropology, sociology, systems, philosophy, clinical psychology, school and mental health counseling, marital and family therapy, social work, and medicine, for example. New perspectives will not invigorate the field if scholarship is informed only from within. The small world of giftedness-related scholarship may become increasingly narrow, simply perpetuating assumptions, with scholars not looking beyond default references. The fields mentioned above can also be enriched by giftedness scholars. This book itself represents a rare collection of voices from within and "without."

I have learned, through collaborative work with Dutch counterparts, that their monograph-like publications of scholarly work are meant to "*begin* the conversation," instead of serving as an end point. When studies related to giftedness appear in refereed journals, perhaps only a few engage in direct dialogue with the original scholar. The Dutch may generate broader impact, hear more disparate voices, and remain more exploratory than U.S. scholars.

Impaired Advocacy

I have heard convention presenters say that others "just don't understand gifted kids." Aside from my immediate thought that it makes sense that 2%–5% of the population isn't readily "understood" by the other 95%–98%, I am uncomfortable with the externalization of the problem (i.e., not self-reflecting about one's own responsibility). As I frequently say to my school counselors-in-training, if colleagues "just don't understand the work of a counselor," it is the counselor's responsibility to take advantage of formal and informal opportunities to educate colleagues about ethics, basic tenets, and the program they have developed. It is unwise to assume that those without counselor training should understand counselor roles without pertinent information, visibility, posting a packed weekly schedule, and additional clarification as needed. Similarly, stakeholders need complex research-based, conceptual, and clinical information related to giftedness. Patiently educating school personnel, without viewing lack of understanding negatively, is the key. Displaying student products, explaining program curricula and schedules, and working closely with teachers to differentiate curriculum can help with advocacy. Stridently blaming "the system" may be driven by dogma.

Nuanced messages are important. Concerns are complex, reflecting characteristics and burdens associated with giftedness. They go beyond the need for a more-and-faster curriculum. The public understands the needs of children with disabilities. Careful language and tone, coupled with genuine concern about the whole child, can make the case for services at the other end of a bell curve of school-oriented cognitive ability as well, without rocking teachers back on their heels by indicting them. As a result of less narrowness of perspective, the conversation can begin about differentiating instruction, curriculum, and counseling.

Recognizing Barriers   When dark, burdensome aspects of giftedness are part of the shared information, and if social and emotional concerns are competently explained and attended to, charges of elitism tend to diminish, support emerges, and resistant colleagues may even offer their services (Peterson, 1993). When common, positive stereotypes prevail, teachers, administrators, legislators, and state officials may not be supportive of crucial services. Moving away from the dogma that narrowly defines giftedness as "high achievement" and "high motivation to achieve," and attending to more than just performance, can generate compassion in colleagues, more sensitive attention to gifted students who are not achieving well, and fewer charges of elitism. "Resistance" in counseling may reflect ignoring a client's "readiness to work" and a need to redirect. The same may be true when hoping to address needs of highly able students collaboratively. Speaking with a "furrowed brow" about threats to well-being may generate compassion not just in teachers, but in legislators as well. Moving away from dogma and acknowledging complex assets and burdens related to giftedness can help when advocating for services.

Fear of the Dark   What makes attention to the asset-burden paradox, beyond academics, uncomfortable for some invested adults—and even to some gifted students? It is puzzling that advocacy typically ignores whole-child aspects, since these represent what people outside of the field might be able to relate to more easily than to language about high-powered academics and amazing accomplishment. One unintended message might be that exceptional talent is intertwined with arrogance and that gifted kids simply want "more." Another is that they are not part of broader humanity—even in facing universal developmental tasks, albeit with a qualitatively different experience.

Embracing a New Curriculum Component   When a five-year study of the implementation of a teacher-led, small-group social/emotional curriculum at a school for gifted children (Peterson & Norman, 2010) began, some were angry about lost study time, some argued that the groups should be only "for kids with problems," and a few felt "insulted" by the emphasis. By the fourth year of the study, with curriculum and format "institutionalized," perceptions had changed. Attention to social and emotional development was as important as attention to academics. Students were comfortable talking about social and emotional concerns with peers, teachers, and parents, and teachers were comfortable talking with them about affective development. Findings argue for paying attention to the whole child in programs for gifted students, and persisting.

Lack of Attention to Social and Emotional Development

The whole child. Narrow dogma does not embrace the whole child, including social, emotional, and career development. Focusing largely on academic performance or non-performance, on celebrating strong performance and fixing low performance, and on securing optimal college placement can send a powerful message not only about who is worthy, but also that there is basically only one way to "demonstrate giftedness."

Characteristics Associated with Giftedness Asynchronous development, with cognitive out of sync with social and/or emotional (Silverman, 2002), may make negative life events, horrendous local or global events, family dysfunction, and peer-relationship problems especially difficult for gifted children. Sensitivities (Mendaglio, 2006) and intensities (Lovecky, 1992) may exacerbate struggles with developmental or family transitions. Expectations of self and others may contribute to debilitating perfectionism (Greenspon, 2000), reluctance to ask for help even when distressed (Peterson & Ray, 2006; Peterson & Rischar, 2000), and no tolerance for mistakes and fear of failure (Greenspon, 2000). A strong moral sense and sense of social justice may make bullying, cruelty, and other societal ills deeply unsettling. Having few or no intellectual peers at school might contribute to loneliness, as a result of not being able to connect with others about areas felt to be important (Boland & Gross, 2007).

Having opportunities to be informed about and talk about stress, fearsome emotions, existential concerns, differentness, interpersonal challenges, anxiety, depression, eating disorders, and perfectionism can normalize for gifted students what may, in fact, feel "crazy." Neither high achievers nor low achievers may have a frame of reference for putting experiences into perspective. Students can examine "fix-yourself" beliefs and ask for help when needed. Providing pertinent findings related to not asking for help (Jackson & Peterson, 2003; Peterson, 2001, 2002) may counter reluctance to add "toxicity" to others' lives or to disturb a positive public image. Learning listening and responding skills through topic-focused, development-oriented small-group discussions (Peterson, 2008) can help gifted youth connect to others and improve social skills. Helping perfectionists learn to "color outside of the lines" can catalyze broader personal change. Learning about the theory of positive disintegration can help struggling gifted youth to be hopeful. Proactively talking about social and emotional challenges of college life can prepare them for that development shift (Peterson, 2000b). Self-reflection and specific guidance can help negatively critical students take responsibility for self-advocacy and stop blaming "the system."

Career Development   A narrow view of what gifted individuals need may also preclude attention to career development throughout the K–12 years. Social skills related to the work world can be emphasized even in kindergarten (e.g., how bullying others can interfere with success in the work world). Career development is more complex than accumulating credits, receiving good grades, and selecting a college. Considering multiple options, reflecting wide-ranging strengths and interests, may even generate a sense of looming loss when needing to choose a college major and university and leave other options behind. Gifted children, depending on circumstances and modeling, may be ready at an early age to consider that interests, personality, and strengths are related to a good career fit and that one does not have to decide until much later. K–12 and college years will continue to raise awareness of potential fit.

Career development for gifted youth is a complex process. Developmental "stuckness" in finding direction can emotionally paralyze an adolescent (Peterson, 2001). In contrast, premature foreclosure, in order to remove intolerable ambiguity, may result in a poor fit with a career. Gifted immigrant teens and others representing cultural minority and low-socioeconomic populations may lack models within the family and information about careers, financial options for higher education, and what "college" requires in preparation and processes. If "gifted education" ignores these needs, many highly able individuals may fall through the proverbial cracks.

Applying Basic Tenets of Counseling   Counselors are trained to enter the world of a client respectfully, nonjudgmentally, and fully present, not distracted by their own personal issues and values. Preparation involves developing tolerance for ambiguity. The counselor focuses on "where the client is" in the present. Here, these tenets offer a frame for moving away from narrow dogma related to education of gifted youth. Dogma precludes exploring non-performance-oriented development and non-asset aspects of giftedness. That kind of attention might actually be life-altering.

Parents and educators who learn to tolerate ambiguity can be less preoccupied with "nailing down the future," less panicked by underachievement or other troubling phenomena, less product-focused and more process-focused, and less likely to forget to use a developmental lens. Psychoeducational information is indeed often helpful for gifted youth who are trying to make cognitive sense of difficult situations. Pertinent, credible information appeals to their cognitive strengths. When adults are knowledgeable about developmental implications of giftedness, they can help kids normalize troubling feelings, thoughts, and behaviors. However, when opportunities arise, invested adults can stop teaching and instead ask to be taught about the child's world, focusing on present emotions instead of expectations that have or have not been met. Fundamentally, gifted kids may feel understood, appreciated for their complexity, and recognized as "a work in progress," needing unconditional support and nurturing while maturing.

Challenging Dogma without Dismissing Crucial Needs

Being less dogmatic about what and who are worthy of attention encourages invested adults to embrace the whole child, embrace potentially complex social and emotional development, and consider cultural values when conceptualizing giftedness. Thinking less narrowly does not ignore pressing curricular concerns. Nor does it challenge the reality that kids at the upper end of the bell curve need services.

A broader view connects non-academic aspects of high ability to academics. The default dogma mode fits the current education climate, with an emphasis on competitive achievement and school accountability. But thinking more broadly about needs embraces humanness and considers less visible, but crucial, concerns. There has been activity in recent decades regarding twice-exceptionality (e.g., Assouline, Nicpon, & Huber, 2006) and underrepresented populations (e.g., Henshon, 2008; Hébert, 1995, 2000a, 2000b, 2001), and federal and foundation funding has been supportive. However, the default mode often prevails, especially in regard to *familiar* motivation and achievement criteria. More conference presentations need to "de-center" audiences. Advocates for gifted education would be wise to send new and different messages to legislators, emphasizing social and emotional concerns, with an appropriately serious face (Peterson, 1993).

Conclusion

Dogma reflects beliefs and attitudes. Narrow dogma related to giftedness seems to run counter to the altruism that has been associated with it. Restrictiveness, in regard to who receives services, limits interaction among highly able students representing diverse ways of being.

The desire for security and certainty in response to perceived threats, and perhaps as "habit," may drive a narrowing of perspectives and foci during complex times. When narrow doctrine is proclaimed as truth, even by well intentioned and well-informed leaders, the field may shift away from multi-faceted, real-world needs in complex populations and sound ever more elitist. Beating the advocacy drum narrowly and stridently also potentially contributes to uncompassionate responses from individuals and groups whose support is needed.

Prevailing dogma seems not to affirm human complexity, not to encourage creative programming for individuals that do not fit common giftedness stereo-types, not to embrace non-asset aspects of giftedness comfortably, and not to be creative in advocacy. Young researchers may not be encouraged to venture into new territory, challenge prevailing assumptions, or correct myopia. As a result, parents, educators, and counselors lack information that might help them differentiate their approaches. Students whose behaviors do not affirm invested adults are often not invited to the table. Even those who are invited may sense that teachers do not see beyond performance or connect the aca-demic and affective. I have observed that high achievers often cannot think of any response when asked, "How are you like all other kids in your grade at school?" Some say, "Not at all." My sense is that it is dangerous when they have not considered that they and their peers are human, "growing up," and trying to figure out who they are, find direction, and be increasingly autonomous.

The special services the field advocates for need to be open to all students with high capability, regardless of level of academic achievement, and to be appropriately and idiosyncratically responsive. A multitude of factors may con-tribute to a student's not demonstrating strengths, including burdens associated with giftedness. However, nothing stays the same. Change is constant. Their future cannot be predicted, even though prevailing dogma may argue that school-age achievement does just that. Collectively and creatively trying to figure out how to respond to gifted students who do not fit common "gifted-kids" stereotypes might actually invigorate the field, help it to embrace the profound complexity of "high intelligence," make a developmental perspective commonplace, embed giftedness in the broad human condition, and contribute to intellectual humility in students, educators, scholars, and leaders. Wisdom, compassion, ethical behavior, comfortable cross-cultural communication, cre-ative expression and problem-solving, and improved well-being may all be in greater supply as a result.

References

Assouline, S. G., Nicpon, M. F., & Huber, D. H. (2006). The impact of vulnerabilities and strengths on the academic experiences of twice-exceptional students: A message to school counselors. *Professional School Counseling, 10,* 14–24.

Boland, C. M., & Gross, M. U. M. (2007). Counseling highly gifted children and adolescents. In S. Mendaglio & J. S. Peterson (Eds.), *Models of counseling gifted children, adolescents, and young adults* (pp. 153–197), Waco, TX: Prufrock Press.

Gardner, H. (2004). Reflections on multiple iintelligences: Myths and messages. *Phi Delta Kappan, 77,* 200–203.

Greenspon, T. S. (2000). "Healthy perfectionism" is an oxymoron: Reflections on the psychol-ogy of perfectionism and the sociology of science. *Journal of Secondary Gifted Education, 11,* 197–209.

Hébert, T. P. (1995). Coach Brogan: South Central High School's answer to academic achieve-ment. *Journal of Secondary Gifted Education, 7,* 310–323.

Hébert, T. P. (2000a). Defining belief in self: Intelligent young men in an urban high school. *Gifted Child Quarterly, 44,* 91–114.

Hébert, T. P. (2000b). Helping high ability students overcome math anxiety through biblio-therapy. *Journal of Secondary Gifted Education, 8*, 164–178.

Hébert, T. P. (2001). "If I had a notebook, I know things would change": Bright underachieving young men in urban classrooms. *Gifted Child Quarterly, 45*, 174–194.

Henshon, S. (2008). Champion of cultural competence: An interview with Donna Y. Ford. *Roeper Review, 30*, 208–210.

Jackson, P. S., & Peterson, J. (2003). Depressive disorder in highly gifted adolescents. *Journal of Secondary Gifted Education, 3*, 175–186.

Lovecky, D. (1992). Exploring social and emotional aspects of giftedness in children. *Roeper Review, 15*, 18–25.

Margolin, L. (1996). *Goodness personified: The emergence of gifted children.* Piscataway, NH: Aldine Transaction.

Mendaglio, S. (2006). Affective-cognitive therapy for counseling gifted individuals. In S. Mendaglio & J. S. Peterson (Eds.), *Models of counseling gifted children, adolescents, and young adults* (pp. 35–68). Austin, TX: Prufrock.

Peterson, J. S. (1993). Peeling off the elitist label: Smart politics. *Gifted Child Today, 16*(2), 31–33.

Peterson, J. S. (1999). Gifted—through whose cultural lens? An application of the postpositivistic mode of inquiry. *Journal for the Education of the Gifted, 22*, 354–383.

Peterson, J. S. (2000a). A follow-up study of one group of achievers and underachievers four years after high school graduation. *Roeper Review, 22*, 217–224.

Peterson, J. S. (2000b). Preparing for college—beyond the "getting-in" part. *Gifted Child Today, 23*(2), 36–41.

Peterson, J. S. (2001). Gifted and at risk: Four longitudinal case studies. *Roeper Review, 24*, 31–39.

Peterson, J. S. (2002). A longitudinal study of post-high-school development in gifted individuals at risk for poor educational outcomes. *Journal for Secondary Gifted Education, 14*, 6–18.

Peterson, J. S. (2006). Addressing counseling needs of gifted students. *Professional School Counseling, 10*, 1, 43–51.

Peterson, J. S. (2008). *The essential guide for talking with gifted teens: Ready-to-use discussions about identity, stress, relationships, and more.* Minneapolis: Free Spirit.

Peterson, J. S., Duncan, N., & Canady, K. (2009). A longitudinal study of negative life events, stress, and school experiences of gifted youth. *Gifted Child Quarterly, 53*, 34–49.

Peterson, J. S., & Margolin, L. (1997). Naming gifted children: An example of unintended 'reproduction.' *Journal for the Education of the Gifted, 21*, 82–100.

Peterson, J. S., & Moon, S. M. (2008). Counseling the gifted. In S. Pfeiffer (Ed.), *Handbook of giftedness in children: Psychoeducational theory, research, and best practices* (pp. 125–148). New York, NY: Springer.

Peterson, J. S., & Norman, M. R. (2011). *A study of the implementation of a small-group affective curriculum in a school for gifted children.* Manuscript submitted for publication.

Peterson, J. S., & Ray, K. E. (2006). Bullying among the gifted: The subjective experience. *Gifted Child Quarterly, 50*, 252–269.

Peterson, J. S., & Rischar, H. (2000). Gifted and gay: A study of the adolescent experience. *Gifted Child Quarterly, 44*, 149–164.

Piirto, J. (1998). *Understanding those who create* (2nd ed.). Scottsdale, AZ: Great Potential Press.

Renzulli, J. S. (2009). Operation houndstooth: A positive perspective on developing social intelligence. In J. L. VanTassel-Baska, T. L. Cross, & F. R. Olenchak (Eds.), *Social-emotional curriculum with gifted and talented students* (pp. 79–112). Waco, TX: Prufrock.

Silverman, L. K. (2002). Asynchronous development. In M. Neihart, S. M. Reis, N. M. Robinson, & S. M. Moon (Eds.), *The social and emotional development of gifted children: What do we know?* (pp. 31–37). Waco, TX: Prufrock Press.

Silverman, L. S. (1993). A developmental model for counseling the gifted. In L. K. Silverman (Ed.), *Counseling the gifted and talented* (pp. 51–78). Denver: Love.

Spindler, G., & Spindler, L. (1990). *The American cultural dialogue and its transmission.* London, England: Falmer Press.

Terman, L., & Oden, M. (1951). The Stanford studies of the gifted. In P. Witty (Ed.), *The gifted child* (pp. 20–46). Boston: D. C. Heath.

Webster, N. S., & Worrell, F. (2008) Academically talented students' attitudes toward service in the community. *Gifted Child Quarterly, 52,* 170–179.

Wells, D., Donnell, A. J., Thomas, A., Mills, M. S., & Miller, M. (2006). Creative deviance: A study of the relationship between creative behavior and the social construct of deviance. *College Student Journal, 40,* 74–77.

Worrell, F. C. (2009). Myth 4: A single test score or indicator tells us all we need to know about giftedness. *Gifted Child Quarterly, 53,* 242–244.

6

DOGMATISM, POLICY, AND GIFTED STUDENTS

James J. Gallagher

UNIVERSITY OF NORTH CAROLINA AT CHAPEL HILL

The field of education of gifted students has had few successes in the world of public policy, where much opposition has been effective in preventing more public support, both politically and economically. In many ways this has been puzzling to outside observers who see such special education of these talented students as a national priority.

It should be clear to the most casual observer that opposition to educational programs for the gifted and talented is irrational and clearly against the public interest. Over the past 40 years a series of reports have been produced that have pointed to this irrationality and the importance of paying some special attention to these students. These reports include:

- *The Marland Report* (1972)
- *A Nation at Risk* (Gardner, 1983)
- *National Excellence* (Ross, 1993)
- *Rising Above the Gathering Storm* (Augustine, 2007)
- *Preparing the Next Generation of STEM Innovators* (Bruer, 2010)

All of these reports point out that it is in our urgent national interest to nurture the special talents that can be found in all segments of our society. We are well aware from past research (Plucker & Callahan, 2008) that early identification and appropriate education of such students with special gifts and talents will reveal a potential that will, in most cases, flower into future leadership and produce major contributions and leadership in the sciences, arts, politics, business, and more.

Rather than write a sixth report reproducing the essence of these five noted earlier, perhaps it is time to pursue the nature of the irrationality being indicated here. Dogmatism, or persisting in ideas despite evidence to the contrary, is the end result of a psychological mechanism designed to protect the individual from stress and anxiety. Dogmatism occurs when there is a gap between what we believe about ourselves or others, and reality. It is important for our psychological health that such gaps be eliminated. A gap can be closed by modifying our perceptions to bring them into line with reality or by insisting there really is no gap, or by denying reality (e.g., evolution is a fraud). However, the attempt to close that gap by denying reality, rather than modifying one's own position, is what results in what we observe as *dogmatism*.

Such a mechanism is rife in the field of education of gifted and talented but is widely seen in other settings as well. Two examples illustrating the widespread nature of this self-protective device may suffice. A couple is surprised to find that they have produced a child with severe disabilities and raise the questions: *How has God allowed this to happen to my husband and me? We are good and proper people. Other less worthy parents have normal children. Why are we being punished in such a way?* This statement represents the crisis between our self-image and the events that occurred. There are many ways of attempting to resolve this gap between perception and reality, but one is certainly the following: *God would never give us a challenge that we could not meet, so he has chosen us as special people who can show others how we can cope with this challenge effectively.* Such a philosophy can well serve the parents through many difficult months and years ahead and effectively shield them from alternative views that they have a defect in themselves that has shown up in their child and can also protect them from the guilt feelings that might overwhelm them for producing such a flawed child.

A second example would be the crisis caused by the gap between a self-image that *I am a generous and caring person who will help others in trouble* and the reality that *I have given, or done, little or nothing for those who are living in poverty in my own city.* It is psychologically intolerable that such a personal inconsistency be allowed to exist without an explanation. The resolution in many cases may be the following: *Those people are in poverty because they are lazy and refuse to do anything to improve their status. It would be a waste of money and resources since they would only spend it on drugs and booze.* This resolves the gap between *self-image* and reality but one now must vigorously oppose any information (be dogmatic) that would tend to upset the balance that one has created. One would therefore reject any information that persons in poverty work hard or are worthy of special attention.

In the field of gifted education, one prime example of dogmatism can be found in the policy of *educational acceleration*, or moving the student more rapidly through the established systems. Traditionally a student is 18 years of age finishing high school, 22 when finishing college, and if they pursue post-graduate work or professional work like medicine or law, 28 to 30 years old. The effects of educational acceleration are a topic that has been studied over five or six decades with the results of such studies being invariably positive for the vast number of accelerated students. These findings have been summarized in an important report (Colangelo, Assouline, & Gross, 2004).

Furthermore, there are strong economic reasons for this policy of acceleration. The brightest of our students would enter the productive workforce 1 year or 2 earlier, extending their productive years to the benefit of all. If they spent 10 years in public schools instead of 12, that would save 2 years of money that would have been spent in public education for such students. If we are in a competition of brains with other cultures (such as China or India), such a policy of educational acceleration would seem to make sense for another reason because these productive intellects would be available sooner to the advantage of the larger society.

Nevertheless, these positive findings on acceleration continue to be ignored by educational administrators, teachers, and parents. One often heard dogmatic statement is that *Such students would be harmed socially by moving them forward. They might lose friends and their own sense of social acceptance.* The research findings absolutely contradict this proposition. The negative effects of educational acceleration are limited to few students. The majority show academic improvement and good social relationships (see Colangelo et al., 2004). So, we are left with the issue as to what is really going on here.

For educational administrators, acceleration might seem to mean greater hassles with parents wanting their children to be considered for this policy and having to turn down a number of parents, with subsequent bad feelings. Why not let the status quo alone, some educational administrators may conclude, and use the potential harm to accelerated students as the rationale?

Teachers, on their part, may dread the loss of one of their best students to acceleration or seeing the student jump over their grade so that they don't get to work with them at all. A teacher may well have the experience of a single student whom they have known to be accelerated and who turned out badly, so they generalize that experience to all advanced students. These bring forth the dogmatic statement that "they will be damaged socially."

Finally, parents faced with the prospect of accelerating their children may well consider that this would mean that the child they love so much will be leaving for college even earlier than they thought, and this loss is an unpleasant prospect. Parents are naturally concerned about whether these changes result in problems or whether the child remains efficient and socially adapted. They tend to be reassured by statements from administrators and teachers that holding their child back is the right thing to do.

These three groups—administrators, teachers, and parents—each have different reasons for rejecting this policy but they can use the same dogmatic explanation "the child will be harmed by this process of acceleration," and so this myth continues in marked contrast to the available evidence. How can we circumvent this?

The famous defense attorney, Clarence Darrow, gave us a strategy. When asked how he was successful in getting his clients acquitted, he said that first he must get the jury to want to acquit the defendant and then he can present the facts that would allow this to happen. Our problem in the education of gifted students is that we are presenting the facts of the case before convincing "our juries" that the acceleration should happen.

The educational administrator can be convinced that acceleration is in our national defense, plus hear the testimony of students who have been through acceleration. Teachers also can be convinced by individual testimony from students who have participated in these accelerated programs. This is particularly true if the teacher had prior knowledge of the students involved. Parents who have concerns about the results of this process can be influenced by the fact that acceleration counts positively in the admission decisions of high-prestige colleges and universities. The data that has been collected on acceleration can then be influential in decision making but often need the subjective arguments presented here to convince the educators and parents.

The more general policy of *special programming for gifted students* also runs into dogmatic and irrational, but powerful, opposition. Again, the available research data on program effectiveness paints a positive picture (Plucker & Callahan, 2008), as does the testimony of gifted students who have had the experience of the special programs or schools (Lubinski & Benbow, 2006).

Such positive research data are swimming upstream against the dogmatic statements that there be "no special privilege for special people." Such special programs violate the principle, to some, that we are a fair and equitable society. To many critics it is akin to creating a "gated community" inside education where only the intellectually wealthy can prosper.

The argument is that programs for gifted students are just a ruse to create a quality education for the children of the privileged citizens in our society. Such parents can then accept low-quality education for the rest of the students knowing that their child, at least, is receiving a first-rate education. Further, such programs have been accused of shutting out students from different ethnic backgrounds and destroying the equity that should be a significant part of public education (Ford & Grantham, 2003). Arguments are heard that such programs will create feelings of superiority for accelerated students over other students.

Again, counteracting these dogmatic statements lies not so much in presenting data such as "the self image of gifted students tends to go down in such special programs, not to go up," which it does (Pyryt, 2008), but instead stress the positive nature of the programs for the community at large. The one argument that has paid off in more resources for such programs in the past rests on national defense and the fear that other nations are pulling ahead of the United States. We then should be developing these human assets as part of a defensive shield around our nation (J. Gallagher, 2006). Of course, *Excellence for All* should be the policy of education. However, excellence for a child with autism and developmental delay is not the same in content or setting as excellence for a child with an IQ of 150.

The one dramatic example of the success of this argument has been the remarkable response of the country to the *Sputnik* Challenge, in which Russia proved itself to have a lead in space programs and caused major questions to be raised about the effectiveness of our educational programs in science and mathematics. This fear, in turn, led to enormous funds being made available through the National Science Foundation for major curricular projects such as the Physical Science Study Project (PSSC), Biological Sciences Curriculum Study (BSCS), Chemical Bond Approach (CBA), School Mathematics Study Group (SMSG), and others that joined this "alphabet soup" of programs (J. Gallagher, 2002).

Once again, the dogmatic insistence on "no special programming for gifted students" was overcome, not by data on their effectiveness, but by the fear of the consequences of continuing to ignore the education of our most talented students who, quite correctly, were seen as the ultimate protectors of our society.

Reducing Dogmatism About Gifted Students

In summary, then, dogmatism is part of a psychological defense mechanism to protect against stress and depression coming from a perceived major gap between personal beliefs and reality. Faced with this incongruity or gap, the individual may attack the "facts" to reduce their potency. This dogmatic reaction can happen at either the individual level or in belief systems held by groups or organizations. Organizations such as teachers' unions or state associations for gifted students can become just as dogmatic as individuals and the same psychological dynamics are at work as they take a position on educational acceleration or grouping. They can be dogmatic and resist reality if they feel that their group's own status or prestige may be threatened.

The dynamics of dogmatism are easily understood and recognized. It is much more difficult to provide the alternative solutions or substitute ideas to break through the barriers that have been established, often over a long period of time. Until we recognize the dynamics at work, we will continue to argue with our critics in a nonproductive fashion.

How does one reduce the dogmatism that seems to be delaying important actions for students with special gifts and talents (SGT), on an individual or group activity? One approach we can put aside is the direct attack spotlighting the gap between belief and facts in the positions supported by our critics. This means we do not need to provide a sixth national study on why gifted students should be provided assistance in the American school system.

This approach, alone, just stirs up resistance on the part of those whose belief system does not include special programming for such students. The facts available from such studies are valuable as secondary aids in reducing the dogmatism, as they give a rational reason for abandoning the false belief system. But there have to be strong emotional reasons for abandoning the belief system in the first place!

We have learned from our work with children who are delinquent that a direct attack on the offending behavior (stealing or fighting) is often less successful than providing the student with substitute or *alternative behaviors* designed to meet the same needs that the earlier delinquent behavior was designed for (Dunlap & Carr, 2007; Sugai et al., 2000). For example, one approach is teaching students verbal arguments to substitute for physical confrontations. So, what are the substitute or alternate behaviors or thoughts that we wish to substitute for the dogmatic approaches of our critics about education of gifted and talented students?

Suppose that what we wish to change is the position that "gifted education is a strategy for the elite and the well-placed in our society in order to gain special privileges for their children." This is a powerful and emotional position and will only be modified if other alternative thoughts and emotions are presented. This belief system about elitism can be counteracted with the introduction of the *Excellence for All* concept. This means support for quality education for children with disabilities and children from poor families, as well as for more favored families. We can recognize that not all students have the same needs or need the same education. We must commit ourselves to the proposition stated by John Gardner (1984) that "We must have educational excellence for both philosophers and plumbers or neither our ideas nor our pipes will hold water" (p. 102). Here are a few thoughts for alternatives or substitutes for the dogmatic approach concerning elitism.

1. *There are negative consequences for holding to these beliefs about elitism.* We know from generations of study that gifted students will, in a generation, be the leadership cadre of their generation in the arts, sciences, politics, etc., who will determine whether we will prosper economically or politically in a threatening world (Augustine, 2007). If they do not receive good preparation, then we all will suffer.
2. *Gifted Students can be the pilot study for educational reform.* Many of the reforms now being considered by general education have come from the work with gifted students. Emphases on creative thinking, in particular, have profited from work in our field (Tomlinson, 1999). In addition, work on complex problem solving has been important in drawing the general curriculum away from fact presentation to thinking processes (S. Gallagher, 2006). New concepts with great potential can be tried out in special populations, such as in schools of math or science, or governors' schools for the arts, without having to try them out on a population of 60 million plus students with consequent major expense.

3. *Education of the gifted can be a cost saving measure.* Increased efficiency can be built into the entire system by an infrastructure or support system that can first be instituted and piloted for gifted students (J. Gallagher, 2008). Students whose talents have been hidden by lack of opportunity and practice can be tutored and then moved into advanced placement or international baccalaureate programs and contribute more to our educational and societal production.

4. *Success for gifted students means success for us all.* We have accepted this argument in athletics, recognizing that everyone on the team must play certain roles for the team to be successful and that it is the excellence in playing all of those roles that is necessary for final triumph for the team and for our American society.

These ideas of *Excellence for All* can receive acceptance only if they are backed up by meaningful action. An educational support system marked by *technical assistance* so that teachers may receive help upon their request, *tutoring services* so that children in trouble can learn effectively, an ongoing *personnel preparation* system to upgrade existing teachers, and *long-range planning* for the system as a whole (Bruer, 2010). Such an infrastructure or ecosystem can point the way forward for all of education (Kirk, Gallagher, Coleman, & Anastasiow, 2011).

Creating changes in public policy is a frustrating and difficult process. The defense mechanism of dogmatism, which protects us all from too much novelty, applied too quickly, plays a major role in this brake on societal change. The result is that major changes in policy require major efforts in *intensity* for particular changes over a significant period of time. Discouragement often accompanies the difficult efforts in this regard so we must remind ourselves of the quote from anthropologist Margaret Mead, "Never doubt that a small group of thoughtful and determined people could change the world. Indeed, it is the only thing that ever has" (cited in Lutkehous, 2008, p. 261).

References

Augustine, N. (Chair) (2007). *Rising above the gathering storm: Energizing and employing America for a brighter economic future.* Washington, DC: The National Academies Press.

Bruer, J. (Chair) (2010). *Preparing the next generation of STEM innovators: Identifying and developing our nation's human capitol.* Washington, DC: National Science Foundation.

Colangelo, N., Assouline, S., & Gross, M. (2004). *A nation deceived: How schools hold back America's brightest students. The Templeton national report on acceleration.* Iowa City, IA: Belin and Blank International Center for Gifted Education.

Dunlap, G., & Carr, E. (2007). Positive behavior support and developmental disabilities: A summary and analysis of research. In S. Odom, B. Horner, M. Snell, & J. Blacher (Eds.), *Handbook of developmental disabilities* (pp. 469–482). New York, NY: Guilford Press.

Ford, D. Y., & Grantham, T. C. (2003). Providing access for culturally diverse gifted students: From deficit to dynamic thinking. *Theory Into Practice, 42,* 217–225.

Gallagher, J. (2002). *Society's role in educating gifted students: The role of public policy* (RM02162). Storrs, CT: The National Research Center on the Gifted and Talented.

Gallagher, J. (2006). *Driving change in special education.* Baltimore, MD: Paul H. Brookes.

Gallagher, J. (2008). Policy and advocacy. In J. Plucker & C. Callahan (Eds.), *Critical issues in gifted education* (pp. 513–522). Waco, TX: Prufrock Press.

Gallagher, S. (2006). Guiding gifted students toward science expertise. In F. Dixon & S. Moon (Eds.), *The handbook of secondary gifted education* (pp. 427–460). Waco, TX: Prufrock Press.

Gardner, D. (1983). *A nation at risk: The imperative for education reform*. Washington, DC: United States Department of Education.

Gardner, J. (1984). *Can we be equal and excellent too?* (2nd ed.). New York, NY: Norton.

Kirk, S., Gallagher, J., Coleman, M., & Anastasiow, N. (2011). *Educating exceptional children* (13th ed.). Boston, MA: Cengage.

Lubinski, D., & Benbow, C. P. (2006). Study of mathematically precocious youth after 35 years: Uncovering antecedents for the development of math-science expertise. *Perspectives in Psychological Science, 1,* 316–345.

Lutkehous, N. C. (2008). *Margaret Mead: The making of an American icon*. Princeton, NJ: Princeton University Press.

Marland, S. (1972). *Education of the gifted and talented*. Report to the Congress of the United States by the U.S. Commissioner of Education Washington, DC: U.S. Government Printing Office.

Plucker, J., & Callahan, C. (Eds.). (2008). *Critical issues and practices in gifted education*. Waco, TX: Prufrock Press.

Pyryt, M. (2008). Self concept. In J. Plucker, & C. Callahan (Eds.), *Critical issues in gifted education* (pp. 595–602). Waco, TX: Prufrock Press.

Ross, P. (1993). *National excellence: A case for developing America's talent*. Washington, DC: United States Department of Education.

Sugai, G., Horner, R. H., Dunlap, G. Hieneman, M., Lewis, T. J., Nelson, C. M., … Wilcox, B. (2000). Applying positive behavioral support and functional behavioral assessment in schools. *Journal of Positive Behavioral Interventions, 2,* 131–143.

Tomlinson, C. (1999). *The differential classroom: Responding to the needs of all learners*. Alexandria, VA: Association for Supervision and Curriculum Development.

7

EQUITY ISSUES AND MULTICULTURALISM IN THE UNDER-REPRESENTATION OF BLACK STUDENTS IN GIFTED EDUCATION

Dogmatism at its Worst

Donna Y. Ford

VANDERBILT UNIVERSITY

> Many people would agree with John Dewey and Bertrand Russell that open-mindedness is one of the fundamental aims of education, always elusive but eminently worth pursuing. For Dewey, it is the childlike attitude of wonder and interest in new ideas coupled with a determination to have one's beliefs properly grounded; and it is vitally important because we live in a world that is characterized by constant change. For Russell, open-mindedness is the virtue that prevents habit and desire from making us unable or unwilling to entertain the idea that earlier beliefs may have to be revised or abandoned; its main value lies in challenging the fanaticism that comes from a conviction that our views are absolutely certain.
>
> Robert Hare (n.d.)

Dogmatism is a construct that has received prominent attention in political and religious arenas. One has only to search the Internet for information on dogmatism and countless links appear on hundreds of subjects, as is evident by the number of chapters and topics appearing in this book.

Rarely, however, has dogmatism been applied to gifted education. But teachers have been found to be dogmatic in their thinking (Kremer-Hayon, Moore, & Nevat, 1985, 1986). The study of dogma, also referred to as the closed mind, is important to include in discussions of gifted education, particularly regarding the most debatable and polemic topics and issues in the field. Included among them are: identification (definitions, theories, instruments, policies and procedures), under-representation of Black and other culturally different students, and underachievement.

This chapter focuses on dogmatism and three manifestations of dogmatism through the lens of: (a) deficit thinking; (b) ethnocentrism; and (c) prejudice, and how these manifestations in isolation or in combination contribute to and/ or exacerbate under-representation and under-referral. In most school districts, gifted education screening begins with referral by teachers and other school personnel (e.g., nomination form) and/or includes input from them (e.g., checklist). Every study on the referral process that considered racial variables has shown that teachers—mainly White and female—under-refer Black students for gifted education screening and evaluation. Importantly, they consistently under-refer and under-estimate the abilities and potential of this student group more than of any other (see summary by Ford, Grantham, & Whiting, 2008, and recent studies by McBee, 2006, 2010).

In this chapter, I argue that dogmatism in the form of deficit thinking— prejudice, ethnocentrism, and/or negative stereotypes—about Black students especially plays *the* prominent role in their under-representation. Stated another way, deficit thinking hinders the mindset, decisions, actions, and policies of school personnel to be culturally responsive (equitable) to the differences and needs of gifted Black students. Deficit thinking is, I believe, *the* fundamental attribution error that affects/hinders all decisions and behaviors—the test or checklist used, interpretations of test results, interpretations of cultural differences, decisions made regarding policies and procedures, refusal to change tests, instruments, criteria, policies, curriculum, and more.

Definitions and Overview

Richard Paul has conducted a substantial amount of work on, and contributed greatly to, discussions, research, and curricula regarding critical or higher-level thinking. According to him, open-mindedness is an intellectual virtue that involves not just ability and skills, but also a *willingness* to take relevant evidence and argument into account in forming or revising one's beliefs and values, especially when there is some reason we might (vigorously and vehemently) resist such evidence and argument. The goal is to arrive at conclusions that are solid and defensible. To be open-minded means to be critically receptive to alternative possibilities—being willing to re-think or reconsider, despite having formed a strongly held opinion, and sincerely trying to avoid those conditions (such as offsetting those factors that constrain and distort our reflections, perceptions, interpretations and attributes). The attitude and habit of open-mindedness is embedded in the Socratic idea of following the argument where it leads and is a fundamental virtue of inquiry (see Hare, 2003a, 2003b, 2004).

On the other hand, dogmatism, or the closed, inflexible, polemic, narrow, rigid mind, makes one resistant to change in system of beliefs. More specifically, even when confronted with contradictions to one's belief system (based on evidence such as research, experience, etc.), the dogmatist is unable (and/or unwilling) to alter or abandon the original belief system and, instead, clings to an illogical or irrational conviction that the contradiction(s) can somehow be resolved, and that solutions can be found within the confines of the belief system (Rokeach, 1960). People may seek the comfort or crutch of dogma, but an open-minded teacher or individual challenges such tendencies by ensuring that claims and theories remain open to critical review and are not viewed as fixed and final—or beyond all possibility of further thought (Hare, n.d.).

A perusal of online dictionaries produced the following definitions of dogmatism: The tendency to lay down principles as incontrovertibly true, without consideration of evidence or the opinions of others: positiveness in assertion of opinion especially when unwarranted or arrogant; a viewpoint or system of ideas based on insufficiently examined premises. Synonyms include: bigotry, illiberalism, intolerance, narrow-mindedness, bias disorder, fanaticism, opinionatedness partisanship, authoritarianism, sectarianism, small-mindedness, rigidity, dichotomized thinking, and a host of other related descriptors. Regardless of one's preferred term, all have in common dogmatism or closed-mindedness—a belief that one's view is the right or only worthy view—accompanied by resistance to change.

Discussions of dogmatism are incomplete without a focus on values and the work of Milton Rokeach, who noted that values are the yardsticks against which both the self and others are judged (e.g., Feather, 1996; Rokeach, 1973; Schwartz, 1992). Rokeach (1968) defined values as abstract concepts "representing a person's beliefs about ideal modes of conduct and ideal terminal goals" (p. 124). Importantly,

> once a value is internalized, it becomes, consciously or unconsciously, a standard or criterion for guiding action, for developing and maintaining attitudes toward relevant objects and situations, for justifying one's own and other's actions and attitudes, for morally judging oneself and others, and for comparing oneself with others.
>
> *(Rokeach, 1968, p. 160)*

Rokeach's definition emphasizes the broad and enduring, as well as entrenched, nature and power of values. Values are broad in that (a) they can function as general attitudes (Biernat & Vescio, 2004) that are related to an array of relatively more specific attitude objects and behaviors and (b) they are applicable across situations and contexts; that is, while beliefs and attitudes are amenable to change, values are less so. Values give rise to specific attitudes and behaviors, defining appropriate courses of action in light of one's personal goals and/or desired end-states. Within a social-cognitive framework, values have been thought of as superordinate constructs in associative networks beneath which a host of related attitudes and behaviors are arrayed (see Biernat & Vescio, 2004; Biernat, Vescio, Theno, & Crandall, 1996).

As Borland (Chapter 2, this volume) notes, the study of dogma in gifted education is important for a number of reasons, but for this chapter, the most significant reason pertains to the reality that far too many educators and decision makers seem to be of an antediluvian mindset that is not only resistant to change, but is also (a) wed to what is familiar and comfortable, (b) hesitant and resistant to challenging the status quo, (c) oblivious to and otherwise not supportive of addressing or reconciling issues associated with equity and, thus, (d) unresponsive to the needs of Black and other culturally different students. It is my belief that dogmatism contributes in significant ways to under-representation, described next.

Status of Under-Representation in Gifted Education

With or without relying on official census data or reports from the U.S. Department of Education and demographers, many educators recognize that their classrooms have changed racially and economically from the time they began teaching, even if that was five or fewer years ago. On an annual basis, schools are becoming more racially diverse (different) than ever before. Looking at decade intervals for two years, the following changes are evident: White students comprised 55.5% of the student population in 1998; but they were less than 40% as of 2008 (U.S. Department of Education, 2010, see Table A-4-1, p. 152). There are also noteworthy regional differences; West Coast schools have the most racially diverse students with the lowest percentage of White students. As of 2008, the West (42.8% White) was the most racially diverse, while the Midwest was the least racially diverse (71.4% White). From both a national and regional perspective, projections show that this trend in racial diversity in public schools will continue. I've yet to find a report that predicts otherwise.

At the same time that we as a nation and educational system are experiencing increases in students' racial and ethnic diversity, the teaching force—teachers and principals—remains pretty much stagnant or racially homogenous. In the 1999–2000 school year, 84.6% of teachers were White; in the 2007–08 school year, this percentage was 83.4. For the latter school year, Blacks comprised 8%, Hispanics were 6%, and Asians were 1.8% of the teaching force (see U.S. Department of Education, 2010, Table A-27-1, p. 237). Essentially, these data show that there is an inverse relationship between the demographics of students and classroom teachers, which is mainly attributable to too few minorities choosing to become teachers due to testing requirements (e.g., Praxis), discouragement from advisors who urge them to enter STEM (science, technology, engineering, and math) fields, perceptions of teaching as low in salary and prestige, and other factors.

Also noteworthy is that females, namely White females, dominate the classroom setting. Specifically, the majority of teachers, some three fourths, are female, while about half of principals are female (U.S. Department of Education, 2010, Tables A-27-1 and A-29-1). I also found that, at least in 1999, gifted education teachers were also likely to be White and female (Ford, 1999).

The aforementioned demographic data—students, teachers, principals—beg the omnibus question—how willing and prepared are educators to work with students who come from backgrounds that are different from their own—racially, culturally, linguistically, economically, and/or by gender? How prepared are they to recognize, understand, value, and nurture gifts and talents in racially and culturally different students (e.g., minority males vs. females; low-income vs. high-income minorities)?

Based on current outcomes among Black students, in particular, the current reality is that too few educators are culturally competent, which includes dispositions, knowledge, and skills (e.g., Ford, 2010a). Furthermore, there is often reticence about changing current measures/instruments, policies, and practices, undergirded by a desire to adhere to, cater to, and maintain the status quo and what is familiar, comfortable, and of personal value.

Gifted Education Under-Representation Data: Thousands Denied Access

The under-representation of African American and other racially different students in gifted education is a national problem that has received decades of attention, and a few cases have come to litigation; under-representation has yet to be resolved or eliminated nationally. Black, Hispanic, and Native American students have been the focus of litigation, discussions, and debates. Progress, by no means sufficient, has been made with Hispanic and Native American students over the years (e.g., Ford et al., 2008). This is not the case for Black students. That is, most problematic—and resistant to change—is the poor presence of Black students referred, identified, and receiving gifted-education services. According to 2006 data from the Office for Civil Rights Elementary and Secondary School Civil Rights Survey (2008), the most recent data at the time of this writing, Black students are the *most under-represented* in gifted education.

This problem has existed throughout the history of gifted education. For example, when using risk ratios, one can compare the number of students in the total school district with their percentage in gifted education. In 2006, while Black students comprised about 17.13% of students in public schools, they were only 9.15% of gifted education—almost 50% under-representation. And when disaggregated by both gender and race, Black males are more under-represented than any group (55%) (Ford, 2010b; Ford et al., 2008).

How students who are viewed as gifted or promising candidates for gifted-education placement come to the attention of educators and end up in the screening pool or the attention of decision makers varies by school district. However, at the beginning stage, referrals by educators first and then test performance trump all other information. Yet, both are riddled with biases that hinder and compromise in negative ways the eventual placement (or lack thereof) of Black students, more than other students, in gifted education (see discussion and debate by Feedler, 2003, and Santelices & Wilson, 2010, as two examples pertaining to the SAT). Dogmatism, described next, matters.

Manifestations of Dogmatism and Under-Representation

> The world we have created is a product of our thinking. We cannot change things until we change our thinking.
>
> Albert Einstein

Dogmatism comes in many guises, some less obvious and others more blatant. While there are certainly more variants, I discuss three manifestations, including (a) deficit thinking, (b) prejudice, and (c) ethnocentrism. Next, I discuss how these dogmatic manifestations, in isolation or in combination, contribute to and exacerbate under-representation.

Mindset Matters Percepts or perceptions are powerful cognitive and behavioral forces. Perceptions influence our views and expectations of others, and our decisions and behaviors. By way of illustration, when we believe something, we often expect certain outcomes and tend to act upon the belief. Thus, if we believe that gifted students are good test takers, we expect them to score high on tests, and we look for test scores to validate our belief. If we believe that intelligence is determined mainly or exclusively by genetics, we focus on "natural" abilities or talent, trivializing the role of the environment and experiences—including education—in fostering or stifling intelligence and achievement. Likewise, if we believe that Black and/or other culturally different individuals and groups are less intelligent than their White counterparts, then we will most likely hold low and/or negative expectations of them. One consequence is that we will not see gifts and talents in them, will not refer them for gifted education screening and identification, will complete forms about them that are not positive or that show beliefs that they could not benefit from gifted education coursework, and/or will educate and treat them in unfair ways in our interactions, evaluations, and classrooms. In these and other contexts, even when there is information to the contrary, information that contradicts our (mis)perceptions is rendered insignificant by the dogmatic mind, especially a mindset that is ethnocentric or racially prejudiced.

It is my strong belief, based on at least 20 years in gifted education, that under-representation represents dogmatism at its worst; much of what takes place with racially and culturally different students is unjustifiable and indefensible. This mindset is the height of irony as our field prides itself on being comprised of intelligent or critical thinkers, which necessarily includes thinkers who are open-minded. Of course, the irony becomes somewhat less puzzling when we consider that intelligent, gifted individuals are not immune to dogmatism (see Elder & Paul, in press). Otherwise intelligent and caring professionals in the field of gifted education can unwittingly do harm if they do not appreciate the confines of their own dogmatism when it comes to underrepresentation.

Dogmatism and Cultural Differences

Rokeach (e.g., 1960, 1973) stated that belief is a powerful determinant of prejudice (thoughts) and racial discrimination (actions and behaviors). In the sections that follow, a brief overview of several beliefs is provided, specifically, deficit thinking in the forms of ethnocentrism and prejudice, with attention focused on under-representation as a function of educator under-referral.

Ethnocentrism

The term *ethnocentrism* was first coined in 1906 by William G. Sumner, a sociologist, based upon his observations of the tendency for people to differentiate between an in-group and out-group. He described ethnocentrism as leading to beliefs about one's own group being superior and, hence, having contempt for outsiders. Stated another way, ethnocentrism is the propensity or tendency to believe that one's racial (or social) group is the ideal, norm, or standard—and all other groups are compared or measured relative to one's own. An individual who is ethnocentric often judges members of other groups in negative, demeaning, and stereotypical ways.

Ethnocentrism has been found to be common among dogmatists (Rokeach, 1960, 1973), and the implications for gifted education are serious and far-reaching. More to the point, if decision makers, the majority of whom are White (e.g., teachers, counselors, administrators) (U.S. Department of Education, 2010), view their own racial and ethnic group as superior, especially in intelligence or potential, they likely will not see gifts and talents in other groups; this mindset compromises referrals and other types of input for screening, assessment, and placement.

Paul (n.d.) includes ethnocentrism in his model of critical thinking. He asserts that critical thinking entails the possession and active use of a set of traits of mind and affective dimensions: independence of thought, fair-mindedness, intellectual humility, intellectual courage, intellectual perseverance, intellectual integrity, curiosity, confidence in reason, and the willingness to see objections, to enter sympathetically into another's point of view, and to recognize one's own egocentricity or ethnocentricity.

Elder (2004) stressed how ethnocentrism is anathema to acceptance of and respect for diversity:

> Most importantly, the major barrier to our ability to reason well through diversity issues is our native egocentrism (and sociocentrism). We natu-

rally operate within the world from our own perspective, and that per-spective is often oriented toward self-serving interests. Thus, if to get what we want, we must discriminate against other people, our egocentric viewpoint easily enables us to rationalize or justify our actions.

(para. 19)

Further, she states that

Due to our egocentric mode of thinking ... we come to believe that whatever we believe is true because we believe it. Moreover, we are crea-tures of mental habit and naturally defend what we already believe. These rigid habits of thought keep us from seeing things from differing per-spectives, leading to prejudice in favor of people or groups whose ideas are like our own and against those whose ideas are unlike our own (or who seem different from us in some way). Thus, humans are not only naturally egocentric but sociocentric as well. We tend to be clannish, and to believe that the groups we belong to are right, privileged, spe-cial. Through systematic self-deception, we maintain our rigid modes of thinking, avoid recognition of our biases, and treat people and groups without due consideration and respect, even when there is ready evidence to refute our point of view.

(para. 24, Elder, 2004)

Also see Cunningham, Nezlek, and Banaji (2004) and LeVine and Campbell (1972) for more detailed discussions.

Deficit thinking about African American students in particular is the pri-mary reason for under-referral and eventual under-representation (e.g., Ford, Harris, Tyson, & Frazier Trotman, 2002). Every study on teacher referral for gifted education services has found that Black students are under-referred more than any group, as summarized by Ford et al. (2008) and found in two large studies of referrals and race by McBee (2006, 2010). Ethnocentrism cannot be ignored or trivialized, and neither can prejudice, discussed next.

Prejudice

Prejudice is very much related to ethnocentrism. Cunningham et al. (2004) make a distinction between the two:

Whereas prejudice may be seen as negative evaluation of and hostility toward a social group, ethnocentrism includes the tendency to form and maintain evaluations and hostility toward multiple groups that are not one's own. Evidence for an ethnocentric disposition comes from con-sistently high correlations between prejudice toward various subgroups.

(p. 133)

Duckitt (1992, 2006) noted that the scientific study of prejudice and dis-crimination has a recent history in that both are 20th-century concepts that emerged during the 1920s. Before this time, prejudice was not viewed as a social problem or a scientific construct; rather, negative in-group or intergroup attitudes were seen as natural and inevitable responses to group differences. Explanations regarding the source of prejudice are complex, with questions, research, and theories focusing on myriad explanations ranging from person-ality factors or individual differences to sociological factors. Ekehammar and Akrami (2007) noted that one line of thought originates from the authori-tarian-personality theory (Adorno, Frenkel-Brunswik, Levinson, & Sanford, 1950; Cunningham et al., 2004) and the other from social-dominance theory.

Prejudice is defined in this chapter as prejudgments and stereotypes (often negative) about an individual or groups who come from backgrounds different than one's own.

One of the earliest theories of prejudice was conceptualized by Allport (1954), with his five degrees of prejudice. He stated: "prejudice is more from an incident in many lives; it is often lockstitched into the very fabric of per-sonality... to change it, the whole pattern of life would have to be altered" (p. 408). His five degrees include antilocution, avoidance, discrimination, violence or physical attack, and extermination. Antilocution is verbal, such as talking negatively to or about an individual or group different from one's own. At its worst, it is a form of hate speech. Avoidance occurs when an individual or group removes themselves from the presence of others to decrease or eliminate interactions with an individual or group from a different background.

For this chapter, avoidance and discrimination are most pertinent in the context of gifted education. It is quite possible that gifted education is used by some to avoid desegregation—to avoid Black and White students being placed in the same classes or schools or social settings (see Ford, 2010a). Further, it is possible that this avoidance can become a type of discrimination when Black students are denied, due to measures, attitudes, policies, and procedures, opportunities to be recruited and retained in gifted education. Title VI of the I Rights Act of 1964 sheds further light on this illegal practice.

Merton's (1968) model, albeit dated, is timely in that it demonstrates that one (fair-weather liberal) can be nonprejudiced in attitudes and beliefs, but still discriminate (policies, practices, behaviors), and one can be prejudiced but not discriminate (fair-weather liberal). Applying Merton's typology to gifted edu-cation, it is clear that one can be prejudiced and discriminate (all-weather bigot) and, conversely, one can be unprejudiced but not discriminate (all-weather liberal). Less apparent, but very impactful, are the other two types. Timid bigot shows that one can be prejudiced but not discriminate; and fair-weather liberal, in which one can be unprejudiced but still discriminate. In this latter situa-tion, Merton focuses on the role of social or group pressure that contribute to individuals acting out of character or acting against their beliefs to minimize or avoid social pressures and becoming outcasts.

Gaertner and Dovidio (1986, 2000) propose that prejudice has three components—affective, behavioral, and conative. They focus on new, newer, or contemporary racism. They argue that contemporary racism looks different from in the past. It is more likely to be covert (subtle, indirect) than overt, and more difficult to capture and sanction than in the past (see work by Sue, Capodilupo, & Holder, 2008; and Sue et al., 2007, 2009 on microaggressions, which captures the myriad of forms that prejudice can take through messages that communicate expectations). Microaggressions are common, daily verbal, behavioral, or environmental indignities, intentional or unintentional, that communicate hostile, derogatory, or negative racial slights and insults often toward Blacks and other culturally different groups. Sue et al. (2007) noted three distinct forms of microaggression in the context of racial microaggressions: (a)"microassault," (b) "microinsult," and (c) "microinvalidation."

Microassault is defined as an explicit racial derogation characterized primarily by verbal or non-verbal attack meant to hurt the intended victim through name-calling, avoidant behavior, or purposeful discriminatory actions. Microinsults are characterized by communications that convey rudeness and insensitivity and demean a person's racial heritage or identity. Microinvalidation is characterized by communications that exclude, negate, or nullify the psychological thoughts, feelings, or experiential reality of a person of color. Regardless of which form microaggressions take, for example, questioning the existence of racial-cultural issues, making stereotypic assumptions, and cultural insensitivity, they have an impact. Some types of microaggressions include colorblindness (e.g., "I don't see color. I treat everyone the same"), denial of personal bias (e.g., "I'm not a racist; I have Black friends"), and minimization of racial-cultural issues (e.g., "I don't think the problem is race or racism; I think it is classism"). Worth noting is that colorblindness ("I don't see color. People are people. I treat everyone the same") has been associated with higher levels of racism, prejudice, and discrimination and, thus, lower levels of empathy (see Sue et al., 2007, 2009, 2009).

African American students, or those who are not part of the mainstream, pay a price academically and socially. Continuing the aforementioned line of thought, I now focus on test issues.

Testing: Dogmatism Matters

The decision of which measure or instrument—test, checklist, or form—to adopt for screening and identification matters a great deal, and it is riddled with subjectivity and one's mindset or dogma (concretized beliefs, attitudes, and values). Sadly, even with data indicating that a given test or measure may be discriminatory, biased, unfair, or have a disparate impact on Black students, educators—teachers, administrators, school boards—are often reticent to change it. *Griggs v. Duke Power* (1971) was a seminal court case argued before the Supreme Court, in December 1970. It concerned employment discrimination and the disparate impact theory, which was decided in March 1971. Relying on the notion of disparate impact (see *Griggs v. Duke Power*, 1971), I always raise this question with educators: If Black students consistently perform poorly on a test, why do decision makers continue to use it? For myriad reasons—familiarity, cost, ease of administration, etc.—even in the face of disparate impact, it seems that once a test is selected, educators become beholden to it regardless of its usefulness, harm, controversy, and impact on Black and other culturally different students (Ford, 2004).

Under the notion of "objectivity," school personnel routinely adopt and use tests on which Black students perform less well than White students, while ignoring and disregarding tests where scores between the groups are similar, as it often the case on non-verbal measures (e.g., Ford, 2004; Naglieri & Ford, 2005). Here, dogmatism rears its ugly head because data showing the efficacy of other tests are ignored with business continuing as usual.

Selection of the Test or Instrument

In our highly litigious society, decisions matter; decisions cannot be made in an arbitrary, haphazard way, without regard to legal and moral implications and repercussions. Gifted education is not exempt from this and has come under the scrutiny of the Office for Civil Rights for both possible and real violations (see cases from Ford, 1996, 2010b). As painful as it may be to admit, discrimination exists in gifted education, with one form potentially being the test that is adopted for identification and placement (*Griggs vs. Duke Power Co.*, 1971).

The Supreme Court ruled against a procedure used by Duke Power when selecting employees for internal transfer and promotion to certain positions, namely, requiring a high school education and certain scores on broad aptitude tests. African American applicants, less likely to hold a high school diploma and averaging lower scores on the aptitude tests, were selected at a much lower rate for these positions compared to White candidates.

The Court found that, under Title VII of the Civil Rights Act, if such tests disparately impact minority groups, businesses must demonstrate that such tests are "reasonably related" to the job for which the test is required. Title VII of the Civil Rights Act prohibits employment tests (when used as a decisive factor in employment decisions) that are not a "reasonable measure of job performance," regardless of the absence of actual intent to discriminate. Since the aptitude tests involved, and the high school diploma requirement, were broad-based and not directly related to the jobs performed, Duke Power's employee transfer procedure was found by the Court to be in violation of the Civil Rights Act.

This case continues to carry significant implications for gifted education. We must be ever mindful of the extent to which the tests and measures or instruments we adopt are fair and equitable—do they have a disparate impact on racially and culturally different students' performance, gifted education access, and eventual representation? Do they unfairly advantage White students?

To say that tests are powerful in decision making is an understatement. High-stakes testing is now the norm in public school settings, be it sanctioned at the school district level or federally with such legislation as the No Child Left Behind Act. Some professionals are obsessed with tests, resulting in a form of reification (Gould, 1994). More bluntly, it is easy to hide behind the notion of "objectivity," whereby one blames tests for under-representation as opposed to acknowledging that a completely unbiased test is impossible. Specifically, an individual or group develops the format, items/questions, responses, and points associated with responses. This is not objective in the most basic sense.

Flanagan and Ortiz (2001) reported that most tests are culturally loaded and linguistically loaded. Those who are familiar with the items have an advantage, which often means middle-class White groups. Here is one case in point. Recently, I was working with a third-grade, low-income Black student on a homework assignment. On one item, she was asked to determine the correct answer (with two options) based on an item that focused on baiting a hook. One choice was fishing—an obvious and easy answer to me! She was lost, confused, stumped. She was clueless. She chose the other response—as I anticipated she might. I asked this intelligent, motivated student if she knew what "bait" meant. She said "no." Of course, this was a teachable moment. But, how would her teacher have interpreted her wrong response had I not been there? Was this student "dumb," ignorant, and not gifted—or was she intelligent but lacking exposure to fishing? This question significantly affects test selection, interpretation, and use. When educators get results on the test scores of students, they are in a powerful position to make (mis)interpretations—and decisions and changes that have far-reaching consequences (Ford & Frazier Trotman, 2000; Ford & Whiting, 2006; Whiting & Ford, 2006).

When racially and culturally different students score lower than White students, what are educators' interpretations *and* decisions? Do they focus on genetics or environment or both? Do they focus on the impact of the environment—meaning schools, families, and communities? Do they believe that intelligence is dynamic or malleable? The response seems to depend on one's view about the origin of intelligence (Ford, 2010b) and the value placed on the role of equity in educational settings. Too often, the genetically oriented deficit view is espoused or adopted with Black students; they are frequently deemed genetically and culturally inferior to White students.

It is clear that the adoption and eventual interpretation of test scores will influence decisions and how the results are used. Too frequently, the interpretations are used to legitimize the denial of Black students' identification and placement in gifted education. The argument goes something like this: "Black students did not score as high as White students; therefore, they should not be identified as gifted or admitted to gifted education. If we admit them, then they will struggle. This would be a disservice to them. Also, higher performing students would suffer if we 'water down' the gifted education class." This paternalistic view is a camouflage and an excuse that hides or detracts from the real problems or issues—deficit thinking and some form of dogmatic thinking, along with subsequent decisions and behaviors.

Summary and Conclusion

The under-representation of Black students in gifted education is a national problem that has been discussed, debated, and criticized for a number of years. Interpretations regarding this discrepancy between their representation in the larger school population and gifted education classes vary. Some explanations adopt some form of a social explanation or interpretation (e.g., prejudice and/or discrimination), while others point to personal interpretations (e.g., poor motivation) or cultural reasons (e.g., family and community do not value achievement). Whatever the interpretation or misinterpretation, under-representation is real, persistent, and pervasive, and thousands of Black and other racially different students do not have access to gifted education classes and services.

In this chapter, I have proposed that dogmatism in all of its forms both contributes to and causes under-representation. Attitudes, beliefs, and values all converge to hinder Black students' presence in gifted education—from referral to testing to placement. With dogma, change and progress—both needed and long overdue—seem impossible. Educators and decision makers, most of whom are White and middle class, have served as the key barriers and gatekeepers. For example, their inflexibility, fear of change, and desire to cater to the status quo resolutely hinder any and all attempts to make necessary changes in measures, policies, procedures, and practices. Just as important and problematic, deficit thinking (prejudicial thinking and negative stereotypes) about Black students suppresses their objectivity and commitment to equity and advocacy for this student group (Cunningham et al., 2004; Duckitt, 1992, 2006; Ford et al., 2002 LeVine, & Campbell, 1972). This affects their referral of Black students for gifted-education screening, assessment, and placement. Thus, while dogmatic thinking, often discussed in the context of politics and religion, is problematic. Such thinking cannot and must not be ignored in gifted education. As in other disciplines, dogmatism matters in powerful and negative ways, as I have attempted to show in this chapter.

References

Adorno, T. W., Frenkel-Brunswik, E., Levison, D. J., & Sanford, R. N. (1950). *The authoritarian personality*. New York, NY: Norton.

Allport, G. (1954). *The nature of prejudice*. New York, NY: Addison-Wesley.

Biernat, M., & Vescio, T. K. (2004). Values and preduice. In C. S. Crandall & M. Schaller (Eds.), *Social psychology of prejudice: Historical and contemporary issues*, (pp. 191–216). Lawrence, KS: Lewinian Press.

Biernat, M., Vescio, T. K., Theno, S. A., & Crandall, C. S. (1996). Values and prejudice: Toward understanding the impact of American values on outgroup attitudes. In C. Seligman, J. M. Olson, & M. P. Zanna (Eds.), *The psychology of values: The Ontario Symposium, vol. 8* (pp. 155–189). Hillsdale, NJ: Erlbaum.

Cunningham, W. A., Nezlek, J. B., & Banaji, M. R. (2004). Implicit and explicit ethnocentrism: Revisiting the ideologies of prejudice. *Personality and Social Psychology Bulletin, 30,* 1332–1346.

Duckitt, J. (1992). *The social psychology of prejudice*. New York, NY: Praeger.

Duckitt, J. (2006). Differential effects of right wing authoritarianism and social dominance orientation on outgroup attitudes and their mediation by threat from competitiveness to outgroups. *Personality and Social Psychology Bulletin, 32,* 684–694.

Ekehammar, B., & Akrami, N. (2007). Personality and prejudice: From big five personality factors to facets. *Journal of Personality, 75,* 899–925.

Elder, L. (2004). Diversity: Making sense of it through critical thinking. Retrieved from http://www.criticalthinking.org/articles/diversity.cfm

Elder, L., & Paul, R. (in press). Dogmatism, creativity, and critical thought: The reality of human minds and the possibility of critical societies. In D. Ambrose & R. J. Sternberg (Eds.), *How dogmatic beliefs harm creativity and higher-level thinking*. New York, NY: Routledge.

Feather, N. T. (1996). Values, deservingness, and attitudes toward high achievers: Research on tall poppies. In C. Seligman, J. M. Olson, & M. P. Zanna (Eds.), *Values: The Ontario Symposium, vol. 8* (pp. 215–251). Hillsdale, NJ: Erlbaum.

Feedler, R. (2003). Correcting the SAT's ethnic and social-class bias: A method for reexamining SAT scores. *Harvard Educational Review, 73,* 1–44.

Flanagan, D. P., & Ortiz, S. O. (2001). *Essentials of cross-battery assessment*. New York, NY: Wiley.

Ford, D. Y. (1996). *Reversing underachievement among gifted Black students*. New York, NY: Teachers College Press.

Ford, D. Y. (1999). *A study of factors affecting the recruitment and retention of minority teachers in gifted education*. Storrs, CT: University of Connecticut, National Research Center on the Gifted and Talented.

Ford, D. Y. (2004). *Intelligence testing and cultural diversity: Concerns, cautions, and considerations*. Storrs, CT: University of Connecticut, National Research Center on the Gifted and Talented.

Ford, D. Y. (2010a). Recruiting and retaining culturally diverse gifted students from diverse ethnic, cultural, and language groups. In J. A. Banks & C. A. Banks (Eds.), *Multicultural education: Issues and perspectives* (7th ed., pp. 371–391). Hoboken, NJ: Wiley.

Ford, D. Y. (2010b). *Reversing underachievement among gifted Black students* (2nd ed.). Waco, TX: Prufrock Press.

Ford, D. Y., Grantham, T. C., & Whiting, G. W. (2008). Culturally and linguistically diverse students in gifted education: Recruitment and retention issues. *Exceptional Children, 74,* 289–308.

Ford, D. Y., & Frazier Trotman, M. (2000). The Office for Civil Rights and non-discriminatory testing, policies, and procedures: Implications for gifted education. *Roeper Review, 23,* 109–112.

Ford, D. Y., Harris III, J. J., Tyson, C. A., & Frazier Trotman, M. (2002). Beyond deficit thinking: Providing access for gifted African American students. *Roeper Review, 24,* 52–58.

Ford, D. Y., & Whiting, G. W. (2006). Under-representation of diverse students in gifted education: Recommendations for nondiscriminatory assessment (part 1). *Gifted Education Press Quarterly, 20*(2), 2–6.

Gaertner, S. L., & Dovidio, J. (1986). The aversive form of racism. In J. Dovidio & S. L. Gaertner (Eds.), *Prejudice, discrimination, and racism* (pp. 61–89). New York, NY: Academic Press.

Gaertner, S. L., & Dovidio, J. (2000). *Reducing intergroup bias: The common ingroup identity model.* New York, NY: Psychology Press.

Gould, S. J. (1994). *The mismeasure of man* (rev. ed.). New York, NY: W.W. Norton.

Griggs vs. Duke Power Co., 401 U.S. 424. (1971).

Hare, W. (n.d.). Open-minded inquiry: A glossary of key concepts. Retrieved from http://www.criticalthinking.org/page.cfm?PageID=579&CategoryID=68

Hare, W. (2003a). The ideal of open-mindedness and its place in education. *Journal of Thought, 38.* 3–10.

Hare, W. (2003b). Is it good to be open-minded? *International Journal of Applied Philosophy, 17,* 73–87.

Hare, W. (2004). Assessing one's own open-mindedness. *Philosophy Now, 47,* 26–28.

Kremer-Hayon, L., Moore, M., & Nevat, R. (1985). Dogmatism in teacher education practices. *The High School Journal, 68,* 154–157.

Kremer-Hayon, L. Moore, M., & Novat, R. (1986). Dogmatism in teacher education practices: Aptitude-treatment interaction effects. *Research in Education, 36,* 19–26.

LeVine, R. A., & Campbell, D. (1972). *Ethnocentrism: Theories of conflict, ethnic attitudes and group behavior.* New York, NY: Wiley.

McBee, M. T. (2006). A descriptive analysis of referral sources for gifted identification screening by race and socioeconomic status. *The Journal of Secondary Gifted Education, 17,* 103–111.

McBee, M. T. (2010). Examining the probability of identification for gifted programs for students in Georgia elementary schools: A multilevel path analysis study. *Gifted Child Quarterly, 54,* 283–297.

Naglieri, J. A., & Ford, D. Y. (2005). Increasing minority children's representation in gifted education: A response to Lohman. *Gifted Child Quarterly, 49,* 29–36.

Merton, R. K. (1968). *Social theory and social structure.* Glencoe, IL: Free Press.

Office for Civil Rights Elementary and Secondary School Civil Rights Survey. (2008). Retrieved from http://ocrdata.ed.gov/

Paul, R. (n.d.). A model for the national assessment of higher order thinking. Retrieved from: http://www.criticalthinking.org/assessment/a-model-nal-assessment-hot.cfm

Rokeach, M. (1960). *The open and closed mind.* New York, NY: Basic Books.

Rokeach, M. (1968). *Beliefs, attitudes, and values.* San Francisco: Jossey-Bass.

Rokeach, M. (1973). *The nature of human values.* New York, NY: Free Press.

Santelices, M. V., & Wilson, M. (2010). Unfair treatment? The case of Freedle, the AT, and the standardization approach to differential item functioning. *Harvard Educational Review, 80,* 106–133.

Schwartz, S. H. (1992). Universals in the content and structure of values: Theoretical advances and empirical test in 20 countries. In M. Zanna (Ed.), *Advances in experimental social psychology, vol. 25* (pp. 1–65). Orlando, FL: Academic Press.

Sue, D., Capodilupo, C. M., & Holder, M. B. (2008). Racial microaggressions in the life experience of Black Americans. *Professional Psychology: Research and Practice, 39,* 329–336

Sue, D., Capodilupo, C. M., Torino, G. C., Bucceri, J. M., Holder, A. M. B., Nadal, K. L., & Esquilin, M. (2007). Racial microaggressions in everyday life. *American Psychologist, 62,* 271–286.

Sue, D., Lin, A. I., Torino, G. C. Capodilupo, C. M., & Rivera, D. P. (2009). Racial microaggressions and difficult dialogues on race in the classroom. *Cultural Diversity and Ethnic Minority Psychology, 15,* 183–190.

U.S. Department of Education. (2010). *Condition of education 2010.* Washington, DC: Author.

Whiting, G. W., & Ford, D. Y. (2006). Under-representation of diverse students in gifted education: Recommendations for nondiscriminatory assessment (part 2). *Gifted Education Press Quarterly, 20*(3), 6–10.

Shortsighted, Narrow-Minded Individuals and Dogmatism-Saturated Contexts

The Warping of Bright Minds

8

THE NOT-SO-INVISIBLE HAND OF ECONOMICS AND ITS IMPACT ON CONCEPTIONS AND MANIFESTATIONS OF HIGH ABILITY

Don Ambrose

RIDER UNIVERSITY

Large-scale contexts strongly shape the aspirations, behaviors, and development of bright young people. Conceptions and manifestations of giftedness and talent are shaped strongly by socioeconomic environments, which are influenced in turn by the theoretical and ideological climates generated by leaders of influential academic and practical fields. Unfortunately, high ability fields such as gifted education and creative studies pay insufficient heed to these contextual influences (Ambrose, 2005b, 2009a). Understanding large-scale contexts requires navigation into disciplines that attend to them: disciplines such as economics, sociology, and cultural anthropology. This chapter explores the nature of economic theory and practice in today's globalized world and derives some implications for high ability, which is operationally defined here as any blend of rare intelligence, talent, and creativity.

Interdisciplinary borrowing can enrich perceptions of big-picture patterns in fields such as creative studies and gifted education. Some recent interdisciplinary analyses have compared the structure and dynamics of disciplines that attend to the nature of high ability (i.e., gifted education and creative studies) with those of other academic fields finding that both creative studies and gifted education fit the pattern of fractured, porous, contested disciplines (e.g., English studies, political science, cultural anthropology) as opposed to unified, insular, firmly policed disciplines (e.g., economics, analytic philosophy) (Ambrose, 2006b; Ambrose, VanTassel-Baska, Coleman, & Cross, 2010). For better or worse, unified, insular, strongly policed disciplines establish and enforce consensus on a favored theoretical perspective and dissenters face huge obstacles in seeking professional acceptance and support for their work. In contrast, fractured, porous, contested disciplines suffer from a lack of internal consensus on key theories and constructs but they also benefit from this lack of absolute dominance by a single body of thought. They are better able to import ideas from other disciplines, thereby enriching their conceptual foundations. In addition, they often feature skirmishes between competing theoretical camps and these battles can be productive by generating creative new theories, or they can be counterproductive by stalling progress (Bender & Schorske, 1997).

The foreign discipline selected for deeper analysis here is economics in its dominant, neoclassical variant: one of the unified, insular, firmly policed disciplines (see Bender & Schorske, 1997). I focus on neoclassical economics (sometimes labeled "orthodox" or "mainstream" economics) because it is the dominant school of thought, providing the core conceptual framework for this unified-insular discipline. Other schools of thought such as Marxist economics, feminist economics, and ecological economics, sometimes collectively labeled as heterodox economics, have had little influence on public policy in the West and are largely excluded from the profession's leading publications and from more than token representation in most academic economics departments. Although it is important to keep in mind the ongoing development of marginalized economic theories, for present purposes I consider orthodox economics, in particular the body of economic theory that has been pressed into service in support of neoliberal policies, because it is the most influential conceptual framework of the discipline. While it may seem more germane to conduct this analysis with a discipline closer to the fractured, contested, porous structure and dynamics of creative studies and gifted education, the choice of economics can provide some insight about high ability because in the last few decades, the worldview and analytical approach it encompasses has strongly shaped the development of bright, creative people, as well as the social, intellectual, and environmental contexts in which they live, learn, and interact.

Neoclassical Economics Dominating Contexts for the Development of Gifted Young People

As a unified-insular, firmly policed discipline, neoclassical economics draws heavily from utilitarian and hedonistic schools of thought. An influential cadre of neoclassical theorists with libertarian leanings (e.g., Friedman, 1962, 1975; Hayek, 1944) argued that the economy could be understood adequately by assuming that participants in the economy (consumers, entrepreneurs) are self-interested, atomistic, rational actors who use complete sets of information to make self-serving decisions in perfectly competitive markets. They used this theoretical edifice to demonstrate that selfish decisions made by actors in the marketplace are maneuvered by the metaphorical *invisible hand* originally posited by Adam Smith (see Lal, 2006; Nozick, 1974; Smith, 1776/1937), into socially desirable outcomes upon which government intervention rarely would be able to improve. They then used this platform to promote radical changes in society's institutions to favor the deregulation of markets and to minimize government's mandate and size.

Most neoclassical economists prefer unfettered markets, support free trade, and see a limited role for government, and these preferences align with the market-worshiping, government-loathing premises of neoliberal ideology. Neoliberal reformers are successful because their policies tend to benefit those who have power and wealth and such policies have been adopted by supra-national entities including the International Monetary Fund (IMF; Gowdy, 2007; Stiglitz, 2004a). For this reason, in examining the influence of main-stream economics on bright young people more broadly, I concentrate on this neoliberal interpretation of neoclassical economics.

Advocates of laissez-faire politics and economics promote the greatest pos-sible freedom of action in the economic sphere. They argue that government should maintain a hands-off position vis-à-vis the economy so rational actors can respond to incentives and operate largely unrestrained to maximize their utility and their private returns; consequently, government regulation of private enterprise is discouraged strongly. From this perspective, government should not attempt interventions in the economy such as those employed in Franklin Delano Roosevelt's New Deal, or Lyndon Johnson's Great Society program for the alleviation of poverty. Instead, wealth is assumed to *trickle down* from the successful to the less industrious or fortunate; all will face a set of incentives that reward initiative.

The advanced industrial market economies have ushered in an era (of ques-tionable sustainability) in which privileged citizens in rich countries enjoy material plenty, conveniences, and unprecedented choices for consumer goods and services. Nevertheless, there are reasons for concern. If the application of policies informed by neoclassical economic theory provided only these benefits and posed no serious problems, and if it represented a plausible and predictive portrayal of economic reality, it would be hard to contest its beneficial influ-ence on high ability, at least to the extent that economic phenomena determine the life paths of bright young people. But there is reason to believe that neo-classical theory in general, its neoliberal interpretation in particular, distorts perceptions of the economy, society, and humanity's relationship with the bio-sphere. Furthermore, there is concern that it harmfully distorts the purposes of social institutions and the incentives that shape the aspiration development of gifted young people.

The Wrinkles Beneath the Cosmetics: Major Flaws in Neoclassical Economics and Neoliberal Ideology

Theoretical advancements over the last few decades have made clear that much neoclassical economic theory is of little relevance to the real world, which is made up of only partly rational human actors whose diverse behaviors are shaped by many non-economic motivations, who each belong to a diversity of social groups, and who interact in complex economies where externalities, information asymmetries and market power are pervasive. An externality is a cost generated by one person's decisions and borne by another person who had no say in the matter (e.g., pollution from a factory damaging a nearby neighborhood). Nevertheless, simplified distillations of neoclassical theory that neglect such confounding factors are harnessed to support neoliberal economic policies (Heilbroner & Milberg 1995; Gowdy 2007; Stiglitz 2006).

The canonical assumption that individuals can be modeled as excessively or exclusively self-interested is not supported empirically, as concern for one's own material payoffs are balanced by concerns for fairness, reciprocity and a willingness to reward cooperation and to punish uncooperative behavior, even at a cost to oneself (Bowles, 2004). Standard economic arguments demonstrating that economic outcomes delivered by free markets cannot be improved upon through government intervention do not withstand scrutiny because market exchanges are plagued by difficulties in policing and enforcing contracts (Bowles & Gintis, 1993), while information is far from perfect (Stiglitz, 2001), the preferences of economic actors are affected by the preferences of others (Bikhchandani, Hirshleifer, & Welch, 1998; Ormerod, 1998) while externalities are known to be pervasive (Daly, 1977/1992). Furthermore, markets are incapable of supplying public goods such as parks, libraries, and a clean atmosphere in sufficient quantity. Public goods are nonexcludable (it is impractical to exclude a person from benefiting from the good) and nonrival (one person's consumption of the good does not diminish another person's ability to consume the good) and hence they are not traded in or supplied by markets. Markets also fail to ensure appropriate signals for the conservation of natural resources, stewardship of the commons and the protection of ecological systems (Dietz, Ostrom, & Stern, 2003; Heal, 1998). I expand on some of these points below.

Some have delved deeply into the works of Adam Smith, the free-market icon neoconservative ideologues and neoclassical economists have used to bolster their arguments that selfishness is an acceptable or even desirable character trait to reinforce in the economic sphere because it is redeemed by the invisible hand. Fleischacker (2004) and Muller (1995) showed how Smith promoted free enterprise as a method for the downtrodden of his time to escape the shackles of his era's elites while also promoting government regulation to prevent the privileged and greedy from running roughshod over the rights of those less powerful. Wight (2007) and Fleischacker argued that Adam Smith's writings on the invisible hand have been misinterpreted and read selectively as embracing human selfishness and justifying the removal of impediments to market freedom. In fact, Smith's writings show that he believed selfish passions should be counterbalanced by social passions and that he believed market interaction should take place in a context of civility and shared mores. In short, neoclassical assumptions that humans can be modeled as actors making rational decisions on the basis of complete information for the sole purpose of maximizing personal utility have been seriously undermined (Beneria, 2003).

Mainstream economists are committed to enabling increased consumption levels through economic growth. They downplay redistribution as a means to redress deprivation, preferring to grow the economic pie rather than to slice it more equitably. This near-religious neoclassical worship of economic growth (Nelson, 2001) raises serious questions. For example, while unchecked growth may bring enormous benefits to a few, neoclassical economics ignores important costs of growth such as environmental degradation. It fails as well to consider how a healthy environment contributes to human wellbeing (Heal, 1998; Vemuri & Costanza, 2006). Unchecked growth also generates severe costs to all in the form of resource depletion, climate change, and other ecological damage; likewise, growth comes with social costs (Hirsch, 1976; Layard, 2005). Stiglitz (2004b), a Nobel laureate economist and former World Bank chief economist, argued that current free-market beliefs represent a form of ideological fundamentalism because they are based on faith instead of viable economic theory.

Although contentious, there is suggestive evidence that the study of economics promotes values and behaviors that are more selfish, less cooperative, and more corrupt (Frank & Schulze 2000; Kirchgassner 2005) while reducing support for measures to protect the environment (Ewert & Baker, 2001). To the extent that this occurs, it has a pernicious effect on the aspiration growth and talent development of the gifted. Particularly troubling from a high-ability perspective is evidence suggesting that although economic theory poorly describes society or human behavior and motivations, by informing the development of policies and institutions, it favors and encourages the self-centered behavior posited by the model. Economic theory thus leads to the design of institutions intended to function in a society of knaves. Ironically, these institutions then beget knaves, leading to a less altruistic, less cooperative society that increasingly fits the dismal predictions of the neoclassical economic model (Bowles, 2004; Ferraro, Pfeffer, & Sutton, 2005).

Even if we were to accept the dubious neoliberal tenets positing materialistic self-interest and unchecked economic growth as good, the theory still fails to deliver the outcomes it promises. The neoliberal promise that private capital would respond to market deregulation and free-trade policies to deliver material prosperity to the masses has yet to be fulfilled. Instead, despite several decades of neoliberal-inspired market and governmental reforms on the world and US stages, too often privatization undertaken in the name of unleashing free enterprise has led to high levels of corruption and the stripping of public assets instead of wealth creation (Stiglitz, 2003). Particularly in the United States, inequality of income and wealth have escalated overall, the middle class has seen its income stagnate and its security erode, and inequality of opportunity has festered over the past few decades (Ackerman & Alstott, 1999; Baker, 2007; Irvin, 2007; Rapley, 2004).

Yet neoclassical economists rarely reflect on how such failures may in fact be linked to their theoretical framework, and such nonreflection is a classic sign of dogmatism. Heilbroner, a noted historian of economic thought, underlined the "inextricable entanglement of economics with capitalism" and its apologism for the excesses of capitalism (Heilbroner & Milberg, 1995, p. 113). As Stiglitz (1996, 2006) has argued, East Asian countries experienced dramatic economic growth in recent decades, not because governments pursued market liberalization policies in accordance with the neoliberal tax-cutting, deregulating, privatizing tenets of the Washington consensus, but because governments intervened actively and pervasively in the economy, regulating markets, investing in infrastructure and technology, promoting education and technological development, fostering cooperation between government and firms and between firms and their workers, and striving for a more equitable distribution of income. In contrast, countries that followed the deregulated markets, hands-off government script laid out by the Washington consensus experienced lower rates of growth, more uneven economic development and worsening gaps between rich and poor.

All of these shortcomings taken together have encouraged dissenting economists to speak out ever more loudly against the hegemony of neoclassical theory and to advocate for more nuanced economic theory that is relevant to the evolving social and ecological issues in the complex real world in which we live. A particularly cogent set of criticisms appear in Fullbrook (2004). Dissenters have even gone so far as to establish a journal whose tongue-in-cheek title for the first half-dozen years was the *Post-Autistic Economics Review* (now renamed the *Real-World Economic Review)*, which compiles diverse critiques of neoclassical theory and its application. The original title of the journal was somewhat crass given the appropriate sensitivities attending this particular dimension of special needs; nevertheless, the metaphor of autism is informative. The post-autistic movement in economics diagnosed mainstream economic theory as autistic because it manifests the following behaviors of an autistic child:

- Serious deficits in communication, interaction, and learning. Economics fails to learn from the real world and from the successes and failures caused by the past application of policies derived from neoclassical theories.
- Preoccupation with abnormal behaviors such as aimless, repetitive acts. Economists fall into counterproductive fixated response patterns such as repeatedly applying failed economic policies to the economic development of third-world nations. Chang (2002) and Stiglitz (2006) documented how influential neoliberal ideologues and neoclassical economists have forced third-world countries to transform their economic systems, making them align strongly with neoclassical tenets as a requirement for international economic aid. These policies have led to economic stagnation and often have greatly expanded the ranks of the poor. In addition, they are not the

same policies developed nations followed when they were modernizing their economies and moving toward prosperity.

- Excessive attachment to certain objects. Neoliberal economists, politicians, lobbyists, and pundits exhibited blind faith in policies promulgated by ideologically bound institutions such as the World Bank and the International Monetary Fund, despite their less than sterling track records (see Daly 2007; Stiglitz 2004a, 2006).

Other disciplines are increasingly looking at economics more critically, identifying shortcomings with the predominant theory and injecting new ideas for ways to create a more credible economic theory. For instance, Kasser, Cohn, Kanner, and Ryan (2007) analyzed the peer-reviewed literature in psychology and found that it rarely has examined the effects of different economic systems on people's lives. They then examined the values that underlie American Corporate Capitalism (ACC), the model being promoted around the world, and reached,

> a provocative conclusion: The values and goals most closely expressive of ACC's ideology and institutions are also those that oppose and potentially undermine people's concern for: (a) promoting the welfare of others in the broader community; (b) developing a sense of connection and closeness to other humans; and (c) choosing paths in life that help them to feel worthy and autonomous.
>
> *(p. 8)*

Implications for Gifted Education

If gifted education and creative studies have been influenced by the far-reaching grasp of neoclassical economic theory and if that theory is seriously flawed as its many detractors increasingly claim, we should consider analyzing its impact in these fields to assess whether corrective measures are required. This analysis illustrates the possibility that many of the brightest young people suffer from warped aspiration development due to the influence of neoclassical economics. It suggests that the neoclassical economic system traps many gifted economists, policy makers, and graduates of business schools within a dangerous form of utopianism that hurts billions worldwide. It raises questions about the worthiness of current conceptions of merit, which exert strong influence in gifted education. It also suggests the need for stronger emphasis on wisdom and panoramic thinking (broad-scope, long-range thinking skills). Such attention to wise, panoramic thinking could provide some insulation for bright young people who otherwise might fall prey to the pernicious effects of the theoretical hegemony that has dominated economics for so long.

It would be surprising if the education system was not influenced strongly by neoclassical economics, which has so thoroughly dominated most of the world's socioeconomic systems for decades. Aside from powerfully shaping the socioeconomic and political contexts of modern societies, which in turn influence the aspirations and talent development of bright young people, there is direct evidence that it indoctrinates them in school settings. Many states offer high-school courses in economics, and these courses strongly adhere to neoclassical tenets (Maier & Nelson, 2007). In American universities, more than a million students per annum take an introductory economics course, which typically is saturated with neoclassical ideology, while fewer than 2% proceed to complete the more advanced courses in economics where the limitations of neoclassical theory are more likely to be discussed (Salemi & Siegfried, 1999). The fact that many programs require economics credits at the introductory level indicates that large numbers of students are exposed to simplistic, utopian perspectives on neoclassical economic theory and its accompanying neoliberal ideology.

Warped Aspirations Emerging From the Dogmatism of Neoclassical Economics

One important way that neoclassical economics can impact education in general, and gifted education in particular, is its portrayal of the individual as an atomistic, self-interested, coldly rational cost-benefit calculator and society as but the sum of such individuals. Strong attention to individual achievement in education may be shaped somewhat by this notion of atomistic individualism. Emphases on selection of students for gifted programs, high SAT scores, and perfect GPAs all contribute to the development and pursuit of highly competitive personal aspirations.

It is the nature of those aspirations that is most vulnerable to shaping by neoclassical economics and neoliberal ideology. Gifted young people face pressure from parents, educators, and the cultural context to become successful pursuers of material gain and self-aggrandizement. The tendency of many to follow high-profile, potentially prestigious, and lucrative career paths without sufficient thought about whether or not these paths fit their dispositions, talents, or value systems (see Frank & Cook, 1995) suggests that many gifted youths do feel strong pressure from dogmatic neoclassical economic influence on culture in industrial societies, which encourages them to become coldly rational, self-interested players in a Darwinian, materialistic economy.

Outside the framework of neoclassical economic theory, this form of development in its most hyper-materialistic, vainglorious forms, looks like warped variations of aspiration growth such as those represented in the life trajectories of aggressive shallow opulence and privileged depravity posited by Ambrose (2003a). In a synthesis of research and theory from sociology, economics, and ethical philosophy, Ambrose discerned socioeconomic barriers to aspiration development and self-fulfillment as well as various life trajectories bright young people can follow as they develop their talents. In the synthesis, these two life trajectories represent obsession with egoistic individualism and they lead to limited self-fulfillment, whereas several other life trajectories escape egocentrism and lead toward highly altruistic forms of strong self-fulfillment. Those who follow the life trajectory of aggressive shallow opulence become egocentric individuals who are driven, highly competitive, exploitative of others, and insatiably materialistic. These propensities enable them to achieve various forms of gratification, but they are incapable of deep self-fulfillment. Those who follow the trajectory of privileged depravity develop very strong but warped aspirations that lead them toward highly aggressive power seeking in pursuit of ego-gratifying domination over others.

It is likely that neoclassical economics, with its dogmatic emphases on selfish individualism and insatiable materialistic gain, pushes bright young people away from altruism and the deeper forms of self-fulfillment, toward egocentric development, which discourages altruism and allows limited self-fulfillment at best. If gifted youth and the educators who serve them were able to resist this form of neoclassical pressure, individual aspiration development might come to resemble the less self-centered, less materialistic, more altruistic forms of personal development espoused by ethical philosophers (see Gewirth, 1998; Layard, 2005).

Dangerous Utopian Dogmatism

Neoclassical economics might be encouraging yet another life trajectory with more pernicious effects. Bright young people who absorb the neoclassical model and see it as an absolute truth can become influential, unyielding proponents of policies derived from the Chicago-school variant of the model. Examples include the professional economists at the World Bank and the IMF who imposed neoclassical rules and structures on third-world nations to the serious detriment of the populations in those nations (see Chang, 2002; Stiglitz, 2006). Although bright, these economists acted dogmatically, ignoring all criticism and any evidence of the harm their policies would generate.

Paradoxically, these economists saw themselves as serving a greater good— emancipating the populations their policies actually were hurting. Such dogmatism suggests entrapment within a utopian thought framework. Utopian thinking revolves around unwavering, absolutist belief in an ideology aimed at bettering the world in some way, but it tends to devolve into blind dogmatism that can generate much human misery up to and including oppression and genocide (see Kumar, 1987; Weitz, 2003). The aggressive, globalized spread of unchecked, free-market ideology in recent decades may be symptomatic of a pernicious neoliberal-neoclassical utopianism (Ambrose, 2008, 2009b).

Nonmeritorious Meritocracies

If neoclassical economics actually provided nondogmatic, accurate guidance for the ideal set of public policies for the organization of market society as its proponents contend (e.g., Friedman, 1962, 1975; Hayek, 1944; Lal, 2006; Nozick, 1974), the result would be a near-perfect meritocracy as a context for the actions of gifted individuals. Those with the most intelligence, talent, and creativity would rise to the top of society, amass considerable wealth, and serve as positive exemplars for others, and some of their wealth actually would *trickle down* enriching everyone else. Without moral qualms, gifted individuals would be free to direct their talent-development toward materialistic pursuits and self-glorification. In actuality, societies whose public policies are shaped by neoclassical economic theory and its attendant dogmatic ideology of neoliberalism, which is closely aligned with neoconservatism, do exert strong pressure on all young people, including the gifted, to acquire and hoard excessive amounts of material goods and to strive for self-aggrandizement (Ambrose, 2002, 2003a, 2005a, 2009b). Whether or not such behavior represents meritorious manifestations of gifts and talents is highly questionable.

Gifted education heavily relies on notions of merit, especially when systems are devised to select the most meritorious students for gifted programs. Given the flaws in mainstream economic theory and practice, conceptions of merit and the prevalent assumption that we live in a relatively pure meritocracy must be challenged. According to Nobel Laureate economist Amartya Sen (2000) merit is underdefined in today's economy. He argued that

> Conventional notions of "meritocracy" often attach the label of merit to *people* rather than actions. A person with standardly recognized "talents" (even something as nebulous as "intelligence") can, then, be seen as a meritorious person even if he or she were not to use the "talents" to perform acts with good consequences or laudable propriety.
>
> *(p. 12)*

Moreover, Sen claimed that conceptions of merit lacking clarification by conceptions of the good society are somewhat vacuous.

Sen's insights about merit connect with arguments about the nature of high ability in the field of gifted education. If we promote the value-free development of gifts and talents without concern for the ways in which gifted young people will apply their considerable abilities when they emerge into the adult world, we may be creating exceptionally creative and clever egocentrists who see others as mere rungs in a tall ladder to climb in their pursuit of materialism and vainglory. If so, our own ill-formed conceptions of merit will reinforce distorted conceptions of merit in societies strongly shaped by neoclassical economic theory and neoliberal ideology. In such conditions, the wrong people may be rewarded as meritorious.

Severe inequalities in neoclassical-neoliberal societies further confound notions of merit. Sen (2000) argued that conceptions of merit require articulation of what a good society entails, and valid notions of a good society must include concern for equality and justice. In highly stratified nations such as the United States, children born into privilege have enormous developmental and status advantages. They have the financial wherewithal in the form of inheritance trust funds, enriching cultural experiences, and other significant benefits that allow them to generate and follow lofty personal aspirations. They enjoy the networks of privilege, which include highly influential relatives and friends who can help with legacy admissions to prestigious schools and, upon maturity, nepotistic appointments to high-status positions in corporations and other organizations. Meanwhile underprivileged children of high ability suffer from considerable barriers to their aspiration development: everything from malnutrition, to dangerous neighborhoods, to lead-paint poisoning in their squalid homes, to under-funded, dangerous schools, to corporations abusing them with environmental racism (locating toxic industrial facilities in poor neighborhoods) (see Ambrose, 2002, 2003a, 2005a; Bullard, 2005; Kozol, 1991, 2005).

With such glaring discrepancies between the prospects for privileged and deprived gifted children, the meritocracy is illusory at best—a cruel joke on those most in need of developmental support. The privileged enjoy substantial face-value merit along life's journey (i.e., unearned merit) while the deprived have little chance to become meritorious. At the very least, educators of the gifted should be more aware of the socioeconomic discrepancies that make meritocracies in dogmatism-saturated, neoclassical-neoliberal-dominated societies a cruel illusion. Fortunately, there has been some attention to this in the field (see Borland, Schnur, & Wright, 2000; Borland & Wright, 1994, 2000; Hébert, 2002; Hébert & Beardsley, 2001; VanTassel-Baska & Stambaugh, 2007). Adequately compensating for the discrepancies will take considerable will on the part of citizens and policy makers.

The Need for Wisdom, Ethical Responsibility, and Panoramic Thinking Skills

Another implication for the development of the gifted is the need to emphasize broader and deeper thinking skills conducive to wise thought and action. Sternberg (2001a, 2001b, 2005, 2009) has argued persuasively for magnifying wisdom in conceptions of high ability by attending to the ways in which wisdom can be synthesized with intelligence and creativity. His insights are particularly relevant to our analyses of the dogmatism plaguing current socioeconomic systems. A number of other insightful scholars have been emphasizing the importance of ethical wisdom in the development of highly able minds (e.g., Gardner, 2007, 2008; Gardner, Csikszentmihalyi, & Damon, 2001;

Seider, Davis, & Gardner, 2009). This attention to ethical responsibility makes room for entrepreneurial innovation while directly addressing the systemic lack of social and environmental responsibility embedded in the dogmatism of neo-classical theory.

Ideally, gifted youth will develop their panoramic-scanning capacities: the ability to perceive and appreciate broad-scope influences on issues and problems as well as the long-range implications of one's actions (Ambrose, 1996). Such enhanced awareness is within the realm of possibility. The Japanese seem to have institutionalized some panoramic-scanning ability within their economic system because their executives, bureaucrats, and workers focus on the long term much more than Westerners who focus on short-term gains in the stock market or on quarterly reports (Locke, 2005). Of course, the Japanese could strengthen their own panoramic-scanning capacities much more by recogniz-ing their own entrapment within the growth at all costs, ignore the human and environmental costs, dicta of neoclassical economic theory.

Employing critical theory in the training of educators who want to work with the gifted, and in the education of the gifted themselves, could represent a good starting point for the strengthening of panoramic scanning. Critical theory reveals the unfairness, corruption, and mindless folly in socioeconomic systems and the ways in which education suffers from its influence (see Apple, 2004, 2005, 2006, 2009, 2010; Berliner, 2006, in press; Bowers, 1995, in press; Giroux, 1997, 1999, 2008, 2009, in press; Kozol, 1991, 1995, 2005; McLaren & Farahmandpur, 2001; Nichols & Berliner, 2007). Engaging students in critical analyses of the socioeconomic and cultural contexts that surround them can make them more aware of the influences on their own aspiration development including the enormous advantages they enjoy or the daunting barriers they face. Such awareness can make privileged, gifted youth more sensitive to the plight of their less privileged peers, thereby magnifying the likelihood that they will develop more altruistic aspirations and life trajectories. It also could make them more resistant to dogmatic entrapment within economic thought frameworks that encourage selfish, egocentric materialism.

Conclusion

All of these implications connect back to the works of Adam Smith, the icon of neoclassical economics and neoliberal ideology. As discussed earlier, neo-liberal ideologues borrowed what they wanted from Smith's work, specifically his championing of free-market dynamics and individual economic freedom, while ignoring his advocacy of cooperation, prudent government regulation, and altruism (see Fleischacker, 2004; Muller, 1995). If Smith could assess today's trends and issues in gifted education, his blending of economic and moral the-ory suggests that he would prefer to see gifted young people integrating their pursuit of self-actualization with strong social responsibility, ethical awareness, and caring for others. He also would lament the inequality of opportunity in the American education system and in the larger society (Ambrose, 2006a).

Finally, we can learn from the dogmatism in neoclassical economic theory and research. Even though gifted education seems to be a fragmented, contested discipline (Ambrose et al., 2010), there have been times when a particular theoretical perspective dominated conceptions of high ability—IQ conceptions of mind for example (see Kaufman, Sternberg, & Grigorenko, 2008; Sternberg, 1985, 1988, 1990, 1997, 1999, 2004, 2007a, 2007b). There also have been times when a research paradigm became hegemonic. Coleman, Sanders, and Cross (1997) and Borland (1990) provided compelling overviews of the ways in which the positivist investigative paradigm has dominated gifted education. Moreover, even in contested disciplines, warring theoretical camps can adhere dogmatically to the tenets of a favored theory or investigative approach while not appreciating the virtues of competing theories or methods. Rather than view a rival theory or investigative approach as totally misguided, it may be more productive to consider it an incomplete perspective on high ability with some possibly virtuous elements that could augment and strengthen one's own perspective. For example, the criticism of neoclassical economic theory in this analysis should be tempered somewhat with appreciation for its magnification of innovation and individual freedom. In gifted education, opponents in arguments over the applicability of multiple-intelligence theory to the field (see Delisle, 2003), for example, could search each other's perspectives for possible common ground.

Looking at the structure, dynamics, and history of economics as a discipline provides an interesting vision of problems and possibilities in high-ability fields such as gifted education and creative studies. Scanning the discipline of economics reveals some strong contextual influences on the development of gifted young people while also giving us some important lessons about scholarly dogmatism. After ascending to positions of dominance in academic disciplines, theories, inquiry paradigms, and philosophical frameworks can become dogmatically entrenched and overgeneralized, resisting countervailing data and alternative perspectives while hampering investigative progress (Ambrose, 1998, 2003b; Borland, 1990; Coleman et al., 1997; Gillespie, 1992; Longino, 1990; Overton, 1984; Williams, 1999). Scrutinizing other disciplines such as philosophy, sociology, or some of the natural sciences likely can provide very different lessons. More attention to insights from foreign disciplines can help us strengthen high-ability fields while refining the ways in which we guide the development of today's brightest young minds.

Acknowledgment

I am deeply indebted to environmental economist Tom Green for his insightful guidance and critiques pertaining to the nuances of economic theory and research used in earlier drafts of this chapter. If any misinterpretations remain they are mine.

References

Ackerman, B. A., & Alstott, A. (1999). *The stakeholder society*. New Haven, CT: Yale University Press.

Ambrose, D. (1996). Panoramic scanning: Essential element of higher-order thought. *Roeper Review, 18*, 280–284.

Ambrose, D. (1998). A model for clarification and expansion of conceptual foundations. *Gifted Child Quarterly, 42*, 77–86.

Ambrose, D. (2002). Socioeconomic stratification and its influences on talent development: Some interdisciplinary perspectives. *Gifted Child Quarterly, 46*, 170–180.

Ambrose, D. (2003a). Barriers to aspiration development and self-fulfillment: Interdisciplinary insights for talent discovery. *Gifted Child Quarterly, 47*, 282–294.

Ambrose, D. (2003b). Paradigms, mind shifts, and the 21st-century zeitgeist: New contexts for creative intelligence. In D. Ambrose, L. M. Cohen & A. J. Tannenbaum (Eds.), *Creative Intelligence: Toward theoretical integration* (pp. 11–31). Cresskill, NJ: Hampton Press.

Ambrose, D. (2005a). Aspiration growth, talent development, and self-fulfillment in a context of democratic erosion. *Roeper Review, 28*, 11–19.

Ambrose, D. (2005b). Interdisciplinary expansion of conceptual foundations: Insights from beyond our field. *Roeper Review, 27*, 137–143.

Ambrose, D. (2006a). Influences of Adam Smith's "invisible hand" on giftedness and talent. [Review of Fleischacker, S. (2004). On Adam Smith's wealth of nations: A philosophical companion. Princeton, NJ: Princeton University Press.]. *Gifted Child Quarterly, 50*, 185–188.

Ambrose, D. (2006b). Large-scale contextual influences on creativity: Evolving academic disciplines and global value systems. *Creativity Research Journal, 18*, 75–85.

Ambrose, D. (2008). Utopian visions: Promise and pitfalls in the global awareness of the gifted. *Roeper Review, 30*, 52–60.

Ambrose, D. (2009a). *Expanding visions of creative intelligence: An interdisciplinary exploration*. Cresskill, NJ: Hampton Press.

Ambrose, D. (2009b). Morality and high ability: Navigating a landscape of altruism and malevolence. In D. Ambrose & T. L. Cross (Eds.), *Morality, ethics, and gifted minds* (pp. 49–71). New York, NY: Springer.

Ambrose, D., VanTassel-Baska, J., Coleman, L. J., & Cross, T. L. (2010). Unified, insular, firmly policed or fractured, porous, contested, gifted education? *Journal for the Education of the Gifted, 33*, 453–478.

Apple, M. W. (2004). *Ideology and curriculum* (3rd ed.). New York, NY: Routledge.

Apple, M. W. (2005). Audit cultures, commodification, and class and race strategies in education. *Policy Futures in Education, 3*, 378–399.

Apple, M. W. (2006). *Educating the "right" way: Markets, standards, God and inequality* (2nd ed.). New York, NY: Routledge.

Apple, M. W. (2009). Can critical education interrupt the right? *Discourse: Studies in the Cultural Politics of Education, 30*, 239–251.

Apple, M. W. (2010). *Global crises, social justice, and education*. New York, NY: Routledge.

Baker, D. (2007). *The United States since 1980*. New York, NY: Cambridge University Press.

Bender, T., & Schorske, C. E. (Eds.). (1997). *American academic culture in transformation: Fifty years, four disciplines*. Princeton, NJ: Princeton University Press.

Beneria, L. (2003). *Gender, development, and globalization: Economics as if people mattered*. New York, NY: Routledge.

Berliner, D. C. (2006). Our impoverished review of educational reform. *Teachers College Record, 108*, 949–995.

Berliner, D. C. (in press). Narrowing curriculum, assessments, and conceptions of what it means to be smart in the US schools: Creaticide by design. In D. Ambrose & R. J. Sternberg (Eds.), *How dogmatic beliefs harm creativity and higher-level thinking.* New York, NY: Routledge.

Bikhchandani, S., Hirshleifer, D., & Welch, I. (1998). Learning from the behavior of others: Conformity, fads, and informational cascades. *The Journal of Economic Perspectives, 12,* 151–170.

Borland, J. H. (1990). Post-positivist inquiry: Implications of the new philosophy of science for the field of the education of the gifted. *Gifted Child Quarterly, 34,* 161–167.

Borland, J. H., Schnur, R., & Wright, L. (2000). Economically disadvantaged students in a school for the academically gifted: A postpositivist inquiry into individual and family adjustment. *Gifted Child Quarterly, 44,* 13–32.

Borland, J. H., & Wright, L. (1994). Identifying young, potentially gifted, economically disadvantaged students. *Gifted Child Quarterly, 38,* 164–171.

Borland, J. H., & Wright, L. (2000). Identifying and educating poor and under-represented gifted students. In K. A. Heller, F. J. Mönks, R. J. Sternberg & R. F. Subotnik (Eds.), *International handbook of giftedness and talent* (2nd ed., pp. 587–594). Oxford, England: Pergamon.

Bowers, C. A. (1995). *Educating for an ecologicaly sustainable culture: Rethinking moral education, creativity, intelligence, and other modern orthodoxies.* Albany, NY: SUNY Press.

Bowers, C. A. (in press). The challenge facing educational reformers: Making the transition from individual to ecological intelligence in an era of climate change. In D. Ambrose & R. J. Sternberg (Eds.), *How dogmatic beliefs harm creativity and higher-level thinking.* New York, NY: Routledge.

Bowles, S. (2004). *Microeconomics: Behaviour, institutions and evolution.* Princeton, NJ: Princeton University Press.

Bowles, S., & Gintis, H. (1993). The revenge of Homo Economicus: Contested exchange and the revival of political economy. *Journal of Economic Perspectives, 7,* 83–102.

Bullard, R. D. (Ed.). (2005). *The quest for environmental justice: Human rights and the politics of pollution.* Berkeley: University of California Press.

Chang, H. J. (2002). *Kicking away the ladder: Development strategy in historical perspective.* London, England: Anthem Press.

Coleman, L. J., Sanders, M. D., & Cross, T. L. (1997). Perennial debates and tacit assumptions in the education of gifted children. *Gifted Child Quarterly, 41,* 103–111.

Daly, H. E. (1992). *Steady state economics* (2nd ed.). London, England: Earthscan. (Original work published 1977)

Daly, H. E. (2007). *Ecological economics and sustainable development: Selected essays of Herman Daly.* Cheltenham, England: Edward Elgar.

Delisle, J. R. (2003). The false security of inclusivity. *Understanding Our Gifted, 15*(2), 3–7.

Dietz, T., Ostrom, E., & Stern, P. C. (2003). The struggle to govern the commons. *Science, 302,* 1907–1912.

Ewert, A., & Baker, D. (2001). Standing for where you sit: An exploratory analysis of the relationship between academic major and environment beliefs. *Environment and Behavior, 33,* 687–707.

Ferraro, F., Pfeffer, J., & Sutton, R. I. (2005). Economics language and assumptions: How theories can become self-fulfilling. *Academy of Management Review, 30,* 8–24.

Fleischacker, S. (2004). *On Adam Smith's wealth of nations: A philosophical companion.* Princeton, NJ: Princeton University Press.

Frank, B., & Schulze, G. G. (2000). Does economics make citizens corrupt? *Journal of Economic Behavior and Organization, 43,* 101–113.

Frank, R. H., & Cook, P. J. (1995). *The winner-take-all society.* New York, NY: Free Press.

Friedman, M. (1962). *Capitalism and freedom.* Chicago: University of Chicago Press.

Friedman, M. (1975). *An economist's protest: Columns in political economy* (2nd ed.). Glen Ridge, NJ: Thomas Horton and Daughters.

Fullbrook, E. (Ed.). (2004). *A guide to what's wrong with economics.* London, England: Anthem Press.

Gardner, H. (Ed.). (2007). *Responsibility at work.* San Francisco: Jossey Bass.

Gardner, H. (2008). Creativity, wisdom, and trusteeship. In A. Craft, H. Gardner & G. Claxton (Eds.), *Creativity, wisdom, and trusteeship: Exploring the role of education* (pp. 49–65). Thousand Oaks, CA: Corwin Press.

Gardner, H., Csikszentmihalyi, M., & Damon, W. (2001). *Good work: When excellence and ethics meet.* New York, NY: Basic Books.

Gewirth, A. (1998). *Self-fulfillment.* Princeton, NJ: Princeton University Press.

Gillespie, D. (1992). *The mind's we: Contextualism in cognitive psychology.* Carbondale, IL: Southern Illinois University Press.

Giroux, H. A. (1997). *Border crossings: Cultural workers and the politics of education.* New York, NY: Routledge.

Giroux, H. A. (1999). Schools for sale: Public education, corporate culture, and the citizen-consumer. *The Educational Forum, 63,* 140–149.

Giroux, H. A. (2008). *Against the terror of neoliberalism: Politics beyond the age of greed.* Boulder, CO: Paradigm.

Giroux, H. A. (2009). *Youth in a suspect society: Democracy or disposability?* New York, NY: MacMillan.

Giroux, H. A. (in press). Dark times: Bush, Obama, and the specter of authoritarianism in American politics. In D. Ambrose & R. J. Sternberg (Eds.), *How dogmatic beliefs harm creativity and higher-level thinking.* New York, NY: Routledge.

Gowdy, J. (2007). Can economic theory stop being a cheerleader for corporate capitalism? *Psychological Inquiry, 18,* 33–35.

Hayek, F. A. (1944). *The road to serfdom.* Chicago: University of Chicago Press.

Heal, G. M. (1998). *Valuing the future: Economic theory and sustainability.* New York, NY: Colombia University Press.

Hébert, T. P. (2002). Educating gifted children from low socioeconomic backgrounds: Creating visions of a hopeful future. *Exceptionality, 10,* 127–138.

Hébert, T. P., & Beardsley, T. M. (2001). Jermaine: A critical case study of a gifted black child living in rural poverty. *Gifted Child Quarterly, 45,* 85–103.

Heilbroner, R., & Milberg, W. (1995). *The crisis of vision in modern economic thought.* Cambridge University Press.

Hirsch, F. (1976). *The social limits to growth.* Cambridge, MA: Harvard University Press.

Irvin, G. (2007). Growing inequality in the neoliberal heartland. *Post-Autistic Economics Review, 43,* 2–23.

Kasser, T., Cohn, S., Kanner, A. D., & Ryan, R. M. (2007). Some costs of American corporate capitalism: A psychological exploration of value and goal conflicts. *Psychological Inquiry, 18,* 1–22.

Kaufman, J. C., Sternberg, R. J., & Grigorenko, E. L. (2008). *The essential Sternberg: Essays on intelligence, psychology, and education.* New York, NY: Springer.

Kirchgassner, G. (2005). Why are economists different? *European Journal of Political Economy, 21,* 543–562.

Kozol, J. (1991). *Savage inequalities: Children in America's schools.* New York, NY: Crown.

Kozol, J. (1995). *Amazing grace: The lives of children and the conscience of a nation.* New York, NY: Crown.

Kozol, J. (2005). *The shame of the nation: The restoration of apartheid schooling in America.* New York, NY: Crown.

Kumar, K. (1987). *Utopias and anti-utopias in modern times.* Oxford, England: Blackwell.

Lal, D. (2006). *Reviving the invisible hand: The case for classical liberalism in the twenty-first century.* Princeton, NJ: Princeton University Press.

Layard, R. (2005). *Happiness: Lessons from a new science.* London, England: Penguin.

Locke, R. (2005). Japan, refutation of Neoliberalism. *Post-Autistic Economics Review, 30,* Retrieved from http://www.paecon.net/PAEReview/issue23/Locke23.htm

Longino, H. E. (1990). *Science as social knowledge: Values and objectivity in scientific inquiry.* Princeton, NJ: Princeton University Press.

Maier, M. H., & Nelson, J. A. (2007). *Introducing economics: A critical guide for teaching.* New York, NY: M. E. Sharpe.

McLaren, P., & Farahmandpur, R. (2001). Teaching against globalization and the new imperialism: Toward a revolutionary pedagogy. *Journal of Teacher Education, 52,* 136–150.

Muller, J. Z. (1995). *Adam Smith in his time and ours: Designing the decent society.* Princeton, NJ: Princeton University Press.

Nelson, R. (2001). *Economics as religion: From Samuelson to Chicago and beyond.* University Park: Pennsylvania State University Press.

Nichols, S. L., & Berliner, D. C. (2007). *Collateral damage: How high-stakes testing corrupts America's schools.* Cambridge, MA: Harvard Education Press.

Nozick, R. (1974). *Anarchy, state, and utopia.* New York, NY: Basic Books.

Ormerod, P. (1998). *Butterfly economics: A new general theory of social and economic behaviour.* London, England: Faber and Faber.

Overton, W. F. (1984). World views and their influence on psychological thoughts and research: Khun-Lakatos-Laudan. In H. W. Reese (Ed.), *Advances in child development and behavior* (Vol. 18, pp. 91–226). New York, NY: Academic Press.

Rapley, J. (2004). *Globalization and inequality: Neoliberalism's downward spiral.* Boulder, CO: Lynne Rienner.

Salemi, M. K., & Siegfried, J. J. (1999). The state of economic education. *The American Economic Review, 89,* 355–361.

Seider, S., Davis, K., & Gardner, H. (2009). Morality, ethics and good work: Young people's respectful and ethical minds. In D. Ambrose & T. L. Cross (Eds.), *Morality, ethics, and gifted minds* (pp. 209–222). New York, NY: Springer.

Sen, A. (2000). Merit and justice. In K. Arrow, S. Bowles, & S. Durlauf (Eds.), *Meritocracy and economic inequality* (pp. 5–16). Princeton, NJ: Princeton University Press.

Smith, A. (1937). *An inquiry into the nature and causes of the wealth of nations.* New York, NY: Modern Library. (Original work published 1776)

Sternberg, R. J. (1985). *Beyond IQ: A triarchic theory of human intelligence.* New York, NY: Cambridge University Press.

Sternberg, R. J. (1988). *The triarchic mind: A new theory of human intelligence.* New York, NY: Viking.

Sternberg, R. J. (1990). *Metaphors of mind: Conceptions of the nature of intelligence.* New York, NY: Cambridge University Press.

Sternberg, R. J. (1997). *Successful intelligence: How practical and creative intelligence determine success in life.* New York, NY: Plume.

Sternberg, R. J. (1999). Intelligence. In M. A. Runco & S. R. Pritzker (Eds.), *Encyclopedia of creativity* (Vol. 2, pp. 81–88). New York, NY: Academic Press.

Sternberg, R. J. (2001a). What is the common thread of creativity? Its dialectical relation to intelligence and wisdom. *American Psychologist, 56,* 360–362.

Sternberg, R. J. (2001b). Why schools should teach for wisdom: The balance theory of wisdom in educational settings. *Educational Psychologist, 36,* 227–245.

Sternberg, R. J. (2004). *Definitions and conceptions of giftedness.* Thousand Oaks, CA: Corwin Press.

Sternberg, R. J. (2005). WICS: A model of giftedness in leadership. *Roeper Review, 28,* 37–44.

Sternberg, R. J. (2007a). Cultural conceptions of giftedness. *Roeper Review, 29,* 160–165.

Sternberg, R. J. (2007b). Who are the bright children? The cultural context of being and acting intelligent. *Educational Researcher, 36,* 148–155.

Sternberg, R. J. (2009). Reflections on ethical leadership. In D. Ambrose & T. L. Cross (Eds.), *Morality, ethics, and gifted minds* (pp. 19–28). New York, NY: Springer.

Stiglitz, J. E. (1996). Some lessons from the East Asian miracle. *World Bank Research Observer, 11,* 151–177.

Stiglitz, J. E. (2001). *Information and the change in the paradigm in economics* (Nobel lecture). Stockholm, Sweden: Nobel Foundation.

Stiglitz, J. E. (2003). *Globalization and its discontents.* New York, NY: W. W. Norton.

Stiglitz, J. E. (2004a). Capital-market liberalization, globalization, and the IMF. *Oxford Review of Economic Policy, 20,* 57–71.

Stiglitz, J. E. (2004b). *The roaring nineties: A new history of the world's most prosperous decade.* New York, NY: W. W. Norton.

Stiglitz, J. E. (2006). *Making globalization work:* New York, NY: W. W. Norton.

VanTassel-Baska, J., & Stambaugh, T. (Eds.). (2007). *Overlooked gems: A national perspective on low-income promising learners.* Washington, DC: National Association for Gifted Children.

Vemuri, A. W., & Costanza, R. (2006). The role of human, social, built, and natural capital in explaining life satisfaction at the country level: Toward a national well-being index (NWI). *Ecological Economics, 58,* 119–133.

Weitz, E. D. (2003). *A century of genocide.* Princeton, NJ: Princeton University Press.

Wight, J. B. (2007). The treatment of Smith's invisible hand. *Journal of Economic Education, 38,* 341–358.

Williams, M. (1999). *Groundless belief: An essay on the possibility of epistemology* (2nd ed.). Princeton, NJ: Princeton University Press.

9

DOGMATISM AND THE KNOWLEDGE INDUSTRY

More Accurately Assessing the Work of Gifted Scholars[1]

Bharath Sriraman

UNIVERSITY OF MONTANA

Preamble: The Dean's Conundrum

We publish while others perish.

Howard Zinn (1922–2010)

Consider the following scenario, which could be a reality in some universities in the world: Three tenure track assistant professors from different disciplines are applying for tenure and promotion. Dr. A works in the area of Algebra, a discipline within pure mathematics. Dr. B works in Bioinformatics, within Computer Science, and Dr. C works in Continental philosophy. The three faculty members all fall undern the umbrella of the College of Arts and Sciences. All things being equal in the domains of teaching and service, the Dean is in the tricky position of granting tenure based on "scholarly impact within the field" and "recognition from peers at the national level" with the additional pressure of having to meet budget cuts due to large deficits. Cutting two tenure lines would be an easy way to get the base budget out of the red; however, decisions regarding tenure and promotion have to be made on the basis of the recommendations of the respective departments, as well as objective means of comparing and ranking faculty within the College of Arts and Sciences.

A has published two 40+ page papers in the prestigious *Journal of Algebra,* one of the oldest peer reviewed journals in mathematics, one based on her dissertation and a second co-authored article that extends her results to a different but significant branch of mathematics. B has published 8 articles in different refereed conference proceedings, contributed 2 chapters in edited books and has one co-authored journal article. All her conference publications and chapters have numerous co-authors. C has been proactive with extramural funding in order to set up a Center for Ethics and Peace Studies and create a systematic program of synergistic research that involves numerous disciplines and significant outreach with First nations. He also has published a lengthy article in the *Philosophical Magazine,* a journal in place since 1798 with contributions from eminent scientists and Nobel laureates. His article addresses the relationship between solid-state physics and 21st-century emergent technologies, and their ethical implications for society.

If the decision were based on simple arithmetic, the Dean simply has to add up the publications and rank them on this basis. This means the ranking is B (11), A (2), C (1); and the decision is to recommend B for tenure, but deny C and A tenure at this stage and grant them an additional year within the faculty so they may find a position elsewhere. If the Dean's ranking hinged on solo articles in peer-reviewed journals (with multipliers based on the number of co-authors) weighted more heavily than conference proceedings or book chapters, the latter two assigned weights of 0.2 and 0.1 respectively, then the ranking becomes B (2.3), A (1.5), C (1) and the decision still favors B.

Now what if the ranking were based on the Thomson Reuters, Journal Citation Reports© "impact" factors of journals in which the publications appeared, and strictly limited to ISI indices such as the *Science Citation Index,* the *Social Science Citation Index,* etc? Both the *Journal of Algebra* and the *Philosophical Magazine* are indexed and have "significant" impact factors in their fields, whereas none of the publications of B are indexed in ISI. The ranking with this new criteria becomes A (1.5), C (1) and B (0), and A is recommended for tenure whereas C and B are not. A is ranked ahead of C because of having 2 publications. However the rankings between A and C are too close to call, so the Dean actually quantifies the ranking based on the impact factors of the journals with multipliers. The *Journal of Algebra* has an impact factor of 0.632, and the *Philosophical Magazine* has an impact factor of 1.273, so the new ranking becomes C (1.273 = 1 × 1.273), A (0.948 = 1.5 × 0.632) and B (0).

We have seen three possible permutations of rankings, namely BAC, ACB, and CAB. In a strictly "bean" counting game, B would win hands down. If we impose the restriction of "quality" as denoted by publications in a particular index, then A wins, and with the added criteria of "impact factor" within the particular index, C wins. Bibliometric measures have somehow justified the "scholarly" ranking in the end. Is it fair to compare impact factors of two journals from completely different areas? Is it sensible to apply this measure to an individual academic who has published in those journals? These two questions are addressed in more detail in an ensuing section of the chapter. What if the area in which Dr. B works is a cutting-edge area of Bioinformatics, and the field is brand new and emerging with conferences serving as focal points to consolidate the efforts of the researchers and eventually launch new journals focused on this area of research? What if, in 5 years time, her two chapters contributed to the edited books, become the standard references for scholars and are the most extensively cited in that field? These subjective constraints further complicate the issue of being "objective" in judging scholarship and the macabre nature of multipliers or weights in quantifying the value of research.

Hopefully, the scenario described above points to the dilemmas inherent in quantifying and comparing scholarship from different disciplines, and how bibliometric measures can sway decision making affecting the futures of scholars. In an ideal academic world, scholars should not become the victims of arbitrary ranking based on formulae involving impact factors. However, scholars do not exist in an ideal world, but in academia, which is increasingly influenced by corporate models, with budgets affected by market forces and changing demographics, and rankings of prestige based on bibliometric measures from the Knowledge Industry. In the remaining sections of this chapter, I address (a) the sociological nuances involved in scholarship moving from the individual to the field using Latour's framework, (b) social-personality and institutional factors that affect citations in scholarly outlets, and (c) use Kant's anti-thesis of dogmatism and criticism to explain the dangers of blindly using bibliometrics to judge scholarship.

The Economics and Sociology of Scholarship

Scholarship can be viewed as a creative contribution made by an individual to one or more fields, having learned and been enculturated in the knowledge, rules, and practices of a field (Csikszentmihalyi, 2000). This contribution can take many forms, but here we restrict ourselves to the written medium (journal articles, books, conference proceedings, book chapters, etc.). Individual and group efforts continually add to "assets" held in bibliographic repositories such as academic libraries, scholarly databases, and sieved by bibliometric indexes. The Knowledge industry consists of large publishing houses (e.g., Elsevier, Springer, Taylor & Francis, etc.), many with publicly traded parent companies listed on stock markets.

The scope of the Knowledge industry is staggering and difficult to comprehend. It ranges from the individual scholar at one end of the scale, engaged in scholarship to advance disciplinary knowledge that feeds into journals and books held by publishing houses that amass large repositories of knowledge accessible and or purchasable via library or database subscriptions. These in turn generate the revenue for publicly traded parent investment firms. For example, Springer Science and Business Media, the third largest publishing company in the world (after Elsevier and Taylor & Francis) currently owns 60 subsidiary publishing houses that hold 13 different subject collections embodied in 2,000 academic journals and 6,500+ new books published each year. In 2009 Springer Science and Business generated total revenue of 845 million Euros,[2] which converts to approximately 1 billion U.S. dollars.

Translating scholarship into dollars is not as bizarre as it may seem, since at the individual level, scholarly productivity is rewarded by institutions in the form of tenure, promotion and associated salary increases. The point being made here is that the sense of scale when we begin investigating the economic power of the Knowledge industry is staggering. For instance, if we take the approximately $1,000 per individual publication reward offered by some institutions (in Europe, Scandinavia, and other countries) for publishing in a prestigious (indexed) journal and $10^{\wedge}(9)\$$ (or 1 billion) dollar revenue of the publishing house that owns that journal, the scale is $1{:}10^{\wedge}(6)$ (or 1 to a million). This puts into perspective what individual scholarship amounts to when viewed from the perspective of the worth of a publicly traded Knowledge company. The relationship between scholarship and its commoditization in the marketplace is prevalent in today's global knowledge economy (Peters, 2002). Francis Bacon's (1561–1626) view that knowledge is power is interpreted differently by critical theorists in the postmodern age as: knowledge is not only power, but also money (Ernest, 2009, p.68).

Barring the economic vicissitudes that govern academic publishing houses, within the vast jungle of intellectual products embodied in the journals and books that represent the space of academic knowledge, citation devices play the role of sieving scholarship into those that have an impact on a given field as opposed to those that don't, both as a function of time. The sieving also has the unintended effect of lending certain journals more prestige than others as a result of their articles/scholarship being valued more by the community in relation to other journals. In many universities and national systems, tiered rankings of journals are found, based on the recommendations of experts within learned academies, and perceived prestige in terms of impact factors.

From the Macroscopic to the Microscopic

If one moves from a macroscopic view of the Knowledge industry in terms of dollars and cents, and away from simply determining the worth of individual knowledge contributions as a measure of how often a journal article is cited, a very different view emerges. Bruno Latour (1987), the French sociologist, proposed a theory of citations in the book *Science in Action*. One of the arguments in this book is that the "boundaries between the social and technical in scientific practice are blurry" (Luukkonen, 1997, p. 29). In Latour's theory, knowledge construction is an inherently collective social process with references in articles serving the purpose of justifying claims. After a period of time, when a critical mass of references accumulates to justify a certain finding by numerous other scholars, this "finding" takes on the aura of scientific fact, and does not need to be justified with warrants to references. For instance, most mathematics textbooks at the school (e.g., Geometry) and undergraduate level (e.g., Calculus) rarely justify facts by alluding to Euclid's Elements or Newton's

Principia, respectively, or to other fundamental references out of which the knowledge was generated, justified and used. The same is true of textbooks in physics and chemistry.

At an even more microscopic level, before a reference is born, enters the chain of knowledge and citations begin to accrue to it (Pendlebury, 2009), one can analyze the sociological process involved in the generation of this piece of knowledge. The actor-network theory of Latour (1987) is relevant. Callon and Law (1997) provide insights into constitutive factors that interact in order to produce a piece of knowledge, and useful and plausible explanations of why some articles are cited more than others. At this level of scrutiny, we encounter a complex adaptive system, that is, heterogeneous and coextensive networks consisting of both social and technical parts. Actor-network theory claims that all actants, whether person, object (e.g., computer software), or organization, are equally important to a social network. In other words, the smooth running of an actor network preserves societal order. For example, the removal of cellular phone providers or busing services within a school may result in a significant breakdown in social order.

In the case of journal and publishing culture, the constituent actants are individual authors, referees, editorial assistants, the editorial board, the editor, as well as objects such as technical manuals for manuscript preparation, associated software, letters, e-mails exchanged between the author, editor, referees, different versions of manuscripts, etc., and the organization can comprise professional societies, committees within departments that oversee publication merit, institutional administrators, citation indexes, etc. There are also power dynamics that form between the various actors, with editors and referees having more power and the ability to resort to "black-box" mechanisms to justify unfair decisions. In other words, the system is not transparent to an individual scholar attempting to make a creative contribution in it (Roth, 2002) and agency is transferred to "black box" entities such as "editorial panels," "we," "aims of the journal," "journal policy" in cases where manuscripts are (sometimes unfairly) rejected. Many academic journals list their acceptance rates in various databases (e.g., Cabbells), and there is a tendency among scholars to view journals with high acceptance rates of lower quality than those with extremely low acceptance rates. Determining a hierarchical pecking order on the basis of acceptance rates is foolish because publishing in a journal with a low acceptance rate does not guarantee high citation counts. An example helps illustrate my argument.

Quantification of Prestige

Within the realm of educational theory or just education in general there are hundreds of high-quality journals. On the basis of acceptance rates, the *Harvard Educational Review* (*HER*; currently in its 80th year of existence), with an acceptance rate of 1%–3% (according to Cabbells) would be at the top of this list. Does publishing in *HER* confer more prestige than publishing in say *Review of Educational Research (RER)*, or *The Oxford Review of Education (OXRE)*? On the basis of acceptance rates, the "prestige" order is *HER, RER, OXRE*. On the basis of ISI journal impact factor rankings, the order is *RER, HER, OXRE*. However, *HER* is typically run by a group of graduate students overseen by faculty at the Harvard Graduate School of Education, and this editorial board values issues that are "hot" or popular for the mainstream, as opposed to a laboriously crafted metareview of a domain of educational research. Publishing in *HER* requires that a scholar have an uncanny sense of what might be perceived as "hot" or "important" or "controversial" or appeal to a certain college demographic. This also explains why 97%–99% of the manuscripts submitted to *HER* are relegated to the slush pile. In the first of the two rounds of editorial screening, most manuscripts are tossed on the subjective basis of "fit." It makes more sense for a scholar to target *RER* or *OXRE* if their review article does not fit into mainstream/pop culture consciousness.

What if a scholar does manage to publish a very influential article in *HER*, but the tenure/promotion committee devalues this work because uncovering the black boxes reveals that it is a student-run journal, with an arbitrary screening process described above, and not really serious scholarship. I do not mean to pick on any particular journal per se, so I provide a different example from mathematics education.

The *Journal for Research in Mathematics Education* (an ISI journal) has an acceptance rate of around 10%, whereas *The Mathematics Teacher* (a non-ISI journal) also has an acceptance rate of around 10%. Both journals are run by a parent professional organization called the National Council of Teachers of Mathematics, the former for researchers (typically university personnel) and the latter for practitioners (university pedagogues, teachers, mathematics specialists, and others). It is as difficult to get published in *The Mathematics Teacher (MT)* as it is in the *Journal for Research in Mathematics Education (JRME)*. The refereeing actants in the case of *MT* are typically high school mathematics teachers in a leadership position within *NCTM*, who determine the worth of a manuscript on the criteria of whether the piece will help other practicing high school teachers in advancing their content knowledge, or present possibilities for pedagogy that improve the teaching and learning of particular mathematics content. In the case of *JRME*, the refereeing actants are panels of mathematics education researchers using an entirely different set of criteria centered on the relevance of a research study, its fit and significance within the canonical literature, the robustness of its methodology, reliability and validity criteria for the significance of the findings/results etc.

A good scholar in mathematics education is expected to be able to publish in both researcher and practitioner journals; however, many universities devalue publications in practitioner journals. In the last few years, when I have been in the position of an external evaluator for tenure and promotion cases at various universities in the United States, my scrutiny of the academic unit standards language for "scholarship" has revealed that publication in practitioner journals is relegated to the realm of service, and not scholarship. The stipulation of publishing exclusively in ISI journals leaves mathematics education scholars only one possible outlet in their field, namely *JRME*, and a handful in the domain of cognition. The upshot of this has typically been denial of tenure and promotion for colleagues at many institutions.

Scholarship for the lofty purpose of discovery, erudition, sharing, and contributing to disciplinary or multi-disciplinary knowledge development becomes irrelevant, even banal, when viewed from the perspective of an individual scholar confronting (a) universities setting benchmark standards for academic units based on the Knowledge Industry's juggernaut of quantifying scholarship, and (b) the Latourian black boxes and subjectivity inherent in the world of publishing and decision making.

Imagine scholarship that engages in opening and analyzing the Latourian black boxes of a particular group of journals within an academic domain. The black boxes take on a sinister note when astronomical sums of funding from research bodies or private corporations are attached to publication in specific journals, using specific methodologies. The field of medicine has been plagued by allegations of publication bias indulged in by editors and researchers affiliated with pharmaceutical companies that misreport experimental results, leading to an overall bias in the published literature (Ioannidis, 2005). In the next section factors that influence journal metrics, impact factors, and citation counts are discussed based on a review of the existing bibliometric literature. The final section argues for a less dogmatic and more pragmatic approach to assessing and comparing scholarship with the hope of less marginalization of potentially gifted scholars and academics within systems of higher education.

On Kant's Anti-Thesis

At a relatively late stage in this chapter, I finally define dogmatism using a misunderstood page from the history of philosophy that concerns the German philosopher Immanuel Kant (1724–1804). Kant, in his critique of the methods used in metaphysical discourses, tried to sharply distinguish or separate his method from those that preceded him. In labeling and criticizing the work of his predecessors as dogmatic, particularly the rationalist Christian Wolff (1679–1754), Kant unknowingly made numerous a priori synthetic judgments himself! In the realm of validity of geometric theorems concerning space, Lovejoy (1906) remarked that

> Kant ... [n]ot only accepts the logical method of the "dogmatists", but even uses it to establish that principle which, so far as mathematical

reasonings are concerned, is in the same sentence supposed to show the illegitimacy of their logical method.

(p. 213)

A dogmatist, as Lovejoy (1906) defines it, "is a philosopher who deliberately goes about making synthetic judgments a priori, without pausing to ask himself, whether, or how, such judgments are logically possible" (p. 193). In other words, the distinction between criticism and dogmatism becomes blurry and nondifferentiable, when the criticizer succumbs to self contradictory or dogmatic statements in the frenzy to criticize. The implication of this definition for a chapter of this nature is to be careful about the judgments being made about the Knowledge industry, and to address its limitations within the confines of what bibliometric measures really mean, and factors that influence their flux and flow.

Unearthing the "Objectiveness" of Bibliometrics

The "science" of bibliometrics (also known as scientometrics) can be traced back to the seminal ideas of Eugene Garfield in the 1950s who proposed citation indexes as a means to identify influential journals in the sciences. In a sense, bibliometrics is a data-driven metascience. Among his most important contributions to the field of bibliometrics are papers in the journal *Science* (Garfield, 1955, 1972) in which the methodology of citation analysis for journals is described. The basic purpose of citation analysis is to rank journals within a given discipline on the basis of their impact factor. The impact factor of a journal is a simple ratio of the number of citations to the journal over the number of possible citable items over 3-year periods. Seen in these terms, the number per se is an objective measure. However there are a number of subjective influences and misuses of this ratio, which are discussed in the following sections of this chapter. In a nutshell, the unintended impact of impact factors (pun intended) on how scholars within disciplines evaluate journals and other colleagues, has led to several professional bodies such as the International Mathematical Union (IMU) (Adler, Ewing, & Taylor, 2008), and the Social Sciences and Humanities Research Council of Canada (SSHRC) to commission reports to be wary of misuse.

Institutional Dogma

Amin and Mabe (2000, as cited by Arnold & Fowler, 2011) write "impact factor has moved in recent years from an obscure bibliometric indicator to become the chief quantitative measure of the quality of a journal, its research papers, the researchers who wrote those papers and even the institutions they work in" (p. 434). Institutional "research" rankings in numerous countries such as the UK are increasingly based on faculty publication output in SSCI journals and the esteem of the journal rankings relative to others within a discipline (Thomas & Watkins, 1998).

I have heard first hand from academics in China, Cyprus, Iran, Korea, Turkey, and numerous countries in Europe about institution-wide mandates to become listed in the Shanghai "world" ranking of universities (Liu, 2004), which entails scholars increasing their publication in SCI and SSCI journals, with tenure and promotion hinging on a critical number of publications in such journals. This has led to panic among numerous gifted scholars, and the "blind" almost dogmatic searching and targeting of ISI journals for the sake of professional advancement within institutions.

The Shanghai ranking assigns a 40% weight to faculty research output in universities split evenly between publishing in either Nature or Science (20%), and research published in SCI and SSCI journals (20%). In this world ranking, Harvard is ranked #1, whereas the University of Wyoming is ranked #491. Now imagine an unrealistic mandate at the University of Wyoming to catch up with the top 10 universities in this ranking. It is unrealistic, almost foolish to compare faculty productivity between institutions within the same country due to the variability in resources, different strengths of faculties, and the foci of different universities. A university with faculty strengths and laboratory funding resources in medical, pharmaceutical, and natural/physical sciences will always have faculty that can publish research of interest to *Science and Nature,* as opposed to a university that is more oriented towards to the liberal arts and humanities.

It becomes even more unrealistic to compare entire universities in different countries with completely different cultural norms and standards regarding scholarship. Yet, bibliometric measures have taken on an ominous life of their own and impacted the academic life of scholars in many places in the blind adherence and drive of their universities to be listed within the Shanghai world ranking. Institutions making a priori judgments about the scholarly caliber or worth of their faculty based on a ranking methodology that can be critiqued easily for its flawed logic, can be said to have succumbed to a dogmatic view of scholarship.

If we shift our perspective again from the macroscopic to the microscopic and analyze the Knowledge industry from an individual scholar's viewpoint, a different Latourian view emerges. Now imagine oneself as a gifted scholar attempting to understand the larger system and promote oneself with citation devices. How would one go about such an endeavor? It requires understanding the nuances of how citation mechanisms work.

Cozzen's Rewards Versus Rhetoric

Cozzen (1989) reminds us that the basic purpose of citations is to lend credence or persuasion to a scientific idea with the idea of communal ownership. However as she points out, a sociological consequence is

Citations acknowledge the community's intellectual debts to the discoverer, just as payments on a licensing agreement acknowledge economic indebtedness to the inventor. Thus a citation etiquette developed, which stipulates that when a new published idea is used, a progenitor should be explicitly stated.

(p. 440)

The previous sentence is a manifestation of this etiquette! According to Cozzen's (1989) framework, citations have an inherent duality—they are rhetoric because they establish links between bodies of scholarship, between the ideas in articles, sometimes even transforming or contradicting the original ideas. On the other hand, they also serve to reward certain authors for the precedence or pecking order to a scientific claim or idea or finding. Referees and editors of journals who act as gatekeepers enforce the etiquette. Let me give a concrete example.

In the Shadows (as Opposed to Shoulders) of Giants

Four years ago, in the task of determining the theoretical foundations of mathematics education as an area of research for a handbook chapter (Sriraman & Törner, 2008), the literature had to be mined to determine scholars that brought philosophical questions into the theory debate. I ended up with a widely cited theorist who published exclusively in English, whereas my co-author whose native language is German, found someone who preceded the widely cited theorist. When the chapter was reviewed by external referees, this "precedence" conflict took on a life of its own, with one of the referees insisting that the non-English reference be dropped and attribution be made exclusively to the widely cited theorist who published in English. When we insisted to the editor of the book that ideas can concurrently or independently develop without scholars being aware of each other's scholarship, particularly since the time period in question was well before the information age, and it wasn't a question of precedence but proper rhetorical attributions made to the canon of literature, other non-English citations found their way into the field, and the scholar was finally "rewarded" albeit posthumously.

Leydesdorff and Amsterdamska (1990) correctly point out that it is difficult to distinguish analytically between rhetoric and reward devices, and I claim that very often referees, editors, and other actants within the system succumb to rewarding the eminent, or already widely cited, and ignoring lesser-known scholars whose work may be worthy of citing. In other words, there is subjectivity in who scholars choose to cite, and why they do so. Self-citation or pointing other scholars to "standard" references by gatekeepers tends to skew citation distributions in favor of eminent scholars (Haslam et al., 2008). Indexes that measure author impact (not journal impact) fortunately use metrics that neutralize self-citations.

This discussion brings to the foreground several devices (among others) that have a major impact on citation counts: (a) the perceived eminence of a scholar within a field, (b) the dogmatic pressure to cite certain scholars over others to please gatekeepers, and (c) language in which the scholarship is published and disseminated.

Impact on the (Local) Culture and Direction of Scholarship

Given the fact that ISI listed journals are predominantly in English, in numerous countries, scholars are increasingly under pressure to publish exclusively in English. There is a tendency to ignore important citations within their own scientific culture, and instead cite the perceived mainstream. In the case of Korean social scientists, an analysis of 321 papers with 11,358 references found that non-Korean literature was cited 65.3% more than Korean literature (Kim, 2004). Furthermore, "despite the particularity and limitations of the social sciences, Korean researchers have a universal non-Korean orientation and have adopted non-Korean knowledge as conceptual knowledge ... [t]o explain a number of social and behavioral phenomena in Korea" (p. 92). Again, based on personal experience and service on doctoral committees in Norway, Germany, Turkey, Iran, and Cyprus, I have observed similar tendencies among scholars to "mainstream" themselves into the citation flow, and purposefully adopt conceptual frameworks and methodologies that provide access to specific journals and indexes. Again bibliometric measures have the power to influence the culture of scholarship in different countries and make scholars adopt ideas dogmatically as opposed to critically.

Concluding Thoughts: Who Is in Control?

This chapter was an attempt to unravel the mechanics of the Knowledge industry, the macro- and micro-forces that govern knowledge generation, and the dangers in policy makers and key decision makers blindly adhering to bibliometrics as a way to rank institutions, journals, and scholars. In a scholarly sense, an exercise such as this has the inherent danger of the writer adopting a dogmatic stand to attack the larger-than-life bibliometric machinery that increasingly influences and directs research, and makes and breaks lives within academia in the cycle of tenure and promotion. However, one cannot view the Knowledge industry as a Hadean beast. It is more of a complex adaptive system that mutates as disciplinary knowledge expands and new fields of inquiry develop. Gifted scholars are ultimately the cellular automata of this system, who contribute to it and sustain it and paradoxically depend on it for sustenance—intellectually, financially, or otherwise.

Ultimately, decision making on the significance of scholarship is in our control and should be made by weighing in the limitations of bibliometrics that objectify and quantify the worth of ideas. In addressing these limitations, I have revealed the dogmatism that can arise when comparing scholars from different disciplines based on citation counts, or impact factors/prestige of journals from different disciplines or even the same discipline, or comparing institutions, using arbitrary ranking systems or norms. The list of citations in this chapter indicates that bibliometricians are well aware of the limitations of their own field. The reader will note the numerous references that address, criticize, and theorize bibliometrics come from the journal *Scientometrics*. It is time the rest of us became aware of the limitations of the system in which we are integral parts. In the words of Adler and colleagues (2008):

> For an individual scientist, an assessment can have profound and long-term effects on one's career; for a department, it can change prospects for success far into the future; for disciplines, a collection of assessments can make the difference between thriving and languishing. For a task so important, surely one should understand both the validity and the limitations of the tools being used to carry it out.
>
> *(p. 18)*

If gifted scholars use the very bibliometric tools they have created, whose limitations they are aware of, to unfairly marginalize, diminish the scope of, and criticize the scholarship of others, we fall prey to Kant's anti-thesis and become dogmatists ourselves under the guise/act of being critical.

Notes

1. The word "gifted" and "gifted education" are broadly interpreted in this chapter to mean scholars within academia and research/publications produced in institutions of higher learning, i.e., new disciplinary knowledge.
2. 2009 Annual Report of Springer Science + Business Media, available at http://www.springer.com/about+springer/company+information/annual+report?SGWID=0-175705-0-0-0

References

Adler, R., Ewing, J., Taylor, P. (2008). *Citation statistics: A report from the international mathematical union (IMU) in cooperation with the international council of industrial and applied mathematics (ICIAM) and the institute of mathematical statistics (IMS).* 26 pp. Retrieved from http://www.mathunion.org/fileadmin/IMU/Report/CitationStatistics.pdf

Amin, M., & Mabe, M. (2000). Impact factors: Use and abuse. *Perspectives in Publishing, 1,* 1–6.

Arnold, D. N., & Fowler, K. K. (2011). Nefarious numbers. *Notices of the American Mathematical Society, 58,* 434–437.

Callon, M., & Law, J. (1997). Agency and the hybrid collectif. In B. Herrnstein Smith, & A. Plotnitsky (Eds.), *Mathematics, science and postclassical theory* (pp. 95–117). Durham, NC: Duke University Press.

Cozzen, S. E. (1989). What do citations count? The Rhetoric-First Model. *Scientometrics, 15,* 437–447.

Csikszentmihalyi, M. (2000). Implications of a systems perspective for the study of creativity.

In R. J. Sternberg (Ed.), *Handbook of creativity* (pp. 313–338). New York, NY: Cambridge University Press.

Ernest, P. (2009). Mathematics education ideologies and globalization. In P. Ernest, B. Greer, & B. Sriraman (Eds.), *Critical issues in mathematics education* (pp. 67–110). Charlotte, NC: Information Age.

Garfield, E. (1955). Citation indexes for science. *Science 122,* 108–111.

Garfield, E. (1972). Citation analysis as a tool in journal evaluation. *Science, 178,* 471–479.

Haslam, N., Ban, L., Kaufmann, L., Loughnan, S., Peters, K., Whelan, J., & Wilson, S. (2008). What makes an article influential? Predicting impact in social and personality psychology. *Scientometrics, 76,* 169–185.

Ioannidis, J. (2005). Why most published research findings are false? *PLoS Med,* 2(8): e124. doi:10.1371/journal.pmed.0020124

Kim, K. (2004). The motivation for citing specific references by social scientists in Korea: The phenomenon of co-existing references. *Scientometrics, 59,* 79–93.

Latour, B. (1987). *Science in action: How to follow scientists and engineers through society.* Milton Keynes, UK: Open University Press.

Leydesdorff, L., & Amsterdamska, O. (1990). Dimensions of citation analysis. *Science, Technology, & Human Values, 15,* 305–335.

Lovejoy, A. O. (1906). *Kant's* antithesis of dogmatism and criticism. *Mind, 15,* 191–214.

Liu, N. C. (2004). *Academic ranking of world universities.* Shanghai, China: Institute of Higher Education, Shanghai Jiao Tong University.

Luukkonen, T. (1997). Why has Latour's theory of citations been ignored by the bibliometric community? Discussion of sociological interpretations of citation analysis. *Scientometrics, 38,* 27–37.

Pendlebury, D. A. (2009). The use and misuse of journal metrics and other citation indicators *Archivum Immunologiae et Therapiae Experimentalis, 57,* 1–11.

Peters, M. (2002). Education policy research and the global knowledge economy. *Educational Philosophy and Theory, 34,* 91–102.

Roth, W. M. (2002). Editorial power/authorial suffering. *Research in Science Education, 32,* 215–240.

Sriraman, B., & Törner, G. (2008). Political union/mathematical education disunion: Building bridges in European didactic traditions. In L. D. English, M. Bussi, G. Jones, R. Lesh, B. Sriraman, & D. Tirosh, (Eds.), *The handbook of international research in mathematics education* (2nd ed., pp. 660–694). New York, NY: Routledge, Taylor & Francis.

Thomas, P. R., & Watkins, D. S. (1998). Institutional research rankings via bibliometric analysis and direct peer review: A comparative case study with policy implications. *Scientometrics, 41,* 335–355.

10

MOTIVATED DOGMATISM AND THE HIGH-ABILITY STUDENT

Jennifer Riedl Cross and Tracy L. Cross

THE COLLEGE OF WILLIAM AND MARY

> I suppose it is tempting, if the only tool you have is a hammer, to treat every-
> thing as if it were a nail.
>
> Maslow (1966, p. 15)

The dogmatic individual is, in many ways, a loss to humanity. Our unique ability to develop hypotheses about the world we live in and, then, to test their
veracity has brought us to this astounding information age. Thinking about
our problems with an ever-widening perspective, from individual to societal to
global, has allowed us to improve the life conditions of nearly everyone on the
planet, albeit some more than others. There is more information available to the
average individual today than ever before in the history of humankind. When
an individual chooses to ignore relevant available information to maintain a position, the unique ability we humans share—to think about a problem—is wasted.

From a psychological perspective, the decision to ignore information is not
arbitrary. A person placing a priority onmaintaining a position over considering
relevant information does so for a reason. Perhaps the information, although
available, is imperceptible to the individual. The message stated loud and clear
to a person with impaired hearing simply will not be heard. The message stated
clearly at a graduate-student vocabulary level may well be unintelligible to a
child. Relevant information is lost. But the hearing impaired or the child in
these examples is not considered dogmatic. The dogmatic individual can hear
or understand the message, but chooses not to listen to or process it. Dogmatism is a behavior, and a behavior that is not reflexive is motivated. These
motivations deserve scrutiny. Although one might imagine high intellectual
ability to provide superior belief systems, there is no evidence for such a devel-

opmental anomaly. There is in fact, evidence to the contrary (e.g., Klaczynski, 1997; Klaczynski, Gordon, & Fauth, 1997; Stanovich & West, 1997) that will be discussed here.

Highly able individuals develop in a complex world made up of widely disparate influences and experiences (Bronfenbrenner, 1979; Coleman & Cross, 2005). As they mature, they are exposed to parents who may or may not be caring and responsive to their needs (Baumrind, 1971). They may grow up in dangerous environments or with schooling inadequate not only for their giftedness, but to meet any child's needs. Erikson (1968) describes the crises that face all individuals as they develop and gifted children experience all of these crises. The combinations and permutations of all factors possible to affect the lives of the developing child are seemingly infinite. As they create their worldviews and belief systems, whatever factors have been influential will have different consequences.

Considering the lack of a common definition of giftedness, individuals who bear the label will have a wide variety of exceptional abilities, but all fall under the umbrella definition of "human" and all are subject to the needs identified by Abraham Maslow (1970) for drive satisfaction. Only when the physiological needs of hunger and thirst are satisfied can a person begin to concern herself with safety needs, "security; structure, order, law, and limits; strength in the protector; and so on" (p. 18). Meeting these safety needs is a precondition for pursuing satisfaction of the needs for belongingness and love, and then of esteem (of self and from others). Integral to attaining the basic needs at all levels is another hierarchy of needs, which Maslow describes as interrelated and synergistic with the first. These are the cognitive needs, in which the "desire to know is prepotent over the desire to understand" (p. 50). A dogmatist may have satisfied her or his desire to know and understand long before a person with a more open mind. Any discussion of dogmatism must consider the motivation behind an individual's choice to inadequately process available information, particularly when that individual possesses exceptional intellectual ability.

Psychological research over the past several decades provides us with a number of perspectives on the phenomenon of dogmatism, the tendency of an individual to ignore evidence while holding firmly to a belief that may or may not be warranted. Dogmatism is a failure to engage in thinking, a premature "settling" on a belief. In this chapter, we discuss several associated avenues of research that apply to an inability or motivation leading to such a failure. The discussion is followed by suggestions for developing open minds among high-ability students.

What Dogmatism Is and Is Not

As we delve into an analysis of dogmatism, it is important to maintain perspective on just what we mean by the word. Dogmatism is a way of approaching information, a means of forming a belief and an attitude. An attitude differs from a belief. An *attitude* is a judgment one has made, whereas a belief is information one has. A *belief* may be factual or not, but it does not include a value judgment about the item. An attitude is such a value judgment, a "general positive or negative feeling toward something" (Petty & Cacioppo, 1981, p. 7). *Values* are "concepts or beliefs … about desirable end states or behaviors … [that] transcend specific situations … [and] guide selection or evaluation of behaviors and events" (Bilsky & Schwartz, 1994, p. 164). Values lay the foundation for the formation of attitudes and beliefs by directing an individual's attention toward information that serves a motivational need. Schwartz and colleagues (Bilsky & Schwartz, 1994; Schwartz, 1994; Schwartz, Sagiv, & Boehnke, 2000) describe these values as existing on opposing continua situated along two dimensions: self-enhancement versus self-transcendence and openness to change versus conservatism.

We can see an example of these value structures in Lakoff's (1996) analysis of different political perspectives. He describes the opposing conservative and liberal value orientations that are emblematic of differing points on Schwartz's dimensions. Lakoff's Strict Father values strength above all else. This self-enhancement ideal is best served by conservative values. Being open to change would permit challenges to one's power. The Nurturant Parent, who exists on the opposite end of both dimensions, is self-transcendent and open to change. These ideals are best served through empathy for others and an acceptance of differing views. The value of strength that is the focus of the Strict Father has been an important one in human history. Real dangers exist in nature and among societies, particularly those that are fearful for their power or safety. The Nurturant Parent, on the other hand, values strength, but only in the protection and nurturance of others. Both value orientations have had a prominent history in a world of two genders.

Individuals with a conservative value orientation are likely to be more dogmatic than those open to change, because an evaluation of relevant information will present challenges to one's belief system. Conservatism—of any type and not necessarily of a political sort—holds to its beliefs and is motivated by a desire for predictability and security. A conservative may be evaluating information very carefully as it relates to those motivations, however. In examining information that would maintain a predictable and secure world, the conservative may make different assumptions than a liberal who looks at the same information as it relates to self-transcendence. These different assumptions were arrived at with deliberation of facts through different lenses. A dogmatist would not consider the facts.

Simply because a person cannot be swayed to our point of view does not make her or him dogmatic. Dogmatism is defined as "1) positiveness in assertion of opinion especially when unwarranted or arrogant[and] 2) a viewpoint or system of ideas based on insufficiently examined premises" (*Merriam-Webster Online Dictionary*, 2010). It is the notions of "unwarranted assertions" and "insufficiently examined premises" that we can explore through the psychological lens. If belief has been obtained through a careful consideration of evidence, dogmatism is not a valid criticism. Value orientations play an important role in the development of belief, but differing values do not necessarily arise from an insufficient evaluation of evidence.

Thinking Dispositions

Stanovich (2001) describes thinking dispositions as different from cognitive ability. He cites Baron (1988) in making the argument that the emphasis on ability in our conceptions of intelligence has distorted our perception of the role dispositions play in individuals' thinking. Kuhn (personal communication, April 3, 2010) suggests that the various thinking dispositions are affective, in contrast to the actual processing of information, which is cognitive. Our processing of information is not limited by our abilities alone. We each have different "goals and epistemic values" (Stanovich, 2001, p. 247) that bring different capacities to bear on any decision making in which we engage. Research on cognition over the past several decades has exposed some of these dispositions. They have received little attention in the research on gifted students, but are highly applicable to a study of dogmatism among the highly able. What follows is a description of a few of the most relevant of these dispositions.

Tolerance of Ambiguity   Through her research in authoritarianism, Frenkel-Brunswik (1949) identified an *intolerance of ambiguity*, a general personality variable found to be associated with dogmatism. Budner (1962) expanded on her work, describing intolerance of ambiguity as "a tendency to evaluate particular phenomena in a particular way ... a tendency to manifest certain modes of response irrespective of the phenomena being dealt with" (p. 31). In other words, intolerance of ambiguity—"the tendency to perceive (i.e., interpret) ambiguous situations as sources of threat"—motivates certain responses to stimuli. Ambiguous situations lack the cues necessary to be structured or categorized by the individual; they are novel, complex, or insoluble. The intolerance of ambiguity scale developed by Budner is correlated with authoritarianism, conventionalism, dogmatism about religious beliefs, and other attitudes or characteristics consistent with an extreme belief system (e.g., Jost, Glaser, Kruglanski, & Sulloway, 2003; Webster & Kruglanski, 1994).

Regardless of ability level, some individuals will prefer more or less ambiguous situations because of the threat they feel from the difficulty in comprehending them. If an individual studiously avoids a situation or opposes a position because of its ambiguity, any decisions made will have been achieved through an insufficient examination of premises. We have found no indications from empirical research that high-ability students have a greater tolerance of ambiguity than their less able peers.

Closed-Mindedness Rokeach's (1960) conception of closed- and open-mindedness is perhaps most closely aligned with a description of a dogmatic or non-dogmatic thinker. The construct of closed-mindedness was developed from his assertion that it is the *structure* of a belief system that leads one to "accept or reject ideas, people, and authority" (p. 8). In Rokeach's definition of an open mind, information is evaluated and acted on without influence from irrelevant internal (i.e., habits, perceptual cues, power needs, etc.) or external (i.e., authority figures, cultural norms, etc.) pressures. A closed mind, on the other hand, is less aware of the relevance of internal and external influence. "The more closed the system, the more is the acceptance of a particular belief assumed to depend on irrelevant internal drives and/or arbitrary reinforcements from external authority" (p. 61). Individuals who score high on Rokeach's Dogmatism Scale differ in their "ability to form new belief systems" (p. 397) from those who score low. Rokeach believed that there are dual motivations behind a closed or open mind: "the need for a cognitive framework to know and to understand and the need to ward off threatening aspects of reality" (p. 67). He saw a closed mind as protection against anxiety. A closed mind serves as "a cognitive system ... designed to shield a vulnerable mind" (p. 70). The certainty of the closed mind is protective against the doubt presented by the outside world.

In more recent research, Stanovich and West (1997) developed a measure of actively open-minded thinking. This instrument indicates openness to belief change and cognitive flexibility. Stanovich and West explore the construct in their research on critical thinking; proposing, and subsequently finding, that one cannot think critically without a willingness or ability to challenge his or her prior beliefs.

Certainty Orientation According to Sorrentino and Short (1986), all individuals have a predisposition towards achieving certainty or avoiding it. An *uncertainty-oriented* individual does not avoid information gathering, he or she avoids reaching a definite or certain conclusion. The certainty-oriented person, on the other hand, will not attempt to find more information if it will challenge her present knowledge; "... uncertainty-oriented people attend to situations that attain clarity, whereas certainty-oriented people attend to situations that maintain clarity" (p. 391). Such statements as "I know what I believe and I believe what I believe is right" (G. W. Bush; Sanger, 2001, in Jost et al., 2003, p. 353) can be interpreted as representing a certainty orientation. This orientation will affect both one's right-left beliefs and their ideological rigidity. The certainty-oriented person is likely to choose the opinions that provide the most certainty. Sorrentino and Short describe the certainty-oriented person this way:

> Self-assessment, social (and physical) comparison, dissonance reduction, causal searches and attributions, possible selves, self-concept discrepancy

reduction, self-confrontation, social justice, and equity are all characteristics that this person does not have or is not susceptible to. This person is likely to be prejudiced, bigoted, opinionated, and a sexist.

(p. 400)

The opposite—open-minded, tolerant of differences, flexible—is much more ambiguous and challenging to process intellectually. The uncertainty-oriented person is identified by these characteristics. Through their open-mindedness and acceptance of ambiguity, a more complex understanding of the world is possible.

Need for Cognitive Closure   In his theory of lay epistemics, Kruglanski (1989) proposes that there are individual differences in the Need for Cognitive Closure, the need to achieve an answer—any answer—to avoid confusion or ambiguity. Situations vary as well, and some situations are more favorable when closure is avoided, as in making an important decision that will mean sacrifice or hardship. Although need for closure can be affected by such situational differences as time pressure, ambient noise, or attractiveness of the task, there is a general tendency for individuals to attempt to achieve closure with similar patterns that vary individually (Webster & Kruglanski, 1994). It is difficult to maintain an open mind when one seeks closure rapidly. This construct is an elaboration of Rokeach's (1960) closed-mindedness and includes aspects of Sorrentino and Short's (1986) certainty orientation. There are times when one must achieve closure quickly, as in situations of time pressure or danger. When this is not the case, however, a high need for cognitive closure will result in dogmatism.

Need for Cognition   Cacioppo and Petty (1982) found that people vary in their enjoyment of thinking; their need for cognition. Whereas subjects with a high need for cognition found a simple task unpleasant and a complex task pleasant, subjects with a low need for cognition reported the reverse. Need for cognition correlated negatively with dogmatism ($r = -.27$, $N = 104$, $p < .05$), indicating that an open mind is one with a preference for activity. An individual high in the need for cognition would tend to be the opposite of the certainty-oriented individual, with a desire to search for more information, even when it challenges his or her present beliefs.

We would hope that the intellectually gifted child has this preference for cognition, particularly if that preference has been nurtured from an early age. Need for cognition has been found to correlate with measures of fluid intelligence in an older sample (Stuart-Hamilton & McDonald, 2001). In a review of the literature on need for cognition, Cacioppo, Petty, Feinstein, Blair, and Jarvis (1996) reported that a relationship between such factors as verbal ability and school achievement covary with need for cognition, but there is no evidence that abstract reasoning shares this relationship. Different types of intellectual ability may be associated with different thinking dispositions.

There is a parallel in the gifted literature to the need for cognition. Dabrowski's (1966) Theory of Positive Disintegration is often proposed as providing the architecture for advanced development. The theory emphasizes intensity, sensitivity, and overexcitability as characteristic of the highly gifted. It is based on the premise that advanced development is possible as people strive toward what ought to be rather than focusing on what is. Overexcitabilities are inborn tendencies to respond to environment stimuli. For example, intellectual overexcitabilities are often considered characteristic of the gifted personality and described as a need to seek understanding, the truth, and to analyze and synthesize information (Dabrowski & Piechowski, 1977). However, Dabrowski's theory claims that one of the types of the five overexcitabilities (sensorimotor, sensual, imaginational, intellectual, emotional) would often exist in the highly gifted personality, not necessarily that intellectual overexcitabilities would exist. Some have argued that all five categories of overexcitabilities would exist in the highly gifted. The research on this theory, while growing, is quite limited and mixed, but it does provide a link between the field of gifted studies and cognitive psychology.

Personal Epistemology

The cognitive orientations described have been studied largely separately from research in personal epistemology. This field has not yet produced a clearly articulated model explaining a person's beliefs about knowledge and knowing (Greene, Torney-Purta, & Azevedo, 2010; Hofer & Pintrich, 1997), although interest in personal epistemology research has been steady. One branch of investigation in this area has generated a description of the development of epistemological understanding that may be useful to us in our examination of motivated dogmatism.

Perry (1970) and Kitchener and King (1990), in their early work on personal epistemology, found that college students developed their knowledge about knowing in stages, from a view of knowledge as absolute and handed down from an authority, to uncertainty, and then a more mature position of the subjectivity of knowledge. Schommer (1994) describes beliefs about knowledge and knowing as centered on "the source, certainty, and organization of knowledge, as well as the speed and control of knowledge acquisition" (p. 302). These beliefs are significantly related to myriad aspects of learning. For example, learners who believe that knowledge is fed to a passive recipient from an authority are less engaged in the learning process (Schommer, 1994). Students who believed that learning should be quick were less persistent in a difficult learning task than those who believed learning is a gradual process. Dweck and Leggett (1988) found that beliefs about ability, intelligence in particular, as either a fixed entity or as incremental and, thus, improvable, affect motivation to achieve. Epistemological beliefs have implications for adequate processing of information in decision making.

In her study of informal reasoning, Kuhn (1991) interviewed 160 subjects of varying ages, genders, and education levels about their beliefs concerning three topics: a student struggling in school, a criminal repeatedly ending up in prison, and unemployment. Subjects were asked to give their opinions concerning the scenario described and then queried about why they believe so, how they might be convinced otherwise, and how they might convince someone with a divergent opinion that they were right. Even with very little information to go on, more than half of the subjects believed very strongly they knew the cause of the problem. Some of these subjects admitted they did not have much knowledge of the topic, but maintained their level of certainty regardless. These subjects fell into the *absolutist* category and held very strongly to the opinion that they could not be swayed from that belief, even when they agreed another person might be right: "... personal commitment to [their] theory is sufficient to ensure its certainty" (p. 175). The large numbers of absolutists in Kuhn's study would be considered dogmatic. They hold unwarranted beliefs acquired through an insufficient examination of evidence.

About a third of Kuhn's subjects fell into the *multiplist* epistemological category. These subjects believed strongly that anyone's opinion could be right. The multiplist may be just as right as an expert or more so, particularly when his or her belief is based on personal experience, as in the school scenario. The multiplists base their beliefs on an "ownership" of the opinion. The multiplist has insufficiently examined the evidence persons with opposing views have used to reach a decision and has seized on her or his own opinion. Dogmatic in their own views, multiplists may not be perceived as such because of their willingness to accept differing viewpoints. The end result, however, is a belief achieved with insufficient evidence.

The remaining 20% of the subjects in Kuhn's (1991) study were categorized as *evaluative epistemologists*. This minority believed that multiple viewpoints may exist and that they can be compared to each other and evaluated to determine how valid or accurate they might be. These subjects did not maintain a high level of certainty in their beliefs and felt that they could be swayed by the arguments of others, especially experts, if sufficient evidence was provided.

Following up on this classification of thinkers, Kuhn (2003) has utilized the research on personal epistemology (see Hofer & Pintrich, 1997, for a review) to describe these categories as developmental, adding a preschool age of *realist*, in which children consider what they know to be just what they see. Table 10.1 describes these levels of epistemological understanding.

To an evaluative epistemologist, it is clear that the development of an evaluative orientation should be the objective of any schooling. A nation made up of multiplists and absolutists will be easily manipulated or, at best, poor decision makers. At this time, we know little about the developmental progression of personal epistemology. Most research on its development has been with college samples (Kitchener, King, Wood, & Davison, 1989; Schommer, 1994). From what we do know about gifted children, it is likely that many of them could

TABLE 10.1 Levels of Epistemological Understanding

Level	Assertions	Knowledge	Critical Thinking
Realist	Assertions are COPIES of an external reality.	Knowledge comes from an external source and is certain.	Critical thinking is unnecessary.
Absolutist	Assertions are FACTS that are correct or incorrect in their representation of reality.	Knowledge comes from an external source and is certain but not directly accessible, producing false beliefs.	Critical thinking is a vehicle for comparing assertions to reality and determining their truth or falsehood.
Multiplist	Assertions are OPINIONS freely chosen by and accountable only to their owners.	Knowledge is generated by human minds and therefore uncertain.	Critical thinking is irrelevant.
Evaluativist	Assertions are JUDGMENTS that can be evaluated and compared according to criteria of argument and evidence.	Knowledge is generated by human minds and is uncertain but susceptible to evaluation.	Critical thinking is valued as a vehicle that promotes sound assertions and enhances understanding.

Reprinted with permission from Kuhn, D. (2003). Understanding and valuing knowing as developmental goals. *Liberal Education, 89*(3), 16-21.

attain higher levels of epistemological development at an early age. Could we expect a gifted absolutist? Multiplist? Almost certainly.

Thinking Dispositions and High Ability

Values, attitudes, cognitive orientations, personal epistemologies—the highly able student possesses all of these. Despite their exceptional cognitive ability, a thinking disposition that does not include an open mind is limiting. A number of researchers have found that cognitive ability does not predict the ability to reason carefully. Klaczynski (1997) found that high intellectual ability did not protect adolescents from biased reasoning. Subjects preferred to look for information consistent with their own prior beliefs regardless of their intellectual ability. These findings have been repeatedly corroborated (Klaczynski & Gordon, 1996; Klaczynski et al., 1997): cognitive ability does not equate with reasoning ability or the use of heuristics in evaluating information. The gifted child may well be an absolutist. Even a high need for cognition was not sufficient to predict unbiased critical reasoning (Klaczynski et al., 1997). Stanovich and West (1997) found that the ability to evaluate an argument independently of prior belief was more reliant on one's open-mindedness than on one's cognitive ability.

Although all these studies of critical thinking (Klaczynski, 1997; Klaczynski et al., 1997; Stanovich & West, 1997) found ways in which ability was associated with the *quality* of reasoning, biases and thinking dispositions were unrelated to cognitive ability. In contrast to these results, Sá, West, and Stanovich (1999) did find a relationship between cognitive ability and the ability to ignore prior knowledge and belief when engaging in a reasoning task. The difference in this study and others is that Sá and colleagues explicitly told their subjects to ignore their prior knowledge or belief. When given these instructions, those with greater cognitive ability were better able to engage in thoughtful reasoning than their less-able peers. This is a very positive finding for those who wish to encourage more open-mindedness among high-ability students. They can be open-minded if they are taught to be.

Developing Evaluative Epistemologists Among the Highly Able

A study of the highly able, by whatever definition is chosen, is a study of individual differences. The sample is selected based on their fit with the selected criteria. The constructs described here are all similarly designed to find individual differences in ways of thinking—those who are more or less tolerant of ambiguity, closed-minded, certainty-oriented, and so forth. From the critical thinking research cited (Klaczynski, 1997; Klaczynski et al., 1997; Stanovich & West, 1997), it is evident that these variations in cognitive ability and dispositions exist in many combinations. The motivation to be open-minded may be weak when one has been encouraged through influence or experience to prefer predictability and heuristics for reasoning. How can educators encourage the opposite? Are there ways of nurturing an open mind?

We propose that it is possible to encourage open-mindedness among the highly able. Dogmatism is, again, defined as "1) positiveness in assertion of opinion … [and] 2) a viewpoint or system of ideas based on insufficiently examined premises" (*Merriam-Webster Online Dictionary*, 2010). First and foremost, educators must teach their students *how* to sufficiently examine any premise. With these skills, it will be difficult for students to be positive in their assertions until they have fully explored the problem.

Those of us in higher education have come to know that the more we learn, the more there is to learn. Our own open-mindedness has developed through learning how to pose a research question and examine it systematically. Science and mathematics education focus on these methods, but all subjects should emphasize the methods needed for sufficiently exploring a premise. Halpern (1998) proposes the following critical-thinking skills as necessary for developing effective thinkers: (a) verbal reasoning skills, (b) argument analysis skills, (c) skills in thinking as hypothesis testing, (d) likelihood and uncertainty, and (e) decision-making and problem-solving skills. These skills should be foundational in learning about any content area.

Many of the motivating epistemic orientations described here have been proposed as protective: Budner's (1962) intolerance of ambiguity protects against the threat of complex situations; Rokeach's (1960) closed-mindedness protects one from the confusion of the outside world; Sorrentino and Short's (1986) certainty orientation protects the clarity one has achieved in a situation. These protections will not be necessary once a student has successfully learned how to analyze a situation. Developing critical thinking skills (Klaczynski, 1997; Klaczynski & Gordon, 1996) and learning how to evaluate an argument (Kuhn & Dean, 2005; Kuhn & Udell, 2003) will provide protection from the anxiety produced by complex situations; students will know how to deconstruct and analyze them.

Learning about one's own "personal theories" of knowledge (Hofer & Pintrich, 1997) is useful for challenging immature epistemological beliefs. For example, the notion of an "omniscient authority" (Schommer, 1990, 1994) and that hands down information must be dispelled if we wish to encourage a complete examination of a premise. The current focus on accountability in education fosters such immature beliefs in students, who must learn "the facts" to be successful on high-stakes tests. Educators and students alike can benefit from an understanding of their own beliefs about knowledge.

Parents and past experience will have played a substantial role in the development of open-mindedness before a student arrives in the classroom. Some students will arrive with a great willingness to explore, while others will be more inhibited, held back by fears of rejection or embarrassment. Educators should consider their students' values of self-enhancement or transcendence and openness to change or conservatism. Forcing a child who values conservatism to step outside the boundaries of tradition and conformity is likely to result in discomfort unless done with sensitivity. Educators should provide a supportive classroom, one where questioning is valued over answers, where exploration is encouraged and rewarded, where the "facts" take a back seat to the methods used to obtain them.

To be most effective in promoting open-mindedness, educators must provide a role model to their students. Modeling a high need for cognition, a tolerance for ambiguity, an uncertainty orientation, a low need for cognitive closure (except when appropriate), and an open mind will go a long way towards reducing dogmatism in their students.

Our goal as educators should be to produce evaluative epistemologists. One must be open-minded to carefully evaluate information, as Stanovich and West's (1997) research demonstrated. This open-mindedness should extend to the dogmatic you encounter. Are you sufficiently examining the evidence of their argument? Or are you relying on your own beliefs to reach that conclusion? Close examination of values may identify the source of differences of opinion. It is important to remember that dogmatism is a way of approaching information. The content of a belief system is not the source of dogmatism, regardless of how much one disagrees.

Although dogmatism has been measured as a stable trait (Rokeach, 1960), there is evidence that dogmatic behaviors are, instead, affected by situations (Kruglanski, 1989) and are motivated (e.g., Cacioppo et al., 1996; Jost et al, 2003) by the satisfaction of basic needs, including safety and cognitive needs (Maslow, 1970), and by individual values. An analysis of the thinking dispositions and personal epistemology literature suggests a path for educators who wish to encourage the development of evaluative epistemology. Providing them with the tools of evaluation will be the greatest protection educators can give the high-ability student. They require more than a hammer to deal with the complex world around us.

References

Baron, J. (1988). *Thinking and deciding.* Cambridge, England: Cambridge University Press.

Baumrind, D. (1971). Current patterns of parental authority. *Developmental Psychology, 4,* 99–102.

Bilsky, W., & Schwartz, S. H. (1994). Values and personality. *European Journal of Personality, 8,* 163–181.

Bronfenbrenner, U. (1979). *The ecology of human development.* Cambridge, MA: Harvard Press.

Budner, S. (1962). Intolerance of ambiguity as a personality variable. *Journal of Personality, 30,* 29–59.

Cacioppo, J. T., & Petty, R. E. (1982). The need for cognition. *Journal of Personality and Social Psychology, 42,* 116–131.

Cacioppo, J. T., Petty, R. E., Feinstein, J. A., Blair, G., & Jarvis, W. (1996). Dispositional differences in cognitive motivation: The life and times of individuals varying in need for cognition. *Psychological Bulletin, 119,* 197–253.

Coleman, L. J., & Cross, T. L. (2005). *Being gifted in school.* Waco, TX: Prufrock Press.

Dabrowski, K. (1966). The theory of positive disintegration. *International Journal of Psychiatry 2,* 229–244.

Dabrowski, K., & Piechowski, M. M. (1977). *Theory of levels of emotional development* (Vols.1 & 2). Oceanside, NY: Dabor Science.

Dweck, C. S., & Leggett, E. L. (1988). A social-cognitive approach to motivation and personality. *Psychological Review, 95,* 256–273.

Erikson, E. H. (1968). *Identity, youth, and crisis.* New York, NY: Norton.

Frenkel-Brunswik, E. (1949). Intolerance of ambiguity as an emotional perceptual personality variable. *Journal of Personality, 18,* 108–143.

Greene, J. A., Torney-Purta, J., & Azevedo, R. (2010). Empirical evidence regarding relations among a model of epistemic and ontological cognition, academic performance, and educational level. *Journal of Educational Psychology, 102,* 234–255.

Halpern, D. F. (1998). Teaching critical thinking for transfer across domains: Dispositions, skills, structure training, and metacognitive monitoring. *American Psychologist, 53,* 449–455.

Hofer, B. K., & Pintrich, P. R. (1997). The development of epistemological theories: Beliefs about knowledge and knowing and their relation to learning. *Review of Educational Research, 67,* 88–140.

Jost, J. T., Glaser, J., Kruglanski, A. W., & Sulloway, F. J. (2003). Political conservatism as motivated social cognition. *Psychological Bulletin, 129,* 339–375.

Kitchener, K. S., & King, P. M. (1990). The reflective judgment model: Ten years of research. In M. L. Commons, C. Armon, L. Kohlberg, F. A. Richards, T. A. Grotzer, & J. D. Sinnott (Eds.), *Adult development: Models and methods in the study of adolescent and adult thought* (Vol. 2, pp. 63–78). New York, NY: Praeger.

Kitchener, K. S., King, P. M., Wood, P. K., & Davison, M. L. (1989). Sequentiality and consistency in the development of reflective judgment: A six-year longitudinal study. *Journal of Applied Developmental Psychology, 10,* 73–95.

Klaczynski, P. A. (1997). Bias in adolescents' everyday reasoning and its relationship with intellectual ability, personal theories, and self-serving motivation. *Developmental Psychology, 33,* 273–283.

Klaczynski, P. A., & Gordon, D. H. (1996). Everyday statistical reasoning during adolescence and young adulthood: Motivational, general ability, and developmental influences. *Child Development, 67,* 2873–2891.

Klaczynski, P. A., Gordon, D. H., & Fauth, J. (1997). Goal-oriented critical reasoning and individual differences in critical reasoning biases. *Journal of Educational Psychology, 89,* 470–485.

Kruglanski, A. W. (1989). *Lay epistemics and human knowledge: Cognitive and motivational bases.* New York, NY: Plenum Press.

Kuhn, D. (1991). *The skills of argument.* Cambridge, England: Cambridge University Press.

Kuhn, D. (2003). Understanding and valuing knowing as developmental goals. *Liberal Education, 89,* 16–21.

Kuhn, D., & Dean, D. (2005). Is developing scientific thinking all about learning to control variables? *Psychological Science, 16,* 866–870.

Kuhn, D., & Udell, W. (2003). The development of argument skills. *Child Development, 74,* 1245–1260.

Lakoff, G. (1996). *Moral politics: How liberals and conservatives think.* Chicago, IL: University of Chicago Press.

Maslow, A. H. (1966). *The psychology of science: A reconnaissance.* New York, NY: Harper & Row.

Maslow, A. H. (1970). *Motivation and personality* (2nd ed.). New York, NY: Harper & Row.

Merriam-Webster online dictionary (2010). Dogmatism. Retrieved from http://www.merriam-webster.com/dictionary/dogmatism

Perry, W. G. (1970). *Forms of intellectual and ethical development in the college years: A scheme.* New York, NY: Holt, Rinehart and Winston.

Petty, R. E., & Cacioppo, J. T. (1981). *Attitudes and persuasion: Classic and contemporary approaches.* Dubuque, IA: Wm. C. Brown.

Rokeach, M. (1960). *The open and closed mind.* New York, NY: Basic Books.

Sá, W. C., West, R. F., & Stanovich, K. E. (1999). The domain specificity and generality of belief bias: Searching for a generalizable critical thinking skill. *Journal of Educational Psychology, 91,* 497–510.

Schommer, M. (1990). Effects of beliefs about the nature of knowledge on comprehension. *Journal of Educational Psychology, 82,* 498–504.

Schommer, M. (1994). Synthesizing epistemological belief research: Tentative understandings and provocative confusions. *Educational Psychology Review, 6,* 293–319.

Schwartz, S. H. (1994). Are there universal aspects in the content and structure of values? *Journal of Social Issues, 50,* 19–45.

Schwartz, S. H., Sagiv, L., & Boehnke, K. (2000). Worries and values. *Journal of Personality, 68,* 309–346.

Sorrentino, R. M., & Short, J-A. C. (1986). Uncertainty orientation, motivation, and cognition. In R. M. Sorrentino & E. T. Higgins (Eds.). *Handbook of motivation and cognition: Foundations of social behavior* (pp. 379–403). New York, NY: Guilford Press.

Stanovich, K. E. (2001). The rationality of educating for wisdom. *Educational Psychologist, 36,* 247–251.

Stanovich, K. E., & West, R. F. (1997). Reasoning independently of prior belief and individual differences in actively open-minded thinking. *Journal of Educational Psychology, 89,* 342–357.

Stuart-Hamilton, I., & McDonald, L. (2001). Do we need intelligence? Some reflections on the perceived importance of "g". *Educational Gerontology, 27,* 399–407.

Webster, D. M., & Kruglanski, A. W. (1994). Individual differences in need for cognitive closure. *Journal of Personality and Social Psychology, 67,* 1049–1062.

11

FACING DOGMATIC INFLUENCES WITH CONSCIOUSNESS WORK

Diane Montgomery

OKLAHOMA STATE UNIVERSITY

> Eighty-five years ago the ghost dancers thought that by dancing they could change the earth. We dance to change ourselves. Only when we have done this can we try to change the earth.
>
> Crow Dog (1990, p. 144)

The dogma of today's society in general and within the American educational system in specific is crippling to advanced development. The aim of this chapter is to call for the inclusion of consciousness work within the educational plans for children and youth, specifically, within gifted education. Consciousness work includes the practices that reveal the rich inner life that is not recognized easily because it may remain in the dark and unknown world. The dark and unknown reality is perpetuated by strict intellectualism or dogmatic influences of society or schooling. Therefore, the consequence of practicing the skills for authenticity, such as the acts of reflection, meditation, the arts, and mindfulness reveal an inner calling that is congruent with educational literature in the interrelated areas of moral development (White, 2003), concern for others (Ingram, 2003; Kane, 2003) and the environment (Hartsell, 2006), character development (Folsom, 1998; Tiiri, 2009), and spirituality in education (De Sousa, 2003). In addition to consciousness work with gifted children, the implementation of strategies to practice consciousness in teacher preparation and professional development assures that children and youth who are gifted will not only benefit society but fulfill their own healthy and holistic development.

The word *consciousness* represents a full range of many meanings in its common and scientific use (Velmans, 2009). Most commonly, consciousness refers to the waking world of what is known, has been directly experienced, or is perceived through the senses. To be conscious of self or conscious of one's surroundings are examples of this use of the word. Yet, what is heard or seen can be blinded or silenced by narrow-mindedness, mindlessness, or a refusal to accommodate new information (dogmatism). Consciousness is often used to denote an initial awareness, such as when a child first develops a consciousness about self. For adults, this type of awareness (self-consciousness) ranges from the experiences of learners who become transformed by new insight, perceptions, or perspectives to those who see themselves as explorers in a realm of knowing that cannot be documented by normative science or logic (Forman, 2010). In teacher-education and development programs, an effort is made to increase the awareness of diversity among learners according to race, class, or gender to heighten the critical consciousness of practitioners (Freire, 1990; Green, 1971).

Consciousness has been variously studied scientifically from the early work of William James (1890, 1897), providing a foundation to the science of consciousness (see Ferrari, 2010) to neurological and technically sophisticated assessments (see Gawryluk, D'Arcy, Connolly, & Weaver, 2010). Descartes defined thought and human special sciences as metaphysics (Hennig, 2010). Some researchers argue that the artificial intelligence of machines may or may not be considered conscious by meeting certain criteria (Dournaee, 2010). Although a review of this vast scientific exploration of consciousness is beyond the scope of this discussion, it is important to recognize the multiple meanings of the result of consciousness studies in our society today.

Not as obvious as the waking awareness or that which is made known through measurable scientific research is the knowing of deeper meanings of consciousness, those that are abstract or covert, such as stigma consciousness, awareness that belonging to one group brings negative views or stereotypes, or moral consciousness (Mustakova-Possardt, 2004), the integration of moral motivation, agency, and critical discernment (Freire, 2006). Yet deeper, consciousness work can represent all that is not immediately known in the waking world, those images from the spirit world, archetypal symbols, or unknown interconnectedness.

For this discussion, consciousness is considered to be the depth of spirit, the daimon as described by Reynolds and Piirto (2005, 2009). It represents the core of being for each individual and for the collective of humanity (Jung, 1970). Schlitz, Vieten, and Amorok (2007) extend understanding of consciousness in this way by saying, "Your consciousness is the context in which all of your experiences, perceptions, thoughts, or feelings converge" (p. 17). Using the term *worldview,* these authors discuss how easily people can become attached to a set of beliefs about reality. They stated that "our worldview determines what we're capable of seeing, and therefore determines our perception of reality" (p. 18). Steeped in the dogmatic context of schooling, students who are gifted and their teachers may not notice what in the universe is missing. The dogma that is created by the sharp focus on learning outcomes, rules of appropriate behavior, structures for exclusion, and lack of creativity are the water in the metaphor of fish not able to describe the liquid in which they swim. Consciousness work alleviates the dire situation of a stagnant and narrow worldview. This work includes those activities or practices that bring the richness of an inner life to the outside, known world. Enriching the inner life and extending a view of world to be inclusive of all cultures, alternative ways of perceiving, and all ways of being results in a transformation of the goals of learning and teaching and the way that one is then able to experience others.

Gifted educators and researchers have a history of advocating for extending and enriching the worldview of students. One prominent voice in the literature calls for more activities associated with global education as a response to the educational needs associated with the characteristics of the gifted learner. For example, Annemarie Roeper (2008) describes global education as a mechanism to respond to the sensitivities demonstrated by the gifted children with whom she has studied and experienced. Gibson, Rimmington, and Landwehr-Brown (2008) offered a curricular plan for the knowledge, skills, attitudes, and values needed to promote world citizenship for gifted learners. Other methods in gifted programs designed to help students learn about others who may differ from the circumstances of self are service learning (Lee, Olszewski-Kubilius, Donahue, & Weimholt, 2008; Terry, 2008; Webster & Worrell, 2008), cultural competence (Ford, Moore, & Harmon, 2005; Ford & Whiting, 2008), and character development (Tiiri, 2009), aspects that build authenticity in learning.

Seeking Authenticity, Becoming Awake

Authenticity denotes a depth of heart, a dimension that adds truth in combination with compassion to increase the positive emotions and empathy that are necessary in relationships. Authenticity contributes to the wholeness of character. Miller (2000) explains this holism as "the whole is greater than the sum of its parts means that the whole is comprised of a pattern of relationships that are not contained by the parts but ultimately define them" (p. 21). When perspective comes from one portion of the whole, a reductionist response resembles dogmatic, partial truth. In other words, a blindness to the whole truth or other possible views is cemented by stagnating, smaller and smaller units of analysis. Miller's description of levels of holism reflects authenticity at each of three levels: knowing all aspects of the developmental needs of self; relating to others in a peaceful society; and being aware of the ways that behavior influences the earth. Interactional authenticity then, is the method of becoming awakened to the world and the role of self, others, and the universe. Knowing the relationship to the universe is the consequence of the acclaimed necessity for the consideration of spirituality in the education for gifted learners (Roeper, 2008; Sisk, 2008). Roeper writes, "It's my conviction that only when we learn to trust the unknown (that which we can't understand or prove) will we get a glimpse of the true reality of this universe" (p. 10).

Awakening is the opposite of being awake. Nakagawa (2000) described two psychologies of holism, one that is the ordinary waking world and the other a deeply conscious, awakened state. This holistic, awakened state is achieved through consciousness work, connecting to the deepest space of soul. Jung (quoted in Spoto, 1995) believed that consciousness was socially constructed in accordance with personality, but the elements grow out of the "virtually time-less, transcultural matrix of the unconscious" (p. 142). Bringing the depth of soul to a conscious knowing required the work of art, contemplative practice, or other psychological strategies, such as active imagination.

Although situated in the religious literature, the need for a combination of imagination and consciousness was argued by Schweiker (2007). This work included conversations designed to bring a global ethic into a moral conscious-ness that enacts an awareness of societal issues of the world's populations. This imaginative consciousness is manifest in education with a pedagogical model offered by Mustakova-Possardt (2004) as a theory for infusing moral conscious-ness into education and learning. The results of her study support four develop-mental dimensions for moral motivation and critical discernment, dimensions which combine the heart and mind. The dimensions were identified as a moral sense of identity, sense of responsibility and agency, sense of relatedness on all levels of living, and sense of meaning and life purpose. Clearly, this type of con-sciousness has vast implications for the work done on a daily basis in classrooms of gifted children and teachers.

Learning and Consciousness

Educational philosophy dictates program choices in gifted education (Johnson, 2005). Johnson describes three philosophical views. Materialistic monism por-trays the world as matter and energy with consciousness resulting merely from regular brain activity. This view is consistent with scientists looking for neu-rological activity to explain dreams (Hori, Ogawa, Abe, & Nittono, 2008) and numerous other ways that science strives to explain consciousness by study-ing neurological correlates (see, for example, the discussion of brain activity and morality in Churchland, 2008). In education this view is true for those who believe that learners respond to environmental stimuli, situations in which behaviorism (stimulus and response relationship) and positivism (objective study of causes) dominate the educators' actions.

The second view is named dualism and portrays consciousness as separate studies of matter and energy. In this view, qualitative methodology and its strategies are used to uncover the personal, subjective meaning and reality of individual consciousness. According to Johnson (2005), consciousness within this view is a personal interpretation of the outer world and constructivism is the dominant educational approach.

The third philosophy is transcendental monism. Within this view, consciousness is the "basic essence" (Johnson, 2005, p. 68) and matter and energy emerge from its reality. Citing Goswami (1993), Johnson presents the world as a representation of what is known in quantum physics and holism becomes the educational foundation. In his way of avoiding the dogma of accepting only one narrow view, Johnson promoted expanding the research methodologies and educational strategies to include all views. This expansion requires teaching holistically and including the concept of wisdom.

Holistic education recognizes the need to assist learners to develop as whole persons rather than separate components experiencing knowing and the world separately. Forbes (2003) described the commonality among several views of holistic education by saying that "holistic education has as its goal the fullest possible human development with fitting into society and vocation having secondary importance" (p. 3). Forbes described ultimacy as the primary goal of holistic education. Ultimacy is an act of seeking in two areas, facilitating the discovery of fulfillment of person and discovery of one's greatest service or calling. Hart (2009) paved a way to move from the currency of information to transformation of self and ego through learning and teaching. Seeking transformative learning goes beyond the knowledge, skills, and abilities in a content area and integrates intuition and analytic thinking for learning. In gifted education, the integration of creative and critical thought is planned across curricula. For example, current guidelines using the parallel curriculum design by Tomlinson et al. (2009) enhances learning beyond a core knowledge to include connections among people, creative awareness of self, and global skills.

Other paths toward consciousness work have been paved with research on wisdom in the field of gifted education. Sternberg (2003, 2010) has made significant contributions weaving the role of wisdom in the identification of giftedness using his extensive research on what wisdom is and how it goes beyond what an individual knows to what is done in life. Wisdom is ability to act toward universal values, an ethical action for the common good (Sternberg, 2009). Wisdom is part of the holistic classroom, one in which the human concerns, social conditions, ethical responses, and convictions to actions are overt.

Closely related to descriptions of wisdom is the bold use of the spiritual in the classroom. Sisk (2008) calls for engaging the unique characteristics of giftedness to heighten global awareness. She combines these exceptional qualities of perception and sensitivity, intuition, and visioning to constitute a spiritual intelligence or higher calling of wisdom for gifted learners.

The dogmatic block to consciousness work in school is the idea that all practices relating to the spirit must be religious education. Yet, the distinction between religious faith and deep spiritual meaning toward others can be delineated within an open-minded context of interpersonal and intrapersonal relationships. As dogmatism is the result of a narrow-minded, behavioral interpretation of learning, the deep spirit and collective unconscious meanings in symbols are neglected in the full development of children and youth. Examples for how to begin to bring creative spirit in the classroom are to infuse the arts and encourage teachers to truly collaborate in planning.

Co-Creation in Curriculum

The implementation of packaged, scripted, or programmed curriculum has been a strategy that educators have used for several years (Gelberg, 2008), particularly in reading (Parsons & Harrington, 2009). The evidence for the effectiveness and value of such programs may exist, particularly from the original authors of the programs; however, when thinking about the consistent results needed in larger-scale research to be able to promote a practice that is evidence-based, mixed results emerge (see Constas & Sternberg, 2006). Each of the innovative ideas for a method, strategy, or other process of teaching reading or learning math facts was tried by one or two people at a school of need. These educators probably witnessed radical results and convinced school or regional colleagues to initiate the practice. Then, success breeds publishers, scripts, standardization, and one right way to conduct the practice that started out as an innovative, creative, and effective idea. Although some teachers prefer having the day mapped out and the strategies scripted, others believe that real teaching includes creativity and joy (Starnes, 2010). Little is known about whether the adoption of programmed curricula leads to success or a dogmatic loyalty.

With the initiators of Project CREATES (Connecting Community Resources Encouraging All Teachers to Educate with Spirit; Montgomery, Otto, & Hull, 2007), a plan was developed to respond to a frustration brought by the many years of experience in public schools working for school reform. In the zealous efforts to quickly solve student achievement problems, school administrators would find programs that promised results and demanded an all-school implementation, all in the name of doing good work for student achievement. The foundation of CREATES was in opposition to such coercion through co-creation, a process that was designed to confront the dogmatic, stifling effects of learning and drilling with a packaged curriculum. As a project with a mission to transform teaching and learning by the infusion of high quality arts instruction in high quality academic instruction, the authenticity of the project was to demonstrate in all work the co-creation dimension. Co-creation as a value to curriculum planning, implementation, and student evaluation can be expressed consciously in all relationships as well.

The official definition of co-creation is the production of something within a team for which each team member sees her contribution taking authorship for the whole and each team member makes the production unique. The product could not have been the same without any one of the members. This co-construction of new understanding in teaching and learning occurs through innovation in collaboration and openness to learning from another person and another discipline. Community artists, arts educators, general and special educators, students, and families participate in the learning process. The core planning occurs with teaching artists working as instructional coaches with artists and teachers, a bridge to making the creative spirit of each child visible to self and to others.

When dogmatism creeps into the co-creative process there are some telltale signs. Observation of co-created lessons revealed that some artists persisted in teaching the same drop-in art lesson to any class. Fully field independent, the artists were functioning as entertainers, not educators. Although the fun part of art (Hull, 2003) has been documented as one of the benefits according to the perceptions of elementary teachers, the greater value of creative expression and domain expertise is neglected. Teaching artists who collaborated with teachers become true coaches (Wilcox, Bridges, & Montgomery, 2010) for unique products based on the same theses, learner outcomes, content learning, or artistic skills.

Curriculum change may create anxiety for teachers; however, one study (Buchanan, 2009) demonstrated how attention to the spiritual dimension of teachers can be fostered through connectedness and reduce stress and anxiety for teachers during change. Written for academic leaders to facilitate connectedness, this study provides a model for the priority of relationship and connectedness among school personnel while transforming instruction. Deep engagement with one another to own the change and be committed to its success brings about the true sustainability that grant money cannot buy without the conscious work of connecting the teachers, the community, the students, and their families in learning.

Classroom Strategies for Contemplation

One type of dreaming is the conscious and waking dream, which uses imagination to inspire achievement of goals. "I dream of one day being able to ..." is a waking thought of hope and aspirations for future accomplishments. On the other hand, there is the practice of guided imagery that encourages complex concepts to be understood and integrated into a knowledge schema. Imagery, metaphors, and symbols occurring in art and in nature teach about the science of the world experienced through our senses.

Other promising strategies for learners and their teachers include mind-body exercises, such as building and walking the labyrinth, learning yoga poses, or practicing Tai Chi or Qigong. Although these practices are not well-known or part of the regular school curricula, it is likely that they can be discovered by investigating who in the community has experience or knowledge. Small towns to large cities have minority populations with connections to materials and experts who can lead lessons. Lessons are easily accessed through library and Internet resources to infuse these wisdom practices in academic units as part of the learning process. Community resources to assist teachers with integration are available in all states. Walking the labyrinth is an ancient tradition encouraging contemplation and integrating a walking meditation. In any meditative activity, including the preliminary work of mindfulness, a concentrated effort to breathe and go through prescribed motions allows the stillness of mind and expansion of heart.

The development of mindfulness, a keen awareness of self and others, and an introspective and reflective practice with a moment of transformation of worldview or perspective promotes authenticity of self and a transcendence of ego. Evidence of this transcendence occurs as individuals engage in the "simple act of drawing novel distinctions" (Langer, 2000, p. 220). Mindfulness may be associated with meditation practices as well. Although meditation may take many forms, one useful practice for classroom application is the contemplative practice of sitting in silence to cultivate a discovery of perception and thought. A close concentration or thoughtfulness, mindfulness toward the breath reveals the mind's hesitation to settle down without constant processing of information.

Starting with small steps of consciousness work brings greater awareness of the needs of students for more holistic practices and more complex activities. First steps might be the physical education teachers working with teachers to bring body movements, stretches, and mind–body exercises before children have to take tests. The success of this strategy may lead to more involvement in physical work as learning occurs, which may lead to learning how to lead yoga, which may lead to other contemplative practices. School personnel who might otherwise resist the use of movement, meditation, or the arts as creative practices will begin to see the results and the transforming process to a greater awareness, greater consciousness. Less dogmatism may result.

Transforming Teacher Preparation and Development

In spite of hearing so much about the problem of teacher retention, we find little in the teacher preparation or development programs that equip teachers for the stress of their work. They balance the structure of the school dictates and student needs, designing curriculum for a vast range of abilities and skills represented in their classrooms. The effect of mindfulness on mental and physical health has been documented for the past twenty years (see, for example, Kabat-Zinn, 1996; Whitehead, 1992; Williams, Kolar, Reger, & Pearson, 2001). In preparing counselors, research (Schure, Christopher, & Christopher, 2008) shows that a college course consisting of yoga, meditation, and Qigong resulted in positive physical, emotional, mental, spiritual, and interpersonal changes for students enrolled in the course. Furthermore, the practices had a considerable effect on counseling skills and relationship developed in therapy. Some exploratory and initial studies of teachers have shown remarkably positive results (see, for example, the September 2006 special issue of the *Teachers College Record*; Gold, Smith, Hopper, Herne, Tansey, & Hulland, 2010; Solloway, 2001). Hoy,

Gage, and Tarter (2006) investigated mindfulness at the collective level and reported the effects of flexibility in thinking, examination of the rules, and thoughtful examinations of the subtle consequences of actions on the trust that was engendered at 75 middle schools among school personnel. The mindfulness served as a transformation of dogmatic thinking and acting into a positive and trusting experience for school personnel. Yet, few educational administrator preparation programs offer or support mindfulness practices.

Miller and Nozawa (2005) describe in case studies how contemplative practices, such as meditation, enrich the life of the teacher. They state the importance of teacher preparation programs that promote teaching as an inner fulfillment by saying, "If teaching is ego-based it can become a frustrating series of mini-battles with students" (p. 43). Relinquishing control to teach from an inner, developed self magnifies the multiple role expected of the teacher, connecting with students on levels deeper than transfer of knowledge cognitively.

Yet, few teachers of the gifted realize that an important aspect of professionalism is meditative self-care that transfers to the loving kindness necessary for creating the learning community that sustains holistic learning. Genoud (2009) leads those who meditate to an understanding of an awareness of "the first instant of perception before the arising of a concept; to be mindful means, precisely, to be present at each moment" (p. 123). The optimal path to healthy professional development includes contemplative practices to encompass a moral consciousness, a critical consciousness, and a global consciousness.

Conclusion

This discussion has as its goal to encourage consciousness work in schools, with gifted children, and in teacher preparation and professional development programs. The concept of dogmatism has been extended to include emotional and spiritual narrow-mindedness. This sort of dogma is a blindness that ignores the images and symbols that teach deeply within an archetypal knowing, and a deafness to natural sounds and words that represent more than the surface-level of meaning. As an anecdote to this dogma, each educator first examines his or her own heart, life skills, meditative practices, and physical and mental well-being. The healthiest of teachers lead to the most aware teachers and the best teachers of the gifted.

References

Buchanan, M. T. (2009). The spiritual dimension and curriculum change. *International Journal of Children's Spirituality, 14,* 385–394. doi: 10.1080/1364436090329348

Churchland, P. (2008). The impact of neuroscience on philosophy. *Neuron, 60,* 409–411. doi: 10.1016/j.neuron.2008.10.023

Constas, M. A., & Sternberg, R. J. (2006). *Translating theory and research into educational practice: Developments in content domains, large-scale reform, and intellectual capacity.* Mahwah, NJ: Erlbaum.

Crow Dog, M. (1990). *Lakota woman*. New York, NY: Harper Collins.

De Souza, M. (2003). Contemporary influences on the spirituality of young people: Implications for education. *International Journal of Children's spirituality, 8,* 269–279.

Dournaee, B. H. (2010). Comments on "The replication of the hard problem of consciousness in AI and bio-AI." *Minds & Machines, 20,* 303–309. doi: 10.1007/s11023-010-9188-9

Ferrari, M. (2010). History of the science of consciousness. [Special issue]. *History of the Human Sciences, 23*(3).

Folsom, C. (1998). From a distance: Joining the mind and moral character. *Roeper Review, 20,* 265–270.

Forbes, S. H. (2003). *Holistic education: An analysis of its ideas and nature.* Brandon, VT: Foundation for Educational Renewal.

Ford, D. Y., Moore, J. L., & Harmon, D. A. (2005). Integrating multicultural and gifted education: A curricular framework. *Theory into Practice, 44,* 125–137. doi: 10.1207/s15430421tip4402_7

Ford, D. Y., & Whiting, G. W. (2008). Cultural competence: Preparing gifted students for a diverse society. *Roeper Review, 30,* 104–110. doi: 10.1080/02783190801955087

Forman, R. K. C. (2010). A conference and a question: Report on consciousness and cpirituality II. *Journal of Consciousness Studies, 17,* 183–188.

Freire, P. (1990). *Pedagogy of the oppressed.* M. Bergman Ramos (Trans.). New York, NY: Continuum.

Freire, P. (2006). *Pedagogy of hope.* New York, NY: Continuum.

Gawryluk, J. R., D'Arcy, R. C. N., Connolly, J. F., & Weaver, D. F. (2010). Improving the clinical assessment of consciousness with advances in electrophysiological and neuroimaging techniques. *BMC Neurology, 10,* Special Section 1-7. doi: 10.1186/1471-2377-10-11

Gelberg, D. (2008). Scripted curriculum: Scourge or salvation? *Educational Leadership, 65*(6), 80–82.

Genoud, C. (2009). On the cultivation of presence in Buddhist meditation. *Journal of Consciousness Studies, 16*(10-12), 117–128.

Gibson, K. L., Rimmington, G. M., & Landwehr-Brown, M. (2008). Developing global awareness and responsible world citizenship with global learning. *Roeper Review, 30,* 11–23.

Gold, E., Smith, A., Hopper, I., Herne, D., Tansey, G., & Hulland, C. (2010). Mindfulness-based stress reduction (MBSR) for primary school teachers. *Journal of Child and Family Studies, 19,* 184–189. doi: 10.1007/s10826-009-9344-0

Goswami, A. (1993). *The self-aware universe: How consciousness creates the material world.* New York, NY: Putnam.

Green, M. (1971). Curriculum and consciousness. *Teachers College Record, 73,* 253–270.

Hart, T. (2009). *From information to transformation: Education for the evolution of consciousness* (rev. ed.). New York, NY: Lang.

Hartsell, B. (2006). Teaching toward compassion: Environmental values education for secondary students. *Journal of Secondary Gifted Education, 17,* 265–271.

Hennig, B. (2010). Science, conscience, consciousness. *History of the Human Sciences, 23,* 15–28. doi: 10.1177/0952695110363353

Hori, T., Ogawa, K., Abe, T., & Nittono, H. (2008). Brain potentials related to rapid eye movements and dreaming during REM sleep: A short review of psychophysiological correlates. *Sleep and Biological Rhythms, 6,* 128–138. doi: 10.1111/j.1479-8425.2008.000358.x

Hoy, W. K., Gage III, C. Q., & Tarter C. J. (2006). School mindfulness and faculty trust: Necessary conditions for each other? *Educational Administration Quarterly, 42,* 236–255. doi: 10.1177/0013161X04273844

Hull, D. F. (2003). *A Q methodological study describing the beliefs of teachers about arts integrated in the curriculum in Oklahoma K-12 schools* (Unpublished doctoral dissertation). Oklahoma State University, Stillwater, Oklahoma.

Ingram, M. A. (2003). The use of sociocultural poetry to assist gifted students in developing empathy for the lived experiences of others. *Journal of Secondary Gifted Education, 14,* 83–90.

James, W. (1890). *The principles of psychology (Volumes I and II).* New York, NY: Holt.

James, W. (1897). *Selected essays in philosophy*. London, England: Dent and Sons.

Johnson, A. (2005). Caught by our dangling paradigms: How our metaphysical assumptions influence gifted education. *Journal of Secondary Gifted Education, 16,* 67–73.

Jung, C. G. (1970) *Collected works*. 18 vols. Princeton, NJ: Bollingen Foundation.

Kabat-Zinn, J. (1996). Mindfulness meditation: What it is, what it isn't, and its role in health care and medicine. In Y. Haruki, Y. Ishii, & M. Suzuki (Eds.), *Comparative and psychological study on meditation* (pp. 161–170). Delft, The Netherlands: Eburon.

Kane, M. (2003). A conversation with Annemarie Roeper: A view from the self. *Roeper Review, 26,* 5–11.

Langer, E. J. (2000). Mindful learning. *Current Directions in Psychological Science, 9,* 220–223.

Lee, S. Y., Olszewski-Kubilius, P., Donahue, R., & Weimholt, K. (2008). The Civic Leadership Institute: A service-learning program for academically gifted youth. *Journal of Advanced Academics, 19,* 272–308.

Miller, R. (2000). *Caring for new life: Essays on holistic education.* Brandon, VT: Foundation for Educational Renewal.

Miller, J. P., & Nozawa, A. (2005). Contemplative practices in teacher education. *Encounter: Education for Meaning and Social Justice, 18,* 42–48.

Montgomery, D., Otto, S., & Hull, D. (2007). *Summative research report for Project CREATES: Learning through the Arts.* Stillwater, OK: New Forums Press.

Mustakova-Possardt, E. (2004). Education for critical moral consciousness. *Journal of Moral Education, 33,* 245–269. doi: 10.1080/0305724042000733046

Nakagawa, Y. (2000). *Education for awakening: An Eastern approach to holistic education.* Brandon, VT: Foundation for Educational Renewal.

Parsons, S. A., & Harrington, A. D. (2009). Following the script. *Phi Delta Kappan, 90,* 748–750.

Reynolds, F. C., & Piirto, J. (2005). Depth psychology and giftedness: Bringing soul to the field of talent development and giftedness. *Roeper Review, 27,* 164–171.

Reynolds, F. C., & Piirto, J. (2009). Depth psychology and integrity. In D. Ambrose & T. L. Cross (Eds.), *Morality, ethics, and gifted minds* (pp. 195–206). New York, NY: Springer Science.

Roeper, A. (2008). Global awareness and gifted children: Its joy and history. *Roeper Review, 30,* 8–10.

Schlitz, M. M., Vieten, C., & Amorok, T. (2007). *Living deeply: The art & science of transformation in everyday life.* Oakland, CA: Harbinger/Noetic Books.

Schweiker, W. (2007). Whither global ethics? Moral consciousness and global cultural flows. *Journal of Ecumenical Studies, 42,* 425–439.

Schure, M. B., Christopher, J., & Christopher, S. (2008). Mind-body medicine and the art of self-care: Teaching mindfulness to counseling students through yoga, meditation, and Qigong. *Journal of Counseling & Development, 86,* 47–57.

Sisk, D. (2008). Engaging the spiritual intelligence of gifted students to build global awareness in the classroom. *Roeper Review, 30,* 24–30.

Solloway, S. (2001). Mindfulness, the hermeneutic imagination and jouissance: Action inquiry and transformations in classroom practice. *Journal of Curriculum Theorizing, 17,* 155–170.

Spoto, A. (1995). *Jung's typology in perspective. Revised edition.* Wilmette, IL: Chiron.

Starnes, B. A. (2010). On carrots and sticks, joyful teaching, and coming to the light. *Kappan, 91*(8), 74–75.

Sternberg, R. J. (2003). *Wisdom, intelligence, and creativity synthesized.* New York, NY: Cambridge University Press.

Sternberg, R. J. (2009). Ethics and giftedness. *High Ability Studies, 20,* 121–130.

Sternberg, R. J. (2010). Assessment of gifted students for identification purposes: New techniques for a new millennium. *Learning and Individual Differences, 20,* 327–336. doi: 10.1016/j.lindif.2009.08.003

Terry, A. W. (2008). Student voices, global echoes: Service-learning and the gifted. *Roeper Review, 30,* 45–51. doi: 10.1080/02783190701836452

Tiiri, K. (2009). Character education and giftedness. *High Ability Studies, 20,* 117–119. doi: 10.1080/13598130903358469

Tomlinson, C. A., Kaplan, S. H., Renzulli, J. S., Purcell, J. H., Leppien, J. H., Burns, D. E., … Imbeau, M. B. *The parallel curriculum: A design to develop learner potential and challenge advanced learners* (2nd ed.). Thousand Oaks, CA: Corwin Press.

Velmans, M. (2009). How to define consciousness: And how not to define consciousness. *Journal of Consciousness Studies, 16,* 139–156.

Webster, N. S., & Worrell, F. C. (2008). Academically talented students' attitudes toward service in the community. *Gifted Child Quarterly, 52,* 170–179. doi: 10.1177/0016986208316038

White, D. A. (2003) Philosophy and theory in the study of gifted children. *Roeper Review, 26,* 16–19.

Whitehead, W. E. (1992). Behavioral medicine approaches to gastrointestinal disorders. *Journal of Consulting and Clinical Psychology, 60,* 605–612.

Wilcox, R., Bridges, S., & Montgomery, D. (2010). The role of coaching by teaching artists for arts-infused social studies: What Project CREATES has to offer. *Journal for Learning through the Arts* (6)1. Retrieved from http://escholarship.org/uc/item/6mw9s8qs

Williams, K., Kolar, M., Reger, B., & Pearson, J. (2001). Evaluation of a wellness-based mindfulness stress reduction intervention: A controlled trial. *American Journal of Health Promotion, 15,* 422–432.

12

DOGMATIC INFLUENCES SUPPRESSING DISCOVERY AND DEVELOPMENT OF GIFTEDNESS AND TALENT IN THE ARABIAN GULF AND MIDDLE EASTERN REGION

Taisir Subhi Yamin

UNIVERSITÉ PARIS DESCARTES, FRANCE

Don Ambrose

RIDER UNIVERSITY

Contextual Factors Contributing to Dogmatism in the Region

Although data don't yet allow firm conclusions about the quality of education in Middle Eastern countries, tentative impressions are that many nations
in the region were doing significantly worse than would be expected by the
year 2000 (IMF, 2011; World Bank, 2011). Furthermore, most of the regions'
countries lack democracy because they have no effective separation of powers,
insufficient respect for the rule of law, and no guarantee of citizens' civil and
political rights. In addition, they do not do well in important dimensions of
human development (e.g., freedom from serious economic deprivation, gender equality, access to knowledge and quality education, adequate health care)
that provide citizens with the freedom and empowerment necessary for self-
actualization (UNDP, 2010; Alkire, 2002). In such conditions bright young
people suffer from suppression and warping of their aspirations and talents (see
Ambrose, 2005).

This large-scale, long-term neglect of human potential in the Middle East
and Arabian Gulf region appears to be a serious macroproblem. A macroproblem is a dilemma that is exceedingly difficult to solve because it is: (a)
international, resisting solution from within the borders of a single nation, (b)
long-term because it took years, decades, or even centuries to create; consequently, it will take a long time to unravel, and (c) transdisciplinary because it

will take the wisdom of experts from more than one discipline to puzzle out (Ambrose, 2009). Examples of macroproblems include:

1. the dogmatic deregulation of the global socioeconomic system, which has enabled creative but unethical individuals to establish corrupt financial innovations that enable them to engage in massive pillaging of the economy (Stiglitz, 2010);
2. the growing divide between rich and poor within nations and between regions of the world (Clark, 2007; Smeeding & Rainwater, 2004; Woodward & Simms, 2006; Yunus, 2008); and
3. possibly the biggest macroproblem of all—climate change, which promises to dramatically transform life conditions on earth (Archer, 2009; Hansen, 2005).

Obviously, humanity will need to devise and use more effective thinking and problem-solving strategies to grapple with 21st-century macroproblems.

The lack of democratic governance and the attendant civil rights for all citizens represent a persistent, regional dogmatism-driven macroproblem harming Middle Eastern and Arabian Gulf nations. For example, Arabian Gulf countries tend to deny rights of citizens to run for elected office. This is especially the case for women. Some countries such as Saudi Arabia go even further and still restrict women's voting rights.

There are notable exceptions to neglect of democracy in the region (e.g., Qatar, Kuwait, Jordan, and the United Arab Emirates). For example, Jordan has made some major strides in politics by establishing a quota reserving a percentage of parliamentary seats for women, thus contributing to a rise in women's participation in the nation's development (Dahlerup & Freidevall, 2005). Nevertheless, democracy is not as well developed in this region (even in nations where it is developing) than in some other parts of the world. Participatory democracy is a remote prospect in many parts of the region. The leaders of the ruling families and other elites, along with their politicians and administrators, are often reluctant to broaden quality educational opportunities on the grounds that educated and qualified people would be more difficult to manage or control (Yamin, 2007; UNDP, 2010; Gavlak, 2008). Such dogmatic attitudes impede human development, preventing the emergence and implementation of provisions for gifted, creative, and talented young people.

Coping with Brain Drain

As if this isn't enough, many nations in the region suffer from brain drain because large numbers of gifted, talented individuals move away from the nations that need them the most. This phenomenon has become an intraregional concern in the Middle Eastern countries since the late 1970s primarily as a result of employment migration to the Arabian Gulf (DOS, 2009;

DOS, 2010). The weakness of democratic processes in the region has resulted in lack of economic opportunities, political instability, corruption, and poor living conditions for most of the population. Consequently, gifted, creative, talented, and skilled individuals leave their homelands and seek entrance into more developed nations. If their migration is successful, they refuse to return to their home countries because the host nations provide some blend of superior democratic stability, social organizations, freedom, economic opportunity, and living conditions.

In essence, many countries in the region find that a significant proportion of their young people become the human capital and the economic drivers for the development of other nations. For example, employment migration affects about 50% of the total Jordanian labor force (DOS, 2009; UNDP, 2010; UNESCO, 2011). According to the Jordanian department of statistics (DOS, 2010), the total estimate of Jordanians working abroad at any given time is 670,000. The majority of them are working in Saudi Arabia and other countries in the Arabian Gulf (DOS, 2010). In contrast, the number of imported laborers and their dependents exceeds that of the native residents of some oil countries (e.g., United Arab Emirates, Qatar) (DOS, 2010, UNDP, 2010).

While many of those migrating are unskilled or semiskilled, the brain-drain phenomenon includes large numbers of the region's most gifted, creative, intelligent individuals. About 750,000 Arab intellectuals with substantial scientific and technological qualifications have moved away from their home nations (UNDP, 2010). Overall, many nations in the region cannot retain their brightest minds because investments in science and technology in general, and gifted education in particular, are inadequate. Consequently, Middle Eastern and Arabian Gulf nations fail to establish the environments (sociopolitical, economic) required for encouraging their gifted, creative intellectuals to become strongly involved in the development of their nations and to assume roles as productive citizens.

Democratic Erosion Suppressing or Crushing Aspirations and Talent Discovery

The problems of talent suppression and stunted aspirations in the region largely derive from lack of democratic dynamics in sociopolitical systems. Figure 12.1 shows the effects of a nation's governance on the discovery and development of giftedness and talent among its citizens. Generated from a synthesis of research and theory in sociology, economics, ethical philosophy, and history (see Ambrose, 2005), the circular model represents the dynamics of democratic growth or erosion, which derive from balances or imbalances in the tension between right-wing and left-wing ideology. A healthy balance between the right-wing tenets of individual economic freedom and limited government on the one hand, and the left-wing tenets of communal distributive justice and

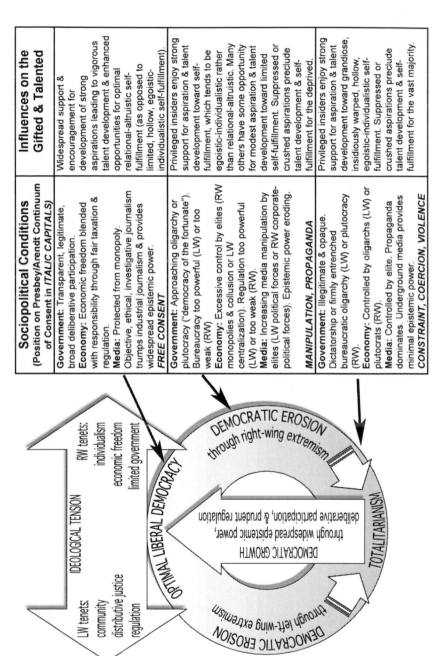

Sociopolitical Conditions (Position on Presbey/Arendt Continuum of Consent in *ITALIC CAPITALS*)	Influences on the Gifted & Talented
Government: Transparent, legitimate, broad deliberative participation. **Economy:** Economic freedom blended with responsibility through fair taxation & regulation. **Media:** Protected from monopoly. Objective, ethical, investigative journalism trumps industrial journalism & provides widespread epistemic power. *FREE CONSENT*	Widespread support & encouragement for development of strong aspirations leading to vigorous talent development & enhanced opportunities for optimal relational-altruistic self-fulfillment (as opposed to limited, hollow, egoistic-individualistic self-fulfillment).
Government: Approaching oligarchy or plutocracy ("democracy of the fortunate"). Bureaucracy too powerful (LW) or too weak (RW). **Economy:** Excessive control by elites (RW monopolies & collusion or LW centralization). Regulation too powerful (LW) or too weak (RW). **Media:** Increasing media manipulation by elites (LW political forces or RW corporate-political forces). Epistemic power eroding. *MANIPULATION, PROPAGANDA*	Privileged insiders enjoy strong support for aspiration & talent development toward self-fulfillment, which tends to be egoistic-individualistic rather than relational-altruistic. Many others have some opportunity for modest aspiration & talent development toward limited self-fulfillment. Suppressed or crushed aspirations preclude talent development & self-fulfillment for the deprived.
Government: Illegitimate & opaque. Dictatorship or firmly entrenched bureaucratic oligarchy (LW) or plutocracy (RW). **Economy:** Controlled by oligarchs (LW) or plutocrats (RW). **Media:** Controlled by elite. Propaganda dominates. Underground media provides minimal epistemic power. *CONSTRAINT, COERCION, VIOLENCE*	Privileged insiders enjoy strong support for aspiration & talent development toward grandiose, insidiously warped, hollow, egoistic-individualistic self-fulfillment. Suppressed or crushed aspirations preclude talent development & self-fulfillment for the vast majority.

FIGURE 12.1 Model of democratic growth and erosion. Reprinted with permission from Ambrose, D. (2005). Aspiration growth, talent development, and self-fulfillment in a context of democratic erosion. *Roeper Review, 28,* 11–19.

government regulation of the socioeconomic system on the other, provides citizens with awareness of the inner workings of the government (epistemic power) as well as opportunities to participate in that governance. In such conditions a society moves upward on the model toward optimal liberal democracy. At this high point on the circle in the model, a nation's government is transparent and legitimate in the eyes of its citizens. The sociopolitical system is guided by the involvement and free consent of the governed. It provides a healthy context for the aspiration development and discovery of talents. In addition, those aspirations and talents are infused with altruism, which contributes to the achievement of long-term, individual self-fulfillment and the creation of a more humane society.

In contrast, when the sociopolitical system of a nation skews emphatically toward either left-wing or right-wing ideological extremism that nation descends down a slippery slope of democratic erosion toward totalitarianism at the bottom of the model. Excessive control of governance and the economy by elites (ideologically extreme left-wing or right-wing oligarchs or plutocrats) robs most of the citizenry of governmental transparency. It also removes opportunities for participation in political decision-making from the masses because, in their attempts to acquire and hoard ever more power for themselves, the elites engage in manipulation and propaganda to deceive and control the general public. In the worst cases, the elites use constraint, coercion, and even violent oppression to control the nation's population. In these conditions, only the children of the elite have significant educational opportunities, and those opportunities tend to lead them toward warped, egocentric versions of aspiration discovery and talent development. The children of the vast majority who do not enjoy political power in an oppressive system usually find their aspiration discovery and talent development suppressed or crushed. To the extent that these dynamics of democratic erosion apply to the Middle Eastern and Arabian Gulf region, and they seem to apply rather well given the plutocratic nature of their governance systems, those who design and implement gifted programs for bright young children in the region must be aware of the contextual, sociopolitical and economic constraints that impinge on the aspiration discovery and talent development of the gifted.

Suppression and Dilution of Gifted Education in a Regional Context that Inhibits Democracy

Most existing gifted programs in the Middle Eastern and Arabian Gulf region are very weak. They suffer from lack of facilities and resources and struggle to function in unfruitful sociopolitical contexts. Excellence in education is ignored by policy makers and most educators in the region, although it is quite different if a program is the initiative of a Sheikh, a prince, a princess, a queen, a president, or a king. In those cases, all the necessary resources are marshaled at public expense to support the program, which is given top priority because it will be employed to nurture the next generation of the ruling families—the "future leaders" of the society.

Gifted programs tend to operate within larger educational systems and the health and vitality of those systems can affect the vitality of provisions for the gifted. Spending on education hovers around 0.2% of the National Domestic Product (NDP) for most nations in the region. For the sake of comparison, spending is about 1% of the NDP of Turkey, 2.4% in Germany, and 3.1% in the United States (UNESCO, 2011). This suggests that the rich oil countries in the Middle Eastern and Arabian Gulf region are not spending enough on education in general and do not invest in gifted education in particular. In essence, the nations in the region have distorted priorities.

Furthermore, when educators do offer constructive suggestions to encourage the development of gifted programs, politicians and administrators ignore or dismiss them while complaining about the lack of necessary resources. Too little attention has been paid to gifted education.

In light of the current situation, how can we be optimists? Based on international comparisons these countries taken together should be spending much more annually to support science, technology, and centers for excellence in education (UNESCO, 2011; Yamin, 2007). In addition, they should be prioritizing innovation in education and the development of provisions for their gifted, talented, creative young people.

However, the story isn't entirely bleak in this region of the world. There are countries that have succeeded in promoting excellence in gifted education. For example, strong programs and innovations can be found in The Jubilee School in Jordan, Centers for Excellence in Israel, and gifted programs in Turkey (Bahar, Ramazan, & Suna, 2009; ICEE, 2009). Nevertheless, far more can and should be done to elevate the life chances and future prospects for bright, young children in the Middle East and the Arabian Gulf.

Revamping Gifted Education in the Region by Shifting Educational Philosophy

In addition to these sociopolitical and economic contextual problems, there are barriers to effective gifted education that derive from the philosophy of education in the region. Several years ago, the International Centre for Innovation in Education (ICIE) recognized that there are two things wrong with gifted education in this region (Yamin, 2009). First, it is not built on strong and reliable foundations. Second, it was created by commercial firms for non-educational purposes.

Educational philosophy in the Arabian Gulf and Middle Eastern region tends to emphasize cognitive development and nebulously aims at enhancing the "mental ability" of children, but it does not recognize more holistic approaches to development. Consequently, the educational systems in the region concentrate on inculcating knowledge, facts, and information. Students are encouraged to learn by heart decontextualized fact-based content that lacks connection with their personal lives. In addition, there is little room for productive, creative thinking or the discovery of aspirations and the development of talents. Philosophically speaking, education in the region is plagued by the same decontextualized-content mania that leading educational scholars have identified in the United States (see Berliner, in press; Bracey, 2004; Nichols & Berliner, 2007).

In the absence of clear vision, the region's countries tend to "import" gifted programs from the West and attempt to force-fit them into contexts without concern for cultural differences. There are serious deficiencies in the ways in which gifted individuals are screened and identified in this region, largely because most Arabian Gulf and Middle Eastern countries import European or American identification tools to be translated literally and then employed in very different cultural settings without any thought of modification. Such lack of attention to cultural context can seriously limit the reliability, validity, and cultural and language compatibility of the initiatives. Persson (in press) provides an extensive treatment of the difficulties created by lack of contextual awareness about phenomena pertaining to giftedness and talent. He shows that this is a very large-scale problem affecting many nations and regions around the globe. In short, it seems clear that it is time to put aside the old screening and identification models and strive to create more context-sensitive ways to identify and address the needs of bright young people in the region.

Excellence, Innovation, and Gifted Education

Quality educational systems and opportunities are keys to (a) development and modernization of national and regional economies, (b) creation of more ethical socioeconomic systems, and (c) discovery of aspirations and development of talents within individuals. Arabian Gulf and Middle Eastern countries need to recognize that the long-term prosperity of the region and the quality of life for its citizens depend on more insightful notions of high ability and gifted education. Rather than ignoring the potential of large segments of the population and borrowing identification practices and programs when gifted education is deemed appropriate, policy makers and educators must develop a more holistic philosophy.

First, they must recognize that preserving the best educational opportunities only for children of the elite is shortsighted and dogmatic. The recent sociopolitical turbulence in several Arab and North African nations provides a reminder that hoarding power to maintain extreme privilege for elites does not last forever. Moreover, spreading opportunities more broadly is an ethical issue. It simply is the right thing to do.

Second, they must think more deeply about identifying and addressing the needs of gifted children. Rather than borrowing instruments and practices from abroad and implementing them without modification they should develop more holistic approaches. They should follow Persson's (in press) advice about attending to the nuances of cultural context and work to develop multiple criteria for culturally sensitive identification of individual students' needs. Attending to the following principles will help streamline the process:

1. Individuals should be screened as early as possible to discover their learning needs and aspirations. The emphasis should not be on labeling individuals, but on recognizing and to responding to their particular needs and abilities.
2. This process should employ both formal measures, with the required psychometric characteristics, and informal measures that have the potential to dig deeper into individual nuances such as the nature of an individual child's embryonic aspirations and the suppressive influences of deprivation on the visibility of that child's potential.
3. Identification measures should align with the intervention programs and special provisions designed to meet the needs of individuals.
4. Equity and poverty reduction should not be add-ons or afterthoughts. Instead, they should be at the forefront of policy design. Putting gifted, creative, and talented students at the center of the educational system is an important part of the process of democratization and political inclusion in a region where democracy has been dogmatically suppressed for decades.
5. Gifted females need special attention in the development of these plans.
6. Only specialized and qualified professionals should be employed in the design and implementation of these processes.

A World Plan of Action

We are in need of a *world plan of action* for transferring up-to-date knowledge and expertise to underdeveloped nations. The ICIE is interested in involving leading scholars in finding ways to develop human potential maximally in order to solve problems of world development. In the context of this action plan, the ICIE, which we envision as the first cornerstone for a global ICIE University, provides a dynamic interaction platform for leading scholars of the East and the West.

In the world of gifted education, regions can be divided into haves and have-nots. The haves include the United States, Canada, Western Europe, some parts of Eastern Europe, Australasia, and parts of eastern Asia. The have-nots include most parts of Africa, Latin America, South Asia, and the Arabian Gulf and the Middle East. Large numbers of children in the have-not regions have impressive hidden potential but lack equal opportunities, support, resources, and facilities.

Underdeveloped nations and regions also tend to suffer from egregious socioeconomic stratification that preserves educational opportunities for the children of elites while fomenting sociopolitical upheavals that can leave no room for gifted education. Consequently, educators and specialized scholars must advocate for the needs of deprived individuals and populations while also arguing that those in control of the levers of power in deprived nations can benefit from expanding the human capital within their borders by attending to the needs of all gifted, creative, and talented young people. If the countries of the Arabian Gulf and the Middle Eastern region are truly concerned about upgrading and improving their educational systems and their economic viability over the long term, their leaders must think about excellence in education for all, which will include provisions for all gifted young people.

Educators and scholars in the have-not nations cannot expand awareness of these needs on their own. International organizations such as the World Council for Gifted and Talented Children (WCGTC) and the ICIE have roles to play in expanding and strengthening gifted education throughout the world. Members of these organizations can take part in advocating for the needs of bright, young, deprived individuals while couching their advocacy in terms that dogmatic, entrenched policy makers can understand (i.e., more effective gifted education for all who need it within the borders of the nation will strengthen the human capital and economic prospects of the nation). Phrasing advocacy in this way could make the message moderately novel to those who most need to hear it, thereby bypassing their dogmatism. While doing this, scholars and practitioners also can magnify the more important aspects of gifted education—the discovery of individual aspirations and talents and the development of more ethical awareness among bright young minds in a complex, threat-filled 21st century.

If the WCGTC and the ICIE provide more vibrant global forums for sharing the latest information about high ability and for providing support and encouragement to those working to strengthen opportunities for the gifted in have-not regions such as large portions of the Arabian Gulf and the Middle East, we might be able to shift the minds of some important leaders and policy makers. But these international organizations can play this important role only if they are supported by ministries of education, leading universities, highly qualified scholars, and very active members. We challenge you to join us in this endeavor.

Conclusion

Gifted education should no longer be considered an option or an afterthought in the Arabian Gulf and the Middle East. Instead, it is a practical and ethical imperative. Vibrant gifted programs aimed at addressing the learning needs of all bright young people, not just the children of elites, represent the region's best option for healthy economic and social development in today's turbulent global, socioeconomic context. Work in the 21st century is shifting from industrial production (manufacturing things) to "mind work" that requires ongoing knowledge acquisition and management of vast amounts of information through the use of creative and critical thought (Ambrose, 2009; Autor, Levy, & Murnane, 2003; Zhao, 2009). Stability and security are disappearing because the new economy is very fluid and unpredictable.

Overall, the 21st-century work environment requires today's young people to tolerate ambiguity, adapt flexibly and frequently, think creatively and critically, work well together with others in ever-shifting collaborative teams, and discover their aspirations and talents. The education of gifted students has never been more important, and this is especially the case for students in the Arabian Gulf and the Middle East. In this region, bright students are trapped within poorly funded schools dominated by rote learning and lacking provisions for the special needs of the gifted. Dogmatic sociopolitical contexts throughout much of the region mire the school systems in outmoded patterns that prevent bright, young children from discovering their aspirations and developing their talents.

The shortsighted, narrow-minded, entrenched thinking of dogmatic leaders and policy makers can suppress the development of the gifted, creative young minds that societies desperately need for successful navigation in the turbulent 21st-century environment. Such suppression is especially prevalent in nations and regions that dogmatically inhibit democratic processes and reserve the best educational opportunities for the children of elites. It is incumbent upon scholars and educators from all nations to shed light on this problem and work toward its correction.

References

Alkire, S. (2002). Dimensions of human development. *World Development, 30,* 181–205.

Ambrose, D. (2005). Aspiration growth, talent development, and self-fulfillment in a context of democratic erosion. *Roeper Review, 28,* 11–19.

Ambrose, D. (2009). *Expanding visions of creative intelligence: An interdisciplinary exploration.* Cresskill, NJ: Hampton Press.

Archer, D. (2009). *The long thaw: How humans are changing the next 100,000 years of earth's climate.* Princeton, NJ: Princeton University Press.

Autor, D. H., Levy, F., & Murnane, R. J. (2003). The skill content of recent technological change: An empirical exploration. *Quarterly Journal of Economics, 118,* 1279–1334.

Bahar E., Ramazan S., & Suna H. (2009). Perceptions of parents with gifted children about gifted education in Turkey. *Gifted and Talented International, 23-24,* 55–66.

Berliner, D. (in press). Narrowing curriculum, assessments, and conceptions of what it means to be smart in the US schools: Creaticide by design. In D. Ambrose & R. J. Sternberg (Eds.), *How dogmatic beliefs harm creativity and higher-level thinking.* New York, NY: Routledge.

Bracey, G. W. (2004*). Setting the record straight: Responses to misconceptions about public education in the US.* Portsmouth, NH: Heinemann.

Clark, G. (2007). *A farewell to alms: A brief economic history of the world.* Princeton, NJ: Princeton University Press.

Dahlerup, D., & Freidevall, L. (2005). Quotas as a 'fast-track' to equal representation for women. *International Feminist Journal of Politics, 7,* 26–48.

DOS. (2009). *Annual report: Employment and unemployment survey.* Amman, Jordan: Department of Statistics.

DOS. (2010). *Statistical yearbook.* Amman, Jordan: Department of Statistics.

Gavlak, D. (2008). Arab education 'falling behind' BBC News. Retrieved March 2011 from http://news.bbc.co.uk/2/hi/7227610.stm

Hansen, J. E. (2005, December). *Is there still time to avoid 'dangerous anthropogenic interference' with global climate?* Paper presented at the American Geophysical Union, San Francisco.

ICEE. (2009). Chais teacher institute summer 2009 training. *Annual report.* Jerusalem, Israel: The Israel Center for Excellence through Education.

IMF. (2011). International financial statistics. Country Report No.: (Qatar, 11/64; Algeria, 11/41; Israel, 11/23). Washington, DC: The International Monetary Fund (IMF).

Nichols, S. L., & Berliner, D. C. (2007). *Collateral damage: How high-stakes testing corrupts America's schools* Cambridge, MA: Harvard Education Press.

Persson, R. S. (in press). Cultural variation and dominance in a globalized knowledge economy: Towards a culture-sensitive research paradigm in the science of giftedness. *Gifted and Talented International.*

Smeeding, T. M., & Rainwater, L. (2004). Comparing living standards across nations: Real incomes at the top, the bottom, and the middle. In E. N. Wolff & J. Levy (Eds.), *What has happened to the quality of life in the advanced industrialized nations?* (pp. 153–183). Cheltenham: UK: Edward Elgar.

Stiglitz, J. E. (2010). *Free fall: America, free markets, and the sinking of the world economy.* New York, NY: W. W. Norton.

UNDP. (2010). *Human development report. The real wealth of nations: Pathways to human development.* New York: The United Nations Development Programme.

UNESCO. (2011). *All global monitoring report 20.* Paris: The United Nations Educational, Scientific and Cultural Organization.

Woodward, D., & Simms, A. (2006). *Growth isn't working: The unbalanced distribution of benefits and costs from economic growth.* London, England: New Economics Foundation.

World Bank. (2011). Ministerial colloquium on quality of education: The Doha Declaration Doha, Qatar (21–22 September 2010). Retrieved from http://web.worldbank.org/

Yamin, T. S. (2007). Intelligence, civilization, and collective creativity. *Al-Mawakif Journal, 18,* 30–37. (in Arabic)

Yamin, T. S. (Ed.). (2009). *Excellence in education 2008: Future minds and creativity.* Proceedings of the Annual Conference of the International Centre for Innovation in Education (ICIE), Paris, France (July 1–4, 2008). Ulm, Germany: ICIE.

Yunus, M. (2008). *Creating a world without poverty: Social business and the future of capitalism.* New York: Public Affairs.

Zhao, Y. (2009). *Catching up or leading the way: American education in the age of globalization.* Alexandria, VA: ASCD.

Combatting Narrow-Minded, Shortsighted Curriculum, Instruction, and Research

13

CURRICULUM AND DOGMATISM IN GIFTED EDUCATION

Joyce VanTassel-Baska

COLLEGE OF WILLIAM & MARY

The field of gifted education is small, fragmented, and porous as documented in a recent article by leading educators within its ranks (Ambrose, VanTassel-Baska, Coleman, & Cross, 2010). Its theories, research, and practice paradigms are often incoherent and unconnected, leaving those outside the field mystified by what it all means. In the field, there are petty rivalries and competitive models that vie for supremacy in schools, the testing ground for much of the practical work of the field. Yet the state of the art of gifted education also produces another disagreeable consequence—dogmatism linked to the authoritarian personality.

This chapter lays out a definition of dogmatism, links the definition to key aspects of the organization, structure, and content of the field of gifted education in the area of curriculum, and concludes by making the case for moving the discussion of models to another level—a level of dialectical discourse where alternative views are entertained and common ground is sought and found, based on reason and logic rather than the cult of personality and glibness.

Definitional Framework

The framework for thinking about the concept of dogmatism and then applying it to our field is based on the work of Rokeach (1954) and more recent work by Johnson (2010). In each view of the concept there is a need to see its multidimensional elements, the need to examine it from various perspectives and fields or disciplines, and the need to understand the characteristics of leaders whose style is authoritarian, which promotes dogmatism rather than free and open inquiry.

Objective reality can be assumed as being represented within a person by certain beliefs or expectations, which to one degree or another are accepted as true, and other beliefs or expectations accepted as false. We can think of all cognitive systems as being organized into these two systems. This belief-disbelief system can further be conceived as varying in terms of its structure and content.

The structure of a cognitive system is shaped by learned experiences, which either provide for open-ended or closed-ended opportunities to learn. If the opportunities are closed, offering a one-right-answer orientation, then the beliefs and expectations resulting set the stage for a dogmatic belief system. If, on the other hand, the experiences are open-ended where inquiry is encouraged, then the resulting cognitive system would entertain a belief system consonant with less rigid expectations for behavior of self and others.

In respect to the content of belief systems, they are fed by the overall perspectives held about people in general and authority in particular. If beliefs about people, for example, hold that they must be shaped and controlled by outer forces in order to be civilized or to function optimally, then dogmatism is fed. If, on the other hand, the belief about people is dominated by a sense that people respond best to situations and leaders that help them see their own potential for optimal acts, then dogmatism is held at bay.

Rokeach's (1954) definition of dogmatism may be useful to consider: "(a) a relatively closed cognitive organization of beliefs and disbeliefs about reality, (b) organized around a central set of beliefs about absolute authority which, in turn (c) provides a framework for patterns of intolerance and qualified tolerance toward others" (p. 195). Dogmatism in any area is a sign that the individual or group has stopped growing, that one's ideas are calcified at a point in time, impervious to change. Kuhn (1970) made the observation in the discipline of science that it takes a new paradigm several years and many adherents to overturn an existing set of ideas. We cling to that which we think we know until it is no more the thing we know (paraphrasing Lucretius). Because it is through how we think about curriculum that we come to reveal our basic beliefs about reality, knowledge, values, and methodology, this definition of dogmatism is particularly relevant for an examination of the general beliefs that drive curriculum in schools and impact the way that gifted learners experience instruction.

Curriculum Beliefs in Gifted Education

In the field of gifted education, curriculum models take on the mantle of dogmatism. They usually have been developed by one person and sometimes a team in response to a perceived need for working with gifted students in a differentiated approach. Yet too often, the models become fixed and unchanging, even as they experience little application in the world of schools. When they are adopted, often it is not fidelity of implementation that results but rather a hodgepodge of activities that may or may not resemble the model from which they are derived. Yet educators remain dogmatic in their beliefs that they are implementing the accepted model, even as they are inconsistent in its implementation.

But dogmatism begins at the ontological and epistemological levels, where the nature of being and the nature of knowledge itself become subverted, where we become so in love with our own beliefs and values that we cannot entertain healthy skepticism. Just as in ancient philosophy, the skeptic was one who rejected both Stoic and Epicurean philosophic systems on the grounds that they narrowed our orientation to the world, so too modern and postmodern views of knowledge present closed systems of thought that are seductive in their holistic attempts to present the truth and then market it to audiences who are eager for the one right answer.

Dogmatism is also closely allied to the messianic impulse, the need to advocate strongly for a belief that is not widely known or shared. In gifted education, many of us are dogmatists by the very nature of the collective belief system we have taken on in respect to gifted children and their needs and the specific ways they best can be met. The desire to convince others of the rightness of our cause sows dangerous seeds of dogmatism as we try hard to fend off objections and argue down critics. Even the open-minded among advocates for the gifted find it difficult to maintain a neutral position in the midst of such argument, as we encounter dogmatism on the other side of the table as well.

Curriculum Orientations

So what are the dogmatic systems of thought that have impacted curriculum for the gifted? They involve predominantly three different orientations to knowledge, each competing with the others for primacy.

One of these is the view of reality as progress, with technology the agent to move us forward. In this view, knowledge is accrual of useful information that will feed the engine of positive change, enhancing our learning in an incremental but constant way. Knowledge is made known by scientific studies that demonstrate this positive change and learning improved by replication of study findings in large scale-up settings. The standards and assessment movement in education is an example of this type of dogmatism, where the system of testing is a closed one linked to the standards, albeit low-level ones and only a fraction of those to be taught at a given point in time (Berliner, in press). Nevertheless, it is a system that assumes that learning is cumulative in a linear way, that some things are more important than others to learn (e.g., reading and math are more important than science or the arts), and that students and teachers can be held accountable for progress each year in these preselected areas and on a predetermined time frame.

The second orientation to curriculum work in education generally and the field of gifted education specifically is nested in a totally constructivist orientation, suggesting that gifted children know what they need to know and the contexts under which they can best learn it. In this view, a standards-based curriculum is anathema, rejected for its dogmatic and authoritarian tenets. Yet the constructivist view ironically also is dogmatic in its insistence on key principles of student-dominated work with the role of the teacher as guide not instructor, and the curriculum as co-constructed around a topic, issue, or theme of interest to individual learners (Reis & Renzulli, 2007).

The third view of curriculum, advocated by several curriculum models, is more multi-faceted, suggesting the complementarity of seemingly opposing viewpoints between content and process and issues/themes (Tomlinson, Kaplan, Purcell, Leppien, & Renzulli, 2008) as well as an emphasis on curricular dimensions that are cognitive, affective, and aesthetic (VanTassel-Baska & Stambaugh, 2006) and instructional processes that honor analytic, synthetic, and tacit knowledge (Sternberg & Grigorenko, 2000). In this curriculum view, reality is multi-dimensional, the nature of knowledge is tentative and changing, the belief in learning suggests the need for systemic interventions, and the methodology is mixed methods in keeping with the orientations advocated.

Yet each of these models has dogmatic aspects to it in structure, function, and content as well as in the voices of its adherents. Table 13.1 shows the core belief aspects of each of these models with respect to ontology, epistemology, axiology, and methodology.

What Allows Curriculum to Be Less Dogmatic?

There are many ways we can reduce the dogmatic emphases of these curriculum views. One of them rests on dialogue and discussion among the scholars who hold these diverse views, focusing on similarities rather than differences across the models. Another is to address the relative importance of valuing each view for its contribution to learning by sharing the studies supporting the particular model or orientation to learning (see VanTassel-Baska & Brown, 2007, as an example).

Perhaps the most critical tactic is to ensure that inquiry dominates the teaching of any curriculum model, especially for the gifted learner. Thus it is in the instructional models that dogmatism can best be addressed at the practice level. Only in scientific reasoning and verbal argument do we have glimpses of the processes that can break down dogmatic thinking if these processes are assiduously addressed in the classroom. In models of reasoning like Paul and Elder's (2003), for example, students learn to question assumptions, analyze how they contribute to stances on contemporary issues, and debunk them through evaluating evidence and data in order to reach a conclusion. In debate models, students learn to examine competing evidence and argue the relevant case for

TABLE 13.1 Core Belief Aspects of Curriculum Models

Views	Beliefs	Ontology	Epistemology	Methodology
Curriculum as Technology	Assumption of learning as linear, steady, and predictable.	Reality is externally derived from a set of planned experiences.	Knowledge is a set of organized experiences within disciplines, learned in a cumulative sequence.	Quantitative designs that track progress.
Curriculum as Constructivism	Assumption of learning as the creation of meaning	Reality is internal to the individual and externalized through products.	Knowledge is constructed by individuals and groups in response to problems.	Product assessment/portfolios that document meaning-making.
Curriculum as Integrative/Multi-dimensional	Assumption of learning as simultaneously multi-faceted	Reality is multiple, involving both internal and external origins.	Knowledge is tentative, based on multiple perspectives, and emphases.	Mixed methods that acknowledge the contribution of both quantitative and qualitative approaches.

either side of an issue. Through such rigorous activities, gifted students may come to see the value in epistemological orientations to the world other than their own, thus breaking down the tendency toward dogmatism (Stanovich, 2001).

Dogmatism and the Development of the Creative Personality

While we cannot say that dogmatism interferes with the development of some aspects of giftedness if it is viewed primarily through an intellectual gauge, we can suggest that it interferes greatly with the development of creative potential because such potential is dependent on certain personality variables that are the direct opposite of what dogmatism requires. As Cross and Cross explain in chapter 10 in this book, characteristics like intolerance for ambiguity, close-mindedness, an orientation toward certainty, and a need for closure characterize the dogmatic mind. It is the exact opposite of these characteristics that define the creative minds of those who make contributions in a society. Moreover, all of the curriculum models for the gifted advocate for the use of creative thinking as a part of the learning to which gifted students should be exposed.

Thus, while various models may be dogmatic in their assertions, there is a common thread of recommended practice that guards against its being replicated at the student level.

Our research on these matters is inconclusive in some ways, but strong with respect to the importance of creative personality variables. According to Silvia (2008), personality variables confound correlations between intelligence and creativity. Personality variables such as openness to experience predict both IQ (DeYoung, Peterson, & Higgins, 2005) and creativity (Feist, 1998). Openness to experience is found to be the most influential factor on intelligence (Furnham & Thomas, 2004; Furnham, Zhang, & Chamorro-Premuzic, 2006), especially on g(c) (crystallized ability) (Brand, 1994) and is even more strongly related to creativity (McCrae, 1987; Miller & Tal, 2007). However, according to Furnham, et al. (2006), openness to experience is positively related to g(f) (fluid ability). A meta-analysis on these personality variables reported that creative people tend to be autonomous and introverted, open to new experiences, norm-doubting, self-confident, self-accepting, driven, ambitious, dominant, hostile, and impulsive (Feist, 1998). After an extensive literature review, Batey and Furnham (2006) concluded that the most common personality traits that are related to creativity are confidence, independence, and openness to new ideas. Eminent creators have had a certain level of knowledge to advance in a field although there is a curvilinear relationship between knowledge and creativity, which indicates that too much knowledge leads to entrenchment and an inability to conceive of the field in a radically different light (Batey & Furnham).

Feist (1998) also found that openness to experience and extraversion were the most strongly distinguishing characteristics of creative scientists In addition, he found that conscientiousness, conventionality, and closed mindedness tend to be negatively related to being a creative scientist. Extraversion was found to be strongly related to creativity as assessed on three measures of creativity—Guilford's unusual uses divergent thinking test, the biographical inventory of creative behaviors, a self-rated measure of creativity, and the Barron-Welsh Art Scale (Furnham & Bachtiar, 2008).

The development of creative potential, then, is most threatened by dogmatism as it subverts the creative personality into compliance and a sense of being constrained rather than freed up for open exploration of ideas. Just as critical inquiry as the basis for instruction is vital for the gifted learner, so too is creative inquiry. Models such as creative problem solving (Treffinger, Isaksen, & Dorval, 2000, synectics (Gordon, 1961), and metaphor development (Lakoff & Johnson, 1980) all provide the basis for open-ended activities that encourage creative thinking in various forms, including fluency, flexibility, elaboration, and originality, all conducted within a collaborative spirit of group problem solving. As noted earlier, the use of these creative-thinking tools as a part of the recommended curriculum diet is central to passing on a greater open-mindedness to gifted students under our tutelage.

The Role of Higher Education in Breeding Dogmatism

There is also the reality of the reward system in higher education, which pays more attention to the single voice advocating a particular model or theory that is well-documented in the literature, well-articulated in various products and in a dissemination plan, and well-adopted by advocates. This approach attracts graduate students to a given program and produces more advocates for the model, based on this process perpetuating itself by using the model as the basis for learning about curriculum in that particular institution. Dissertations of these same students take aspects of the model and apply them to their questions of interest, thus ensuring a steady stream of publications about the importance of the work.

Yet we rarely question these tactics, even labeling them as examples of success in the world of higher education, even as they serve to corrupt an open system of inquiry and debate about how the models can be viewed as complementary rather than competitive.

Studies of epistemological orientations have suggested that intelligence is not an important factor in respect to people's clinging to a particular set of beliefs about knowledge (see Hofer & Pintrich, 1997; Greene, Torney-Purta, & Azevedo, 2010). Rather, it is their orientation to thinking itself as a closed rather than open activity. For example, Cooper (2009) found in his study that the study sample of both creationists and evolutionists both manifested some absolutist dogmatism in their thinking even though their belief systems were polar opposites. Frequently, then, these people are logical within the system they are advocating. It is only possible to debate the merits of the proposal on its underlying assumptions, not on the logic of its main ideas. Often research evidence is used to support aspects of an approach not really tested or a model not fully understood in operation.

Application of Key Features of Dogmatism to Curriculum Models in Gifted Education

As Rokeach (1960) suggested in his seminal work, there are some key features contained in dogmatic viewpoints that are important to acknowledge. I assert that these features are present in the current climate around curriculum models in the field.

One of these features is a desire to make the dogmatic belief as different as possible from others, constantly pointing out its distinctive features. In speaking of curriculum in this field, we often emphasize the ways that a model is distinctive and dwell more on those features than on the ones that are common to all models. For example, the Integrated Curriculum Model (ICM) and the Parallel Curriculum Model (PCM) share almost the same components for development except for a few aspects. Where the models diverge is on the issue of integration of the multiple components of each model. The ICM was conceived to be integrative in design and implementation while the PCM has deliberately put the components on parallel tracks. They also diverge with respect to the treatment of affective development. In the PCM, the affective emphasis in the curriculum is separated out and focused on with respect to identity development. In the ICM, the affective emphasis is woven into the fabric of the design by the use of activities, questions, and assessments that stress student reflection and establishing personal relevance of the curriculum for one's life. By choosing books for discussion that employ gifted characters who face problems and issues similar to gifted students, the curriculum also promotes self-understanding in the context of the real world.

The PCM is a model for curriculum planning based on the composite work of Tomlinson et al. (2002). The heuristic model employs four dimensions, or parallels, that can be used singly or in combination. The parallels are: the core curriculum, the curriculum of connections, the curriculum of practice, and the curriculum of identity. It assumes that the core curriculum is the basis for all other curricula and it should be combined with any or all of the three other parallels. It is the foundational curriculum that is defined by a given discipline. National, state, and/or local school district's standards should be reflected in this dimension. It establishes the basis of understanding within relevant subjects and grade levels. The second parallel, the curriculum of connections, supports students in discovering the interconnectedness among and between disciplines of knowledge. It builds from the core curriculum and has students exploring those connections for both intra- and interdisciplinary studies. The third parallel, the curriculum of practice, also derives from the core curriculum. Its purpose is to extend students' understandings and skills in a discipline through application. The curriculum of practice promotes student expertise as a practitioner of a given discipline. The last parallel, the curriculum of identity serves to help students think about themselves within the context of a particular discipline; to see how a particular discipline relates to their own lives. The curriculum of identity uses curriculum as a catalyst for self-definition and self-understanding. The authors suggest that the level of intellectual demand in employing all elements of the PCM should be matched to student needs.

The VanTassel-Baska (1986) Integrated Curriculum Model (ICM) was specifically developed for high-ability learners, based on research evidence of what works with the gifted in classroom contexts. It has three dimensions: (1) advanced content, (2) high-level process and product work, and (3) intra- and interdisciplinary concept development and understanding. VanTassel-Baska, with funding from the Jacob Javits Program, used the ICM to develop specific curriculum frameworks and underlying units of study in language arts, social studies, and science. The model was designed to demonstrate a way to use the content standards but go beyond them, using differentiation practices for the gifted.

The content dimension is the first component of the model and represents, in the unit development process, a total alignment with national and state standards. However, it also represents the use of appropriate advanced content that goes beyond the standards, often calibrating unit activities or reading choices to what typical students can do at higher grade levels in the content area. In addition to being aligned with standards, the content dimension was designed to represent the most exemplary curriculum in that subject area by using the research-based pedagogical practices that are effective and national reports emanating from the various subject areas. Thus the content of the standards is the core area for beginning the differentiation process with respect to acceleration, adding complexity and depth, incorporating creativity demands, and increasing the challenge level.

The process-product dimension of the ICM focuses on the importance of designing curriculum that incorporates higher-level processing skills as a part of the challenge for students. Units of study systematically use a reasoning model, a research model, and some use a problem-solving model to ensure that students can manipulate these thinking skills within specific subject areas. In some instances, like science and literature, the subject area already incorporates higher-level thought in the use of the scientific research model in the case of science and the study of literary elements that move from the concrete elements of character, plot, and setting to the abstract elements of theme, motivation, and structure. As students manipulate these skills, they are encouraged to generate a meaningful product that demonstrates their capacity to apply these higher-level skills effectively. In most units of study, the product or series of products are research oriented.

The third dimension of the model emphasizes the use of a higher-level macroconcept that has meaning within and across subject areas and serves to provide an interdisciplinary pathway to bind the curriculum together. It is the integrative glue that allows the model to be cohesive in design and implementation. The concepts used in the unit development process were those identified by scientists as the most critical for today's students to understand—concepts like change, systems, models, and scale. These concepts and their underlying generalizations guide the learning of specific content and amplify the use of higher-level skills and processes. Students continue to apply these concepts to their learning across subject areas and across grades, and to see ways they apply to their own lives.

Advocates of these models do not deliberately show the common elements. Nor do they acknowledge each other's work as a routine way to build on the prior work in a field rather than isolating one's own work as wholly original.

Another disturbing feature of dogmatism is the tendency toward rigidity of the people who hold absolutist orientations, never shifting even as new data are available to challenge beliefs. This too is a feature found in our curriculum orientations. As data suggest, for example, that replication of positive progress cannot be done in all settings with all learners, we ignore the finding and its implication for a faulty system of standards and assessments and merely try to refine our efforts to make it work as seen in the retooling of No Child Left Behind around a technical-assistance model rather than the overhaul so badly needed. This situation is emergent because we cannot challenge the assumptions on which the legislation is based—all children can learn the same things at the same time, teachers are the single variable responsible for student progress, and successful schools should show incremental student growth each year in predetermined areas. Denial of competing data then becomes another strategy in dogmatism, ignoring the funding of projects that do not support the "party line." Regrettably, this is a bipartisan problem as the education agenda has not changed in the light of a new administration.

Willingness to compromise is another feature not often present in the laying out of dogmatic systems of thought. Rather than compromise, co-opting and distorting is the viable alternative employed. The aspects of the nonbelief system that have shown credibility in the public sphere are then incorporated into the dominant dogmatic system. The best example of this in gifted education is how acceleration has been co-opted to feed a classroom practice called "compacting," which allows for basic material to be learned quickly so that students can work on independent projects that adhere to the belief system of student independence in learning (Reis & Purcell, 1993) Compacting perverts the intent of acceleration to advance students along a continuum of study in their areas of strength in favor of the enrichment option of project work in an area of interest. Advocates would argue that the use of compacting is beneficial in removing gifted learners from routine and even remedial work that they already know. Thus the mechanism of preassessment is a positive act for the gifted while the resulting intervention is debatable, with the research support favoring acceleration in content over generic enrichment.

Isolation of the belief system from the nonbelief system is another tactic used to enhance dogmatism of thought. This can be accomplished in many ways. One way would be through associating with disciples only, and never interacting directly with those who do not share your belief system. Another is through publications that cite only one point of view on a subject, work from the recognition of only one thought system, and systematically exclude work on the topic if it presents an alternative picture of reality. This tendency again is supported by the mechanisms of higher education, where professors are encouraged to collaborate with those whose ideas resonate with their own and to engage graduate students in the research process as early as possible, often before they have read widely or thought deeply about the relevant ideas. The publication inclusion-exclusion game is tolerated and even encouraged by journal editors who often assign manuscripts to people who are adherents to a given belief and who encourage the reification of the model and its originator through citations and commentary. Those who review a piece and do not share the closed view, often have their critiques not taken seriously at the revision stage of manuscripts.

Cognitive narrowing is another feature of dogmatism whereby a field is reduced to a single set of ideas as opposed to being represented in diverse ways by a broad array of scholarly perspectives. Gifted education, I believe, has been narrowed in this way by the dominance of a single model that purports to be both a program and a curriculum, an identification system, and an assessment and evaluation model that is appropriate for everyone whether the individual is gifted or not. The School-wide Enrichment Model (Reis & Renzulli, 2007) has been refined through an additive process as the field has shifted from one direction to another, based on the political fads that continue to impact all of education. The prominence of the adherents to this model have drowned out the voices of others whose ideas are different or represent the disbelief continuum at uncomfortable positions.

Authoritarianism, including force, based at least partially on a belief in the need to have changes made now, often accompanies the implementation of dogmatic views. Camus once observed: "To insure the adoration of a theorem for any length of time, faith is not enough; a police force is needed as well." There is a need to bully educators into submission to protocols for implementation, forms to complete for specific purposes, organization of classrooms and students to meet the expectations of the espoused ideas. Teachers and administrators often submit to these tactics, only to change them once the pressure is gone. There is a need to rid these schools of competing views, including the use of curriculum materials that do not adhere to the belief system, professional development not based on the model, and maverick educators who might voice objections.

The role of tolerance in our field is also threatened by dogmatic views. The downside of truth is the danger of fanaticism. Because absolutistss brook no alternatives, conservatives are tempted to invade their neighbor's autonomy and try to force truth down their throats. Liberals face the opposite problem, for the danger that stalks relativism is that it could lead to nihilism. At that extreme, relativism collapses into the view that nothing is better than anything else. This is an unlivable philosophy, but the indiscriminate championing of tolerance has moved our society in its direction while debasing the meaning of tolerance in the act (Brown, 2001, 2006).

Tolerance used to mean that people of strong convictions would willingly bear the burden of putting up peacefully with people they regarded as plainly in error. Now giving voice to alternative views is not widely practiced nor even tolerated in many quarters. Alternative views are not cited in the literature of the field and often do not find a voice in the journals or the published material of the field. We no longer conduct debates at national meetings, partly because we do not want to appear as out of line with the prevailing beliefs in particular niches of the field.

Antidotes to Dogmatism

What are the counters to prevent any set of ideas, models, and theories from becoming dogmatic? What can we do to entertain more openness in the field, more sensitivity to the contributions of multiple models rather than just our own? I would suggest the following approaches as a set of principles to apply to our work in the field.

- Ensure that courses in gifted education include multiple approaches to curriculum development, based on different assumptions about the schooling process.
- Conduct discussions at conferences that tackle the areas of agreement and disagreement about provisions for gifted learners. Unpack the belief systems that govern our thinking.
- Prepare balanced manuscripts that acknowledge relevant work done by those with competing viewpoints.
- Work toward a higher level of synthesis as an approach to creativity rather than clinging to an existing model or feeling the need to diverge from current models.
- Employ inquiry techniques as a major tool to enhance gifted student learning at all levels.
- Challenge our own assumptions about reality, knowledge, values, and methods with regularity. Use a critical friend to prod us in the right direction.

Conclusion

The rise of dogmatism as an orientation to advanced learning, aided and abetted by the informal rules of higher education, is a concern especially for a field like gifted education which is small, pre-paradigmatic, and susceptible to fads. The signs are everywhere in the area of curriculum that there are personalities that drive this orientation and make others adhere to a belief system not widely representative of the field's thinking nor open to entertaining other viewpoints. Yet there is hope that open-ended thinking can be retained and practiced in the pursuit of answers to difficult questions regarding the education of the gifted. Research agendas can test alternative approaches rather than a single intervention and build on current conflicting research as opposed to ignoring the lack of coherence. Practice paradigms can be experimental, using different models and approaches with different kinds of gifted learners. And practitioners at all levels can be more reflective about what works, why, and under what set of conditions. Advocacy then can be truly focused on the gifted student, not particular and rigid ways to meet her needs.

References

Ambrose, D., VanTassel-Baska, J., Coleman, L. & Cross, T. (2010) Unified, insular, firmly policed or fractured, porous, contested, gifted education? *Journal for the Education of the Gifted, 33,* 453–478.

Batey, M., & Furnham, A. (2006). Creativity, intelligence and personality: A critical review of the scattered literature. *Genetic, General and Social Psychology Monographs, 132,* 355–429.

Berliner, D. (in press). Narrowing curriculum, assessments, and conceptions of what it means to be smart in the US schools: Creaticide by design. In D. Ambrose & R. J Sternberg (Eds.), *How dogmatic beliefs harm creativity and higher-level thinking.* New York, NY: Routledge.

Brand, C. (1994). Open to experience-closed to intelligence: why the "Big Five" are really the "Comprehensive Six". *European Journal of Personality, 8,* 299–310.

Brown, W. (2001). Reflections on tolerance in the age of identity. In A. Botwinick & W. E. Connolly (Eds.), *Democracy and vision: Sheldon Wolin and the vicissitudes of the political* (pp. 99–117). Princeton, NJ: Princeton University Press.

Brown, W. (2006). *Regulating aversion: Tolerance in the age of identity and empire.* Princeton, NJ: Princeton University Press.

Cooper, G. W. (2009). *Creationist and evolutionist dogmatism.* Retrieved February 12, 2011, from http://www.creationism.org/csslis/v04n3p15.htm

DeYoung, C. G., Peterson, J. B., & Higgins, D. M. (2005). Sources of openness/intellect: Cognitive and neuropsychological correlates of the fifth factor of personality. *Journal of Personality, 73,* 825–858.

Feist, G. J. (1998). A meta-analysis of personality in scientific and artistic creativity. *Personality and Social Psychology Review, 2,* 290–309.

Furnham, A., & Bachtiar, V. (2008). Personality and intelligence as predictors of creativity. *Personality and Individual Differences, 45,* 613–617.

Furnham, A., & Thomas, C. (2004). Parents' gender and personality and estimates of their own and their children's intelligence. *Personality and Individual Differences, 37,* 887–903.

Furnham, A., Zhang, J., & Chamorro-Premuzic, T. (2006). The relationship between relationship between psychometric and self-estimated intelligence, creativity, personality and academic achievement. *Imagination, Cognition, and Personality, 25,* 119–145.

Gordon, W. J. J. (1961). *Synectics.* New York, NY: Harper.

Greene, J. A., Torney-Purta, J., & Azevedo, R. (2010) Empirical evidence regarding relations among a model of epistemic and ontological cognition, academic performance, and educational level. *Journal of Educational Psychology, 102,* 234–255.

Hofer, B. K., & Pintrich, P. R. (1997). The development of epistemological theories: Beliefs about knowledge and knowing and their relation to learning. *Review of Educational Research, 67,* 88–140.

Johnson, J. J. (2010). Beyond a shadow of doubt: The psychological nature of dogmatism. *The International Journal of Interdisciplinary Social Sciences, 5,* 149–161.

Kuhn, T. S. (1970). *The structure of scientific revolutions* (2nd ed.). Chicago, IL: Chicago University Press.

Lakoff, G., & Johnson, M. (1980). *Metaphors we live by.* Chicago, IL: University of Chicago Press.

McCrae, R. R. (1987). Creativity, divergent thinking, and openness to experience. *Journal of Personality and Social Psychology, 52,* 1258–1265.

Miller, G. F., & Tal, I. R. (2007). Schizotypy versus openness and intelligence as predictors of creativity. *Schizophrenia Research, 93,* 317–324.

Paul, R. W., & Elder, L. (2003). *How to study and learn a discipline: Using critical thinking concepts and tools.* Dillon Beach, CA: The Foundation for Critical Thinking.

Reis, S. M., & Purcell, J. H. (1993). An analysis of content elimination and strategies used by elementary classroom teachers in the curriculum compacting process. *Journal for the Education of the Gifted, 16,* 147–170.

Reis, S. M., & Renzulli, J. S. (2007). *Enriching curriculum for all students* (2nd ed.). Thousand Oaks, CA: Corwin Press.

Rokeach, M. (1954). The nature and meaning of dogmatism. *Psychological Review, 61,* 194–204.

Rokeach, M. (1960). *The open and the closed mind.* New York, NY: Basic Books.

Silvia, P. J. (2008). Another look at creativity and intelligence. Exploring higher order models and probable confounds. *Personality and Individual Difference, 44,* 1012–1021.

Stanovich, K. E. (2001). How to think straight about psychology (6th ed.). Boston, MA: Allyn & Bacon.

Sternberg, R. J., & Grigorenko, E. L. (2000). *Teaching for successful intelligence.* Arlington Heights, IL: Skylight Training and Publishing

Tomlinson, C. A., Kaplan, S. N., Purcell, J., Renzulli, J., Leppien, J., & Burns, D. (2002). *The parallel curriculum: A design to develop high potential and challenge high-ability learners.* Thousand Oaks, CA: Corwin Press.

Tomlinson, C. A., Kaplan, S. N., Purcell, J. H., Leppien, J. H., & Renzulli, J. S. (2008). *The parallel curriculum: A design to develop learner potential and challenge advanced learners.* Thousand Oaks, CA: Corwin Press.

Treffinger, D. J., Isaksen, S. G., & Dorval, K. B. (2000). *Creative problem solving: An introduction.* Waco, TX: Prufrock Press.

VanTassel-Baska, J. (1986) Effective curriculum and instructional models for talented students. *Gifted Child Quarterly, 30,* 164–169.

VanTassel-Baska, J., & Stambaugh, T. (2006). *Comprehensive curriculum for gifted learners II* (3rd ed.). Needham Heights, MA: Allyn & Bacon.

VanTassel-Baska, J., & Brown, E. (2007). Towards best practice: An analysis of the efficacy of curriculum models in gifted education. *Gifted Child Quarterly, 51,* 342–358.

14

PARALYSIS FROM ANALYSIS

Arguing for a Break from Traditional High School English

Kathleen M. Pierce

RIDER UNIVERSITY

Laurie R. Kash

OREGON STATE UNIVERSITY

To start, it is important to acknowledge that the genesis of American schooling springs from the religious instruction provided to the children of New England Puritans and Congregationalists. The reading curriculum of the American colonies was what John Locke called "the ordinary road of the Hornbook, Primer, Psalter, Testament, and Bible," texts that were used for the dual function of teaching both reading and religion (see Monaghan, 1989, p. 53). Early American schooling was synonymous with religious education; learning to read meant learning to read the Psalms, prayers, the Bible. Eventually, the common school evolved, and so did private and religiously affiliated schools. However, it is not a stretch to understand how the heritage of the American high school English classroom accounts for its striking resemblance to classrooms of yore that used canonical religious texts for paving the way to reading as well as to righteousness. It is also easy to understand how current practices are rooted in the fervent, unassailable belief that meaning is imbued in text and that text is indeed sacred.

The high school English class that relies primarily on literary analysis as its teaching and learning strategy is not sinister, but it is myopic. A curriculum defined by single texts and students' reading, writing, and discussions of those texts is a dogmatism-bound, restrictive course of study that requires limited student engagement with curriculum or with each other. Using Amabile's concept of the creativity intersections, Ambrose (2009) suggested that the workplace with its "carrot and stick" motivation can thwart intrinsic motivation, the driver behind creative and technical and motor skills that combine for optimal creative productivity (p. 176). An English class that employs the single methodology of literary analysis is the classroom analogy for Henry Ford's assembly line with its fragmented yet repetitive work processes.

Operating Under the Influence of Tradition

English teachers in training at the university level attend classes in both English and education. Regardless of the particular undergraduate experience, English majors intending to teach English usually take some kind of requisite "methods" course in addition to their classes in literature. Usually taught through a school or department of education, the methods course surveys various teaching methods for integrating and teaching the English curriculum that includes literature and varied language arts like writing and speaking. Methods courses foster the entry-level English teachers' skills and dispositions in using the English language arts—reading, writing, listening, speaking, and viewing—to create instructional plans for students' learning that align with national and state curriculum standards. In addition to content knowledge, preservice candidates must become fluent with various pedagogical strategies as well before they begin practice. Little (2009) says that teacher preparation programs should help teachers ingrain various approaches to teaching in order to "… use and encourage higher-level thinking and … employ metacognitive approaches like concept mapping as strategies for teachers' use throughout their teaching and not just with special populations" (p. 360).

Once teachers leave university to begin careers teaching English in high schools, they often start by replicating practices that they themselves experienced as English students at the high school and university levels. Schools of education, professional associations at state and national levels, and individual state departments of education promulgate the need to address subject-area standards and skills. Therein lies the rub: it is possible to plan lessons that nominally address standards but do little to engage students in actively complex, meaningful ways. The college-level literature course seems to be the prevailing model from which many contemporary high school English courses have been drawn. Said one student teacher, "Even if I had a creative English teacher in high school, it was undone by four years of uncreative college professors who just 'professed' about books" (M. Benson, personal communication, July 18, 2010). Having been English majors, most English teachers come by this model of teaching honestly—or naively. The long heritage and status quo of many high school departments of English inadvertently or deliberately conspire to restrict possibilities for the beginning English teacher and make creation of new practice formidable.

The default, traditional approach to teaching English is problematic because it enacts a single strategy for teaching and learning: reading an assigned piece of literature and analyzing it through verbal and/or written discussion. Why does such a limited methodology of literary analysis continue to hold sway in so many high school English classrooms? One block to innovative teaching in the English classroom might just be teachers' fear, habit, and familiarity, in that order. Once hired into high school English departments, beginning teachers likely eschew the newer, integrated methodologies of their teacher education programs in favor of local methods in order to assimilate into the culture of their new workplace and adhere to the expectations of students, parents, and fellow teachers. Beginning teachers generally follow the status quo of their local school; the immediate need to keep a teaching job and earn tenure win out over risking new implementation or different practices (Pierce, 2007). For a beginning teacher, following the practices and advice of experienced English faculty is a highly visible way of ensuring professional survival among students and peers alike. Classroom teaching that begins as imitative or even as homage to other English teachers becomes habit after enough practice. With veteran teachers often assigned as untrained mentor teachers, beginning English teachers are guided into institutional practice by peer mentors who often operate under the direct supervision of the school administration.

Theorists and practitioners question the usefulness of literary analysis as a way to help students learn much of anything—especially about literature and literary criticism (Graff, 2009; Smagorinsky, Daigle, O'Donnell-Allen, & Bynum, 2010). Graff suggested that a certain kind of literary analysis might actually be a way to keep students out of meaningful critical conversations about novels and poetry. Graff further argued that the "standard literature essay" is based on a monological model that is not engaged in any meaningful way with the views of others. He sees the literary essay as closely related to the five-paragraph essay that might ask students to include supporting ideas from others—but in reaction to a predetermined theme (pp. 8–9). Denied choice and voice in their writing, students muddle on best as they might and writing or saying what they believe their teacher expects them to say.

Wiggins (2009) noted an irony with regard to writing in school and English class particularly because "… in the real world, Audience and Purpose matter in ways that school often shields writers from … It just has to be on topic, handed in on time, and be four–five pages" (p. 30). The methodologies employed in too many English Language Arts (ELA) classes require low-level recall of plot and character and analysis of theme—all of which can be easily procured from one of many of today's online versions of CliffsNotes, SparkNotes, or myriad assistance websites that help students respond to their teachers' prompts with little, if any, real analysis at all. Given that many texts and activities for the acquisition of new knowledge and skills in English class remain the same throughout time, is it any wonder why gifted students are bored in many ELA classes, why the light of creative intelligence is dimmed, and why the spark of the teacher's energy is dampened in this static environment?

It seems, however unwittingly, English teachers have clung to a dogmatic notion that writing about literature helps students think, reason, appreciate culture, and write more intelligently despite little evidence to suggest that is the case. Nevertheless, many English teachers persist in a teaching practice that does little to encourage reading, illuminate literature and controversies, or engage students' original thinking.

Under the Influence of Testing

In varying degrees, high stakes state testing, the Advanced Placement (AP) exams, and the SATs all employ the same methodology by requiring students to read and analyze texts and then write about the text or select the best answer among a multiple choice list. Often, the very texts selected for classroom study are those likely to appear on AP exams or those that can be found in basal texts and anthologies. In and of itself, there is nothing sinister about the AP test format except that, perhaps because it is externally assessed without contextual knowledge of the writer, it tends to employ the vacuous kind of prompt and predetermined theme that encourages students to engage in writing that lacks originality or meaningfulness. Graff (2009) argued that students are not engaged in controversy or literary criticism at all when they are forced to write pseudoarguments in literature classes and AP tests that "compare and contrast" poems by Emily Dickinson and Robert Frost, for instance, while "analyzing the significance of dark and night in each." Graff faults this sort of traditional writing assignment because:

> assignments like those ... actually train students in how to be pointless, that there is nothing at stake in academic writing, that there are no consequences as there are in the rhetorical world outside of school. So don't ask questions, just do whatever the teacher wants and get on with it.
>
> *(p. 9)*

But the AP and SAT tests are a couple among many standardized tests in students' careers. In this age of accountability that has emerged from the 1990s' push for teacher accountability and standards-based education, federal legislation has prompted states to initiate testing at nearly all levels of the K–12 spectrum in most subject areas. Federal programs like No Child Left Behind (2002) and Race to the Top (2009) have intensified the importance of testing because incentives and funding are tied to successful test performance considered tantamount to student achievement. For schools facing unprecedented budget cuts, every dollar counts; and for administrators, whose faces sometimes grace the local papers when their schools do not meet the national measure for success, Adequate Yearly Progress (AYP)—the stakes are high. While the push toward testing satiates community desires to improve the educational system by making more public the relative success or failure of schools and their teachers, it has compromised flexibility in the curriculum and the time in the year to deliver it.

Teachers are more pressed than ever to prepare students for successful performance on standardized testing and are often asked to repeat the testing for the best results up to three times in a school year for each subject area. Hart and

Teeter (2002) found that 73% of adults surveyed supported testing to determine student achievement and supported holding schools and teachers accountable for those scores. External and internal pressures on teachers and students to perform well on standardized tests can diminish creative intelligence in the classroom.

This is not to suggest that students cannot both learn the skills and content necessary to perform successfully on state testing and master them through creative and inventive means (Feng, VanTassel-Baska, Quek, Bai, & O'Neill, 2004). But school districts are adopting textbooks less frequently (Howard, 2008), are adopting fewer single title texts, have less money to spend on students because more is being spent on employee insurance and retirement, and districts are less likely to provide much needed professional development for the teachers to encourage creative conveyance of curriculum in the classroom.

Hart and Teeter (2002) found that 91% of adults surveyed supported programs to encourage teacher professional development and growth because all groups in the study recognized the vital importance of effective teaching to the overall quality of education. But as budgets tighten, administrators make difficult choices that may include reduction in professional development and elimination of non-contact days for peer collaboration and planning. It is no wonder then that according to U.S. Department of Education statistics, about 269,000 of the nation's 3.2 million public school teachers quit the field in the 2003 2004 school year with over half of those leaving because they felt dissatisfied with teaching (Parker-Pope, 2008). Without the fire of professional development to inspire teachers and keep them current on best practice, without funding to invest in new technology, relevant single-title texts or innovative software, what can teachers, beginning and veteran, do to enliven their practice and to engage creative intelligence in the classroom for themselves and their students? Darling-Hammond (2010) asserted:

> To improve education through the use of standards and assessments, it is critically important to invest not only in well-designed assessments, but also in teacher expertise—through professional development, instructional assistance, and improved hiring and retention of teachers—and well-designed and plentiful curriculum resources ...
>
> *(p. 73)*

Engaging with the English Curriculum

With very little, if any, direct professional development, teachers can loosen the bonds of their own pedagogical dogmatism, reinvigorate their own teaching practice, and light fires beneath learners of all kinds. It begins with a shift in thinking from teacher-centered inquiry to student-centered inquiry. Wiggins (2009) reminded us that the "majority of Americans will not write academic papers for a living. The writing tasks that are required of us in the real world are … context-bound precise and focused tasks …" (p. 31). Students could use and develop their language arts to forge investigations, create original work responses, explore and explain various disciplines, as well as speak meaningfully for themselves by employing an array of language arts in projects that go beyond mere textual analysis and extend into creating original work. Students enjoy role-playing and problem-based learning, which can develop myriad communication skills. By capitalizing on this generation's desire for collaboration and social exchange (Howe & Strauss, 2000), teachers can use problem-based learning to broaden understanding of texts and, perhaps even more importantly, contexts at little or no additional cost to the teacher, building, or district. These methods are especially powerful for gifted children because of their heightened awareness of their world. As Cohen and Frydenberg (1996) reminded us, gifted children:

> are profoundly concerned about their world. They feel that they must DO something to make it better, to preserve it, to alleviate suffering. This energy, commitment and compassion needs to be focused on making a difference—a harnessing of "child power."
>
> *(p. 36)*

Problem-based learning plays into this desire of gifted children to make and do and solve for the betterment of society.

Considering that professional development is somewhat limited during times of economic hardship, teachers tend to fall back to what they know both pedagogically and textually. Using texts that teachers already have available in their classrooms or available affordably or for free through web-based resources, and without any additional expenditure for new materials, teachers can employ more student-centered strategies like Socratic Seminars to bring texts to life in new ways for their students. In Socratic Seminars, first developed by Mortimer Adler in the early 1980s, teachers typically bring a text to class that may be consumed in one sitting (Adler, 1982, 1998). This may be a selection from a longer work studied by the class like a chapter of a novel or a selection or may be a shorter independent work like a poem or essay. The teacher has the students read the selection, often marking it with notations that will assist in the seminar to come. Then students, usually seated with the teacher in a circle to represent the importance of every voice, are asked to share with each other what they found within the text, sometimes related to a prompt established at the outset of the seminar. At no time does the teacher validate or invalidate student comments, rather, through questions à la Socrates' gadfly method, the teacher can help guide the student-centered inquiry. Because the teacher is not in possession of "the right answer" in this type of discussion, students begin to rely on themselves and each other to understand the significance of what they have read rather than waiting out the teacher. Students become more independent learners and thinkers and more creative in their connections to learning because they are not limited by the typical classroom guessing game of ELA discussions where students know they are simply trying to find the answer they think the teacher wants to hear. Strategies such as the Socratic Seminar create authentic purposes and audience for students.

Students become more independent learners and thinkers and more creative in their connections to learning because they are not limited by the typical classroom guessing game of ELA discussions where students know they are simply trying to find the answer they think the teacher wants to hear. Little (2011) says that a key element of Socratic questioning is the teacher's skill at probing student responses to the questions with further questions, moving among the questioning levels to elicit deeper, more carefully reasoned and complex thoughts from students. Strategies such as the Socratic Seminar create authentic purposes and audience for students and can be especially effective with gifted learners.

Another powerful pedagogical method shown to be effective with students of all intellectual levels is Problem-Based Learning (PBL). PBL allows students and teachers to engage in real-world scenarios in order to master skills and content. Students are given a role in the scenario and empowered to learn what they need in order to successfully answer the questions posed by the scenario. The need for learning arises from the students' needs to right the disequilibrium of the "ill-structured problem" (Gallagher & Stepien, 1996) rather than from the dictates of the teacher, something very appealing to most gifted learners. PBL encourages cross-curricular connections and higher-level thinking while promoting active and hands-on learning. One reason this is especially vital with gifted students is their existential leanings prompt them to ask the relevance of studies and are not satisfied with pat answers.

The real-world problem solving of PBL can answer the question of relevance for the students through the execution of exercise. Problem-based learning is focused, experimental learning "minds-on, hands-on," which centers on real-world issues and problems and their solutions (Torp & Sage, 2002). PBL curriculum encourages vocabulary acquisition by creating disequilibrium and a desire to know in order to complete the role successfully and perform within the scenario. For example, a student in the role of a first-aid provider at a swimming pool might need to know that paramedics glove-up to prevent the spread of bloodborne pathogens—and consequently—what a bloodborne pathogen is (Kash, 2009).

Even in a language arts class, a student participating in PBL might become anything from a doctor, to a nuclear engineer (Gallagher & Stepien, 1996), to a lawyer or an archaeologist. For example, in an exercise designed to teach inductive and deductive reasoning, students may be asked to play the role of a CSI, or crime scene investigator. Here students could be handed actual evidence bags filled with belongings of a victim of a crime whose identity is unknown. Students must organize the evidence into categories, make assumptions, develop hypotheses, and submit their ideas about the person's identity or cause of death to the "lead investigator," in reality, the teacher, in the form of a crime report. Imagine the authenticity a writing teacher can have teaching the importance of audience and purpose when students are playing the role and writing for an audience other than the teacher and in a rhetorical form other than the five-paragraph essay. Teachers can begin to meet the demand of career-related learning standards being adopted in many states by using writing in real-world contexts. Layer on to that an element of literature being studied in an English class. In a five-minute warm up activity, students might share a weather report from the witches in *Macbeth;* or in a ten-minute free writing exercise, students may provide an excerpt from a letter home by one of the sailors on the *Pequod* in *Moby-Dick;* or in an entire class period, students can don a toga and portray Aristotle as they decry violations of his *Poetics* in Arthur Miller's *Death of a Salesman.* Wolf and Brandt (1998) remind us of the importance of integration of various disciplines, something PBL does with relative ease and with tremendous implications for integration in the ELA classroom.

What is helpful for students in this case is also helpful for teachers. The majority of the work for teachers when using PBL is spent in preparing the question, scenario, and roles as well as securing resource materials for the student researchers. The Internet has greatly improved the teacher preparation and student inquiry processes. Once the students engage in the scenario, the teacher becomes a facilitator and guides student inquiry; classroom management becomes easier as more of the students are more engaged throughout. The pace of the PBL class is lively, and the energy is contagious. Homework can be minimal as PBL can be employed in the classroom setting with little or no preliminary set up by the students. Grading can be conducted through myriad means: observation, self-reflection, peer feedback, and write-up of results of inquiry just to name a few. PBL provides a perfect foil to this age of Internet plagiarism since the more authentic a role and scenario can be, the less likely students will be to borrow whole-cloth from the web. For teachers experiencing the grind of teaching the same prep multiple times in one day, PBL is reinvigorating because the authentic inquiry is always new, different, and dependent upon the interests and prior knowledge of the students in each class.

Though students benefit in many ways from methods like PBL, perhaps the greatest benefit to students is the benefit to teachers. By using creative means of curricular conveyance like PBL, teachers and students are freer to become more creative and engaged in learning in the moment (Kash, 2009). Instead of relying on teacher-initiated inquiry, which is tiring to both the teacher and the students, and consistently puts the teacher in the spotlight, methods like PBL inspire students to initiate the learning and the inquiry. It does not sacrifice the building of foundational skills assessed in most state testing. And learning through PBL is simply more fun. Cohen and Frydenberg (1996) say that gifted students excel in identifying patterns and relationships necessary for complex activities like PBL and Socratic Seminar. The ability to recognize patterns and relationships is also fostered for gifted learners in English class through varied activities that promote the study of language itself and elements like grammar, poetics, and vocabulary. Little (2011) says that language study "… encourages the habits of mind of the critical reader and the practiced writer …" deepens understanding of literary texts through aesthetic and linguistic appreciation, and helps gifted learners develop the tools and skills of the discipline (p. 157). Such varied strategies increase the likelihood of creative productivity in classrooms.

So literary texts themselves can indeed provide inspiration and curricular springboards for creating units of study that explore and critique our worlds and perspectives. Posing an essential question to frame a unit of study and "design backward" (Wiggins & McTighe, 2005) from the intended learning is a useful way to plan instruction while also planning for students to use various language arts skills and tools in meaningful, artful, and relevant ways. For instance, using Rachel Simon's *Riding the Bus with My Sister*, a memoir about the year the author spent with her sister Beth, a woman with intellectual disabilities, the following essential question could frame a unit of study in English class: "How can one relationship affect the trajectory of a life?" Such a question invites analysis of the relationship between Rachel and her sister Beth or between Rachel and her mother or between Beth and one of the bus drivers, and so on. A good essential question transcends place and time, so in this case, the essential question invites students' exploration of a significant relationship within their own lives, someone as intimate as a family member or perhaps a childhood hero; this activity might result in the development of an essay or poetry, small group discussion, or photography exhibit with narrative. Backward design allows the teacher to plan instruction as well as create strategic opportunities for students to create original work inspired by a single text but that helps students to:

- use new skills and knowledge across the English language arts to go well beyond the text itself;
- explore and construct meaning in various modes;
- investigate a variety of diverse content and disciplines, literature, genres, modalities, and media;
- work independently and collaboratively with others;
- use and explore a variety of the language arts and multimodal forms of expression to create responses;
- make personal meaning and knowledge from exploration of literature, self, others, and the world;
- extend and tier the curriculum for gifted learners.

Backward design, promoted since the standards-based movements of the 1990s, has seen a resurgence of popularity as education reformers (Marzano,

2007; Wiggins & McTighe, 2005) emphasize the importance of establishing a clear objective and essential question, but encourage student creativity in demonstrating mastery of learning. Such encouragement takes its shape in teacher-designed, strategically structured assignments or curricular scaffolding. VanTassel-Baska (2011) insists that 20 years of research provide evidence that higher-level instruction and flexible curriculum delivery challenge gifted learners and all students as well.

Implications for Gifted Students

Inspiring gifted students to rise to higher cognitive levels by requiring more authentic and complex work can lead to developing students' creative intelligence. More generally, educators the world over are familiar with Bloom's Taxonomy from the 1950s. Some 40 years later, educational psychologists led by Lorin Anderson, himself a student of Bloom, revised Bloom's Taxonomy to reflect the movement toward outcomes-based education (Anderson & Krathwohl, 2001; Forehand, 2005). The revision puts greater emphasis on the creation of new knowledge. Marzano (2000) revised Bloom's Taxonomy further to include: knowing, organizing, applying, analyzing, generating, integrating, and evaluating. Relative to a taxonomy that encourages higher levels of thinking and complexity in teaching and learning, the "teaching to the test" methodology reduces the band of creativity and original work since multiple-choice tests cannot assess higher-level thinking and performance in testing formats that include a series of content question stems, each followed by its correct answer and three optional distractors. In theory, expansion of the literary canon and the pedagogical toolkit are necessary to keep students engaged; in practice, budgets are tight, and principals are not buying new texts or professional development for teachers (Howard, 2008). Standardized testing does not inspire teachers or students; but in practice, standardized tests are accountability measures for evaluating schools, teachers, and students considered, for reasons financial, practical, and political, to be an educational priority at this time.

Interestingly, Darling-Hammond (2010) observes that when state testing consisted of performance assessments, a hallmark of early and mid-1990s standards-based education, "teachers assigned more writing and more complex mathematical problem solving, and that achievement on these higher-order skills improved" (p. 69). The problem seems to be not with the tyranny of testing and accountability but in what *kind* of test is administered and what the test asks students to do. Performance assessments and preparation for performance assessments require more complex, authentic work. And so the nettlesome problem of the traditional English class format is not with literature or with writing; it is what teachers ask students to do with literature and writing about literature. Greater reliance on student-centered pedagogical and curriculum approaches like problem-based learning and backward design promote movement toward synthesis and creation, highlighting and strengthening creative intelligence and allowing gifted children to shine and inspire while maintaining their need for choice and personal power (Dredger, 2008).

Recommendations for Practical Application

English teaching that integrates interdisciplinary and conceptual learning with varied modes of curricular engagement can open avenues for higher-order thinking, complexity, creativity, and manipulation of skills and ideas for gifted learners. When the 3 o'clock bell rings, and the planning for tomorrow begins, teachers need more than theory to prepare for their lessons. Little (2011) suggests starting with the literature selected for instructional purposes and being thoughtful regarding the types and levels of questions asked about the literature for discussion and writing (p. 152). This is indeed a start. From provocative, challenging literature, English teachers can scaffold the English curriculum throughout Bloom's taxonomy, and its more recent iterations, and create opportunities for student-centered performance assessments. These strategies use literature to promote greater student achievement and engagement.

What hope is there, then, for English Language Arts teachers seeking to engage their students, especially their gifted students, and encourage them to aspire to the heights of creativity? Crossing boundaries and breaking with the dogmatic disciplinary traditions of the high school English classroom seem to be a good place to begin the revision. Borrowing from the fields of curriculum studies and gifted education, English teachers can open their students' learning potential and creativity by unlocking the paralytic constraints of a discipline that privileges literary analysis as a primary method for teaching and learning in English. Pedagogical inventiveness across the secondary English curriculum may well ignite the fire of creative intelligence within all students … and do no less for their teachers.

References

Adler, M. J. (1982). A revolution in education. *American Educator, 6,* 20–24.

Adler, M. J. (1998). *The paideia proposal: An educational manifesto.* Clearwater, FL: Touchstone.

Ambrose, D. (2009). *Expanding visions of creative intelligence: An interdisciplinary exploration.* Cresskill, NJ: Hampton Press.

Anderson, W., & Krathwohl, D. R. (Eds.). (2001). *A taxonomy for learning, teaching, and assessing: A revision of Bloom's educational objectives.* New York, NY: Longman.

Cohen, L. M., & Frydenberg, E. (1996). *Coping for capable kids.* Waco, TX: Prufrock Press.

Darling-Hammond, L. (2010). *The flat world and education: How America's commitment to equity will determine our future.* New York, NY: Teachers College Press.

Dredger, K. (2008). Incorporating student choice: Reflective practice and the courage to change. *English Journal, 98,* 29–35.

Forehand, M. (2005). Bloom's taxonomy: Original and revised. In M. Orey (Ed.), Emerging perspectives on learning, teaching, and technology. Retrieved from http://projects.coe.uga.edu/epltt/

Feng, A., VanTassel-Baska, J., Quek, C., Bai, W., & O'Neill, B. (2004). A longitudinal assessment of gifted students' learning using the integrated curriculum model (ICM): Impacts and perceptions of the William and Mary language arts and science curriculum. *Roeper Review, 27,* 78–83.

Gallagher, S., & Stepien, W. (1996). Content acquisition in problem-based learning: Depth versus breadth in American Studies. *Journal for the Education of the Gifted, 19,* 257–275.

Graff, G. (2009). The unbearable pointlessness of literature writing assignments. *The Common Review, 8,* 6–12.

Hart, P. D., & Teeter, R. M. (2002). *A national priority: Americans speak on teacher quality.* Princeton, NJ: Educational Testing Service.

Howard, J. (2008, September). Textbook sales drop, and university presses search for reasons why. *The Chronicle of Higher Education,* Retrieved from http://chronicle.com/article/Textbook-Sales-Drop-Puzzli/1132/

Howe, N., & Strauss, W. (2000). *Millennials rising: The next great generation.* New York, NY: Vintage.

Kash, L. R. (2009). *Perceived risk curriculum for at-risk learners.* Oregon State University. Retrieved from http://hdl.handle.net/1957/13091

Little, C. A. (2009). Always pushing the rock uphill—An interview with Joyce VanTassel-Baska. *Journal of Advanced Academics, 20,* 356–368.

Little, C. A. (2011). Adapting language arts curricula for high-ability learners. In J. VanTassel-Baska & C. A. Little (Eds.), *Content-based curriculum for high-ability learners* (2nd ed., pp. 151–186). Waco, TX: Prufrock Press.

Marzano, R. J. (2000). *Designing a new taxonomy of educational objectives.* Thousand Oaks, CA: Corwin Press.

Marzano, R. J. (2007). *The art and science of teaching: A comprehensive framework for effective instruction.* Alexandria, VA: ASCD.

Monaghan, E. J. (1989). Literacy instruction and gender in Colonial New England. In C. N. Davidson (Ed.), *Reading in America: Literature and social history* (pp. 53–80). Baltimore, MD: The Johns Hopkins University Press.

No Child Left Behind Act of 2001. (2002). (20 USC 6301). (Public Law 107-110).

Parker-Pope, T. (2008, January 2). Teacher burnout? blame the parents. *New York Times,* Retrieved from http://well.blogs.nytimes.com/2008/01/02/teacher-burnout-blame-the-parents

Pierce, K. M. (2007). Betwixt and between: Liminality in beginning teaching. *The New Educator, 3,* 31–49.

Race to the Top. (2009). *American Recovery and Reinvestment Act of 2009 (ARRA),* Section 14005-6, Title XIV, (Public Law 111-5).

Smagorinsky, P., Daigle, E. A., O'Donnell-Allen, C., & Bynum, S. (2010). Bullshit in academic writing: A protocol analysis of a high school senior's process of interpreting Much Ado about Nothing. *Research in the Teaching of English, 44,* 368–405.

Torp, L., & Sage, S. (2002) *Problems as possibilities: Problem-based learning for K-16 education* (2nd ed.), Alexandria, VA: Association of Supervision and Curriculum Development.

VanTassel-Baska, J. (2011). An introduction to the Integrated Curriculum Model. In J. VanTassel-Baska & C. A. Little (Eds.), *Content-based curriculum for high-ability learners* (2nd ed., pp. 9–32). Waco, TX: Prufrock Press.

Wiggins, G. (2009). Real-world writing: Making purpose and audience matter. *The English Journal, 98,* 29–37.

Wiggins, G., & McTighe, J. (2005). *Understanding by design* (2nd ed.). Alexandria, VA: Association for Supervision and Curriculum Development.

Wolf, P., & Brandt, R. (1998). What do we know from brain research? *Educational Leadership, 56*(3), 8–13.

15

LOOSENING DOGMATISM BY USING DISCIPLINED INQUIRY

Laurence J. Coleman, Margie Spino, and Charles Rop

UNIVERSITY OF TOLEDO

> It is the mark of an educated mind to be able to entertain a thought without accepting it.
>
> Aristotle

> It is what we think we know already that often prevents us from learning.
>
> Claude Bernard, French Psychologist

Dogmatism comes in various guises. It is a serious problem in the development of creative intelligence in any field, and this text discusses several of its forms. Here, dogmatism is defined as a point of view based on insufficiently examined premises, which is associated with rigid adherence to a standpoint. Having a strong position is not dogmatism when it is based on logical reasoning and empirical evidence, and corresponds to reality. A position might not be one with which we agree, but disagreement does not make it dogmatism.

We describe a process of disciplinary inquiry that individuals or groups can use to impede the growth of dogmatism. The procedures evolved as a means to make sense of statements about what is known about high ability and has since been taught to students from other fields/disciplines. The process begins with an analysis of an author's writings in order to derive the conceptual structure and clarify terminology. It continues with a process for unlocking the basic ideas that moves toward creating a research program to test out the worthiness of the idea. Specific procedures are described with examples to show the process in action.

Forces Pushing Toward Dogmatism

In a pluralistic, Internet-driven world where marketing and number of hits are taken as indicators of the significance of an idea, subtle and largely unintentional forces push us toward dogmatism. We are all subject to becoming dogmatic and we are usually unaware of it. Like all fields, ours is dominated by accepted views. Much of what is accepted about giftedness rests on the writings of well-known scholars, conventional wisdom, and an assortment of theories associated with the field. Because accepted views are infrequently examined, ideas get repeated in textbooks, and they become unquestioned statements making the situation ripe for dogmatism.

The second force is paradigm enchantment, which is the belief that there is one best way to view social reality. Paradigm enchantment leads to what are considered the appropriate questions to ask about a phenomenon, willingness to use a particular methodology, and receptiveness to alternate sources and kinds of evidence (Coleman, Sanders, & Cross, 1997). Enchantment in itself is not necessarily dogmatism, but if it prevents one from considering alternate warrants about a phenomenon, it can lead to dogmatism.

A third force is theory-ladenness. In any intellectual endeavor, a person enters the situation laden with a priori thoughts about a phenomenon, or more generally what counts as important. We cannot rid ourselves completely of these thoughts; hence, our thoughts are impregnated with the propensity to accept similar ideas. Thus, the primary control over this possibility is awareness of what unspoken thoughts or unexamined theories are influencing our thinking.

The fourth force is insufficient practice examining our beliefs or authors' assertions about phenomena. Opportunities in training programs to examine the validity of accepted theoretical claims made by others as well as one's own beliefs is not common. Although we have not studied this situation systematically, the experience of the first author as an editor and in conversations with graduate students at roundtable events at the National Association for Gifted Children and at the American Educational Research Association meetings shows it. Commenting on her experience in a class composed of graduate students from various fields, the second author has noted,

> Along the way I discovered theories and theoretical perspectives. It was an amazing feeling. As if I had just discovered that I was wearing a pair of glasses that I could now take off, and that there were different glasses I could try on that would allow me to see the world differently. These theories took a plethora of information and organized it into coherent forms that could be used to think even more deeply about the world.
>
> When these forces are interwoven, we can become their prisoners, creative intelligence can be stunted and dogmatism can thrive. These forces make it apparent that a means for examining assertions, accepted

beliefs, theories, and one's own thoughts would be a valuable tool for building a habit of mind to impede the growth of dogmatism.

The process of warding off dogmatism is time consuming and troublesome. It requires questioning ideas with which one is usually comfortable. Our goal is to present a conceptual basis for systematic examination of statements of various types that undergird inquiry. We are not directly interested in the standards of evidence, but rather in a means for getting to the point of asking that question. In this chapter we examine one theory as an example for demonstrating the operation of the system, although the same process can be used to dissect one's own beliefs, or other forms of accepted knowledge. For a field or a person to mature, it needs to own up to its conceptual foundations in a transparent manner and practitioners should be socialized to adopt a skeptical manner armed with tools such as this one, to guard against dogmatism.

Overview of Our System

We propose a system designed to expose the underpinnings of an author's conceptual stance by reorganizing it into a form that produces researchable questions, which can be compared to the available evidence in order to reveal what is known and unknown about that author's position. The process frees the analyst to apply his or her creative intelligence to resolution of the unknown.

Our method is not foolproof; rather, it is a tool to clarify what is being said or claimed. The procedure has been developed in collaboration with students who have reported that the process raised their sense of agency as independent thinkers and gave them freedom to approach new learning with a beginner's mind. The genesis of this system began in graduate school, where as part of the first author's training, his teacher, Louis Fleigler pushed him to think more deeply about what authors were saying. This system is an extension of that experience; it has evolved into a course of study taught with the third author in which the second author participated.

Presumptions of the System

The process of analysis rests on some presumptions. We believe a rational process can be used to understand phenomena of scientific interest. Transparency is the goal. Making something open makes it more likely the actual "reality" may be found. Implicit in the analytic process is the recognition that writers have "a world view, a general perspective, a way of breaking down the complexity of the real world [sic] … (Patton, cited in Lincoln, 1990, p. 80).

Among those concerned with the education of high-ability or gifted persons, Coleman et al. (1997), building on Guba (1990), showed how three world views or paradigms (i.e., empirical-analytical, interpretive, and transformative) influence the field. Each has its own way of framing how one looks at the world, understanding what is known and how to study it. Each paradigm not only affects what is seen and believed about high ability and creativity but also ultimately guides inquiries about the world. One's world view influences what we "see," what counts as evidence, the types of questions we ask, and the research methods we choose. A writer's paradigm is embedded in her writings, so that it is often hidden. Our system of analysis makes the hidden and tacit observable.

Definition of Terms

The system uses familiar terms in specific ways drawn initially from Marx's (1963) work, and they later evolved in conversations amongst ourselves and in our experiences teaching students. The terms describe steps in our system that work together to seek out and make visible the particulars of a body of work, a position or a theory. A web of statements are created that can be used to examine the validity of the position. In essence, the system extracts *assumptions* that form the foundation for *postulates* and then more specific *hypotheses* leading to *a line of inquiry* about the phenomenon. We define these terms more specifically with examples.

Assumptions   These are ideas that form the foundation of thinking on any topic by the person or theorist. These ideas are neither researchable nor measurable; yet, without them, the person's web of reasoning is less apparent. Another way to think of assumptions is that they are the premises that set the stage for an argument for further discussion. The analysis uncovers these ideas, if not stated explicitly, and uses them to understand the writer. Here is an example of an assumption: Development does not lie exclusively within an individual; rather it is an inseparable melding of person and domain of human activity. Note that the statement makes explicit that which cannot be studied, but it sets the stage for the next step.

Postulates   These are generic statements derived from one or more assumptions that have the potential to be put to some kind of empirical or logical test. Postulates tend to be broad, general statements of relationships between constructs or concepts related to the phenomenon of interest. Here is an example of a postulate: Domains of human activity are on a continuum from universal to nonuniversal. The inference is that activities can be categorized in this manner.

Hypotheses   These are specific statements describing conditions and associated outcomes. These statements make clear the variables, forces, or influences occurring in a particular situation or group of situations and what happens as a consequence of their influence. Here is an example of a hypothesis: Mastering a domain of human activity (drawing) means a person goes through an identifiable sequence and the person can be located at a point of development in that sequence.

Line of Argument/Research   The analytic process moves toward creating inquiries that are conducted for the purpose of increasing understanding about the phenomenon and validating the author's claims. It is the concluding part of the process.

The Process of Analysis

The process begins by identifying a phenomenon of personal interest and a scholar of gifted education who is associated with one's interest. The analytic process proceeds through steps in a recursive fashion to a point where statements are produced that are researchable and for which the outcomes can be used to verify the position. The process does not mean that all aspects of a writer's claims or assertions are researchable at any point in time, but it does enable one to study some aspects of the position. In that manner, it will shed light on its utility, value, and validity.

In essence, we are trying to enter the mind of the person to make his or her thinking transparent. This objective means reading and thinking about what the person is saying while resisting an inclination to evaluate it. The basic query is: What does the person mean and how does she say it. As one goes through the process, this question reemerges and haunts the inquiry-

Becoming knowledgeable enough to engage in the process necessitates reading the person's writings, either published or online. Obviously, an exhaustive reading is the ideal. That is an appropriate and worthy goal for a scholar who wants to specialize in understanding a particular person's work. That is not our purpose in this chapter; rather, our goal is to provide a methodology for understanding a theory or model in order to impede the growth of dogmatism and to fit the theory/model into the analyst's research program. Any reading or paper can be a starting point in the person's bibliography; however, the most advantageous move is to find the work or publication that is cited most frequently as a starting point and then work backward and forward.

There are no shortcuts in getting to know a person's work; time must be spent reading original sources. One can shorten the process by reading summaries or synopses, but that assumes the others' interpretation is complete. In our experience, accounts that appear in compendiums or textbooks are often shallow or simplistic renditions that miss the subtlety of the person's thinking. In analyses of a person's theorizing about high ability, such as Vygotsky, Dambrowski, Gardner, and Winner, the synopses miss the profound subtleties of their writings.

While reading a scholar's major works, one eventually needs to name the theory. While this may appear self-evident, it is not always an easy task. For some scholars, their work has evolved over time, and they do not provide an explicit summary. Other scholars, such as Sternberg, write about several phenomena, such as intelligence (1985), love (1988) or wisdom (1990), and it is challenging to isolate one particular theory within that body of work. If you're lucky, the theorist has a name for his or her theory (such as Andrew Meltzoff's theory of infant development called "theory theory") and has written a book that describes the theory (such as Gopnik & Meltzoff's, 1997, book, *Words, Thoughts, and Theories*).

In this chapter, we use the work of David Henry Feldman, who has written extensively about human development. His most well-known work is *Beyond Universals in Cognitive Development* (1980/1994). Feldman has been selected as an example because his work touches many topics surrounding creative intelligence, such as precocity, domain-specific learning, the interplay of learning and development, cognition, creativity and motivation. Furthermore, his theory encapsulates the meaning of the often misused, but not in this case, phrase—paradigm shift. Non-universal development is where giftedness takes place and creative intelligence flourishes.

Feldman has argued that typical developmental theory requires that four criteria be met: universal achievement, spontaneous acquisition, invariant sequence, and hierarchical integration toward transition. The first two assumptions effectively move non-universal development, also known as domain-specific development, which is where high-ability persons achieve or perform, outside typical developmental theory; in effect, removing the study of gifted behavior and creative intelligence from developmental theory. Feldman proposed that one could still conceptualize non-universal or domain-specific accomplishments as belonging to developmental theory by dropping the first two assumptions (universality, spontaneity) and keeping the last two assumptions (invariant sequence and hierarchical integration).

Finding Assumptions

After identifying the writer's (Feldman) theory, the process is directed toward finding the fewest assumptions possible to explain the theory. The principle involved here is the law of parsimony, which is a well-known injunction to favor the simpler of two equally plausible hypotheses. Few writers provide a list of assumptions with their work, so this is much like an excavation process where the analyst must dig deep into the person's words to uncover his meanings. In our example, the analysis of Feldman's ideas began with reading *Beyond Universals in Cognitive Development* and continued into other writings, some of which are listed at the end of the chapter. By reading, making notes, and eventually positing a possible assumption, the process begins and as the reading continues, a list of tentative assumptions is produced.

Feldman is dealing with a broad area of human life. From our definition of assumptions, we see that none of his assumptions are measurable directly. The assumptions are listed below. A1 denotes the first assumption. The number 1 does not mean that is the most important assumption. Feldman's assumptions include:

- A1. The special qualities of human experience set us apart from other organisms: "humanity is capable of influencing its own future development" (1984, p. x).
- A2. People have proclivities for the development of a talent.
- A3. Development exists in two general forms: universal and non-universal domains.
- A4. Development does not lie exclusively within an individual; rather, it is an inseparable melding of person and domain.
- A5. "People have the potential to be creative." The tendency of minds to be creative is called the "transformational imperative" (1986, p. 95).
- A6. Although there may be hundreds of vectors, and the developmental process is complex and changeable, it is lawful and controlled (1984, p. 109).

The assumptions suggest the potential of the theory. In short, Feldman is proposing that people are unique, have creative potential, develop using similar processes across two broad areas of human activity (universal and non-universal), which occurs in a lawful, not haphazard manner, in the context of individual and socially constructed domains.

A Sideways Step: Metaphors or Graphic Representations

Trying to understand another person's thinking is a complex task. One tool is available to help get beneath the surface of a writer's words. A window into another's thinking was pointed out by Lakoff (1993) who demonstrated that metaphor is at the root of human thought. If we can find and understand a person's metaphor, it increases the likelihood we can understand another's meaning. Our analytic system looks for metaphor that may be driving the person's thinking. Some of our most famous scholars had a model or metaphor in mind. Two examples are Darwin's tree of life and Freud's notion of the iceberg. Once a metaphor is identified, if that is possible, the thinking of the writer becomes clearer.

Another window into someone's thinking is to look for graphic representations or diagrams such as webs or concept maps that represent what has been read. Has the person produced a diagram? Or can one be created to illustrate the idea and relationship between variables or constructs, which help with the

FIGURE 15.1 Feldman's continuum of domains

next steps? Feldman has produced representations of his idea. He has proposed a continuum of domains that are ordered from universal to unique. The one presented here in Figure 15.1 has undergone some changes since 1994 with the inclusion of pancultural.

The diagram illustrates six kinds of developmental domains, that is, integrated knowledge and skills, which humans may learn and create. At the most general level is the universal domain, which represents knowledge that is known by persons living a normal life. It happens spontaneously in the course of growing up. All of the other domains are developmental too, yet are not accessible to everyone, which distinguishes them from the universal. The diagram shows by the size of each block that fewer persons have access to that knowledge; so, the least number have access at the extreme right. The arrow represents the possibility over time that the unique knowledge will become more and more accessible to growing numbers of persons. Reading is an example of a domain that has moved toward the universal. At one time few could read, yet now this domain is widely, not unanimously, accepted, which illustrates the movement, note the arrows, from unique to universal.

Finding Postulates

Often writers make statements about the relationship among constructs and variables. These come in the form of statements such as, if this occurs, then that will happen. Or, under these conditions expect to see this happening or this associated phenomenon. These are postulates. Reading and rereading the original sources looking for such statements makes them apparent. Sometimes they are direct statements; other times they are restatements. Writing postulates helps to flesh out Feldman's theory and builds toward researchable actions.

Emanating from Feldman's assumptions, we constructed postulates and found it useful to try to link the postulates back to the referent assumptions or assumptions as much as possible. Eight groups of postulates were noted: Development, Domains, Cultural Organism, Creativity, and Natural Proclivities and Talent. Each group has multiple postulates associated with it. Below are examples around the group, Domains (Do). We have presented a reduced group of postulates to illustrate the point of generating postulates, not to show an exhaustive list. Thus, the numbering below is not continuous in the examples. Note that the postulates can be observed or measured in some form.

Examples of Postulates about Domain (PDo)

- PDo1. Domains of human activity are on a continuum from universal to non-universal
  - The regions of the continua are: UNIVERSAL, PANCULTURAL, CULTURAL, DISCIPLINE BASED, IDIOSYNCRATIC, UNIQUE
- PDo3. Fewer persons master a domain as the continuum of development proceeds toward unique.
- PDo6. Domains have qualities or characteristics, not necessarily all, such as:
  - Undergo transformation (more than once?);
  - Have special terminology;
  - Have symbol systems;
  - Have "established and accepted pedagogical techniques, institutions and technologies";
  - Recognize signs of early potential. (Feldman, Csikszentmihalyi, & Gardner, 1994, p. 8)

Notice how the meaning of domains is becoming clearer. These postulates can also be traced to the graphic organizer. We can see the outlines of possible hypotheses.

Another Side Step: Corollaries

Sometimes postulates lead rather quickly to hypotheses. However, in some instances narrower statements of relationships between constructs are necessary in order to make plain the postulates before stating hypotheses. Corollaries serve as a bridge in specifying the web of relationships among variables. The analyst may create corollaries to make sense of the postulates. For example, given the vast number of domains of human activities, we created a corollary for the purpose of creating boundaries among domains to increase the comprehensibility of the meaning of domain and to simplify the process of studying them. Based on postulate 2 about domains we stated this corollary: The universe of domains may be divided further into groups of fields of knowledge and skills. These fields are: Academic, Aesthetic, Practical, and Folk. (The terms are not defined further in this example.)

Hypotheses

By reading the postulates, the outlines of the theory become more visible. Deriving a set of postulates sets the groundwork for the specification of hypotheses. A good hypothesis is one that makes clear what is happening and can be traced to the earlier postulates. The objective is to make the statements as concrete or as visible as possible. Hypotheses can be established in three ways. First, search the works of the person for such statements. Second, probe the literature for studies done by peers on the topic. Third, construct hypotheses that follow from the growing understanding of the work and are consistent with it.

Feldman's theory asserts that development takes place in domains that have properties enabling them to be classified as to their level of sophistication and in environments with qualities that support advanced development. These particular hypotheses are not meant to be exhaustive or even the best hypotheses, but rather to show how the process moves forward. These examples make apparent that there are researchable questions that have the potential to validate the theory.

Examples of hypotheses from the domain (Do)

- Hyp1. After conducting a search for domains and classifying them on the continuum, the incidence of persons in each domain will decrease, or increase, corresponding to their region of the continuum.
- Hyp2. Mastering a domain means a person goes through a sequence that can be identified and then the person can be located as to her or his level of development.
- Hyp3. The more qualities a domain has, the more likely that domain will identify and support prodigies.

Specialized Vocabulary: A Third Sidestep

Writers in the course of explaining themselves use terms in ways that suit their purposes. Sometimes they create new terms; sometimes they use common terms in a more specific or specialized way. As stated previously, our process is continually asking, "What does it mean?" and trying to concisely capture the writer's meanings. A section on definitions of terms clarifies the meanings of terms mentioned in the assumptions, postulates and hypotheses. In our example, the term *prodigy* was introduced in Hypothesis 3 so it has to be defined. The definitions of terms section not only helps with communicating clearly about the theory, but also assists in gaining a deeper understanding of the theory.

Line of Inquiry

The entire analytic system is intended to set the groundwork for deliberative future study. Line of inquiry describes future series of studies to be carried out over an extended period of time. Armed with the hypotheses, a line of inquiry directs the search for evidence confirming or disconfirming them.

While any part of Feldman's theory could be the focus of a line of inquiry, in order to continue our example we look at development. We take postulate 6 on domains (PDo6) and associated hypothesis to design a line of inquiry. Hypothesis 1 states that domains can be classified according to the qualities (i.e., undergo transformation; have special terminology, have symbol systems, have established and accepted pedagogical techniques, institutions, and technologies, and recognize signs of early potential.) Accordingly, two studies illustrate one possible line of inquiry.

> Study 1. Do library/document research into the records of organizations, such as professional groups, learned societies, sports federations, ethnic arts organizations, and so forth, to gather information on practices that illustrate the organizations exhibiting the qualities of domains.
>
> Study 2. Using the designation of the 4 field/domains (academic, aesthetic, folk, and practical), interview recognized experts in any domain to determine how and on what basis they recognize signs of advanced development among their members.

By conducting these studies, we are assembling evidence about the hypotheses and, indirectly, we are providing evidence on the utility, value, and validity of the larger theory. Obviously, two studies cannot confirm or disconfirm Feldman's' theory. Our example illustrates how a line of inquiry is derived from the larger analysis. At this juncture the next step is up to the analyst about whether to continue research on this path based on Feldman's work, pick another part of the theory to study, or be satisfied with the level of understanding he has achieved and be ready to move on to another phenomenon.

Summary and Conclusions

Dogmatism, in this chapter, is defined as a point of view based on insufficiently examined premises, which is associated with rigid adherence to a standpoint. Four forces push individuals toward dogmatism: accepted views, paradigm enchantment, theory-ladenness, and lack of practice examining beliefs and claims. The chapter directly addresses the latter force and indirectly the other three forces by providing a system for examining statements. We have proposed a system of analysis for impeding the growth of dogmatism that can free the individual's creative intelligence. Our approach may seem contradictory because we propose a structure for increasing flexible thinking. Yet, using structure to release creativity is a staple in the repertoire of technique for increasing creativity.

Our purpose was to outline a strategy for blocking the development of dogmatism. Our system for combating that progression has been taught successfully to graduate students and teachers. In general, this process is useful for understanding claims about what is known about giftedness, one's own beliefs, and formal theories.

In this chapter we illustrated the system by focusing on David Feldman's non-universal theory of development. Definitions and examples were presented for the four key elements of the analytic process: determining assumptions, extracting postulates, generating hypotheses, and building a line of inquiry with sidesteps to enable the process. The analytic system has the effect of uncovering the network of relationships among constructs and variables and clarifying meanings. The line of inquiry creates a research program to support or disconfirm a claim. The process leads to a richer and deeper understanding of the idea, theory, or statement being considered by providing a vehicle for deliberating over various claims. The process liberates the person from the bounds of the statement and can enable creative intelligence to flourish. The analyst can see the gaps in the claim, the implications of the idea as well as opportunities to further understand the phenomenon. Engaging in this process develops a sense of agency and self-empowerment in the analyst because one can locate his or her interests within the analytic matrix and find a place for their own development.

References

Coleman, L. J., Sanders, M. D., & Cross, T. C. (1997). Perennial debates and tacit assumptions in the education of gifted children. *Gifted Child Quarterly, 41,* 44–50.

Feldman, D. H. (1980). *Beyond universals in cognitive development.* Westport, CT: Albex.

Feldman, D. H. (1994). *Beyond universals in cognitive development* (2nd ed.). Westport, CT: Ablex.

Feldman, D. H., Csikszentmihalyi, M., & Gardner, H. (1994). *Changing the world: A framework for the study of creativity.* Westport, CT: Praeger,

Gopnik, A., & Meltzoff, A. N. (1997). *Words, thoughts, and theories.* Cambridge, MA: MIT Press.

Guba, E. (Ed.). (1990). *The paradigm dialog.* Thousand Oaks, CA: Sage.

Lakoff, G. (1993). The contemporary theory of metaphor. In A. Ortony (Ed.), *Metaphor and thought* (2nd ed., pp. 202–251). New York: Cambridge University Press.

Lincoln, Y. S. (1990). The making of a constructivist: A remembrance of transformations past. In E. G. Guba (Ed.), *The paradigm dialogue* (pp. 67–87). Newbury Park, CA: Sage.

Marx, M. (1963). The general nature of theory construction. In M. Marx (Ed.), *Theories in contemporary psychology* (pp. 4–43). New York, NY: MacMillan.

Sternberg, R. (1985). *Beyond IQ: A triarchic theory of human intelligence.* New York, NY: Cambridge University Press.

Sternberg, R. (1988). *The triangle of love: Intimacy, passion, commitment.* New York, NY: Basic Books.

Sternberg, R. (1990). *Wisdom: Its nature, origins, and development.* Cambridge, England: Cambridge University Press.

SECTION 4

Concluding Thoughts

Patterns in the Analyses of Dogmatism and Giftedness

16

DOGMATISM AND GIFTEDNESS

Major Themes

Robert J. Sternberg

OKLAHOMA STATE UNIVERSITY

Why do some fields progress at a rapid rate, some progress slowly, and others seem to progress hardly at all? This is the question that kept coming into my mind as I read the chapters for this volume. And how quickly does the field of gifted education progress? In this discussion, I attempt to address these issues and also why the answers are what they are. Comprehensive accounts of gifted education can be found elsewhere (e.g., Heller, Mönks, Sternberg, & Subotnik, 2000; Pfeiffer, 2008; Phillipson & McCann, 2007; Renzulli, Gubbins, McMillen, Eckert, & Little, 2009; Sternberg, Jarvin, & Grigorenko, 2011; Sternberg & Reis, 2004).

Some fields move quickly, others, slowly. A field that has moved quickly is cognitive psychology. I received my graduate degree in 1975 in cognitive psychology. As my wife and I finished revising a cognitive-psychology text (Sternberg & Sternberg, in press), I marveled at how quickly cognitive psychology has changed during the time period of the six editions of the text, beginning in 1996 (Sternberg, 1996). The field has changed even more since I received my PhD. The fields of cognitive science and cognitive neuroscience have changed the face of the field of cognitive psychology.

The field of cognitive psychology of today is almost unrecognizable in comparison with the field when I left graduate school. The theories, research paradigms, and research methods have changed greatly. In the mid-1970s, the majority of research projects were done through behavioral studies where, for example, someone might read strings of letters and have their reaction time measured, or learn strings of words and have their performance scored in terms of percentage correct. Today, such studies are rare. Cognitive psychology went through a period where it was supplemented (some might say almost "replaced") by cognitive science, which was based on the metaphor of people as computational devices; this metaphor in turn has given way to cognitive neuro-science. Powerful forces were exerted on the field to move it in these directions.

One factor that propelled cognitive psychology forward was grant support. Federal government support was better in the cognitive-science and then the cognitive-neuroscience area, and investigators went where the money was. Another factor was thought leaders. Powerful scientists such as Herbert Simon, Marvin Minsky, and John Anderson in the cognitive-science days, and then Michael Posner, David Rumelhart, and Jay McClelland, in the more recent cognitive-neuroscience days, helped propel the field forward. Scientists followed the thought leaders and so did jobs. Traditional cognitive psychologists of the kinds found in the 1970s found it progressively harder to gain employment at top research institutions.

Although I have not edited a textbook on giftedness, I have coedited two editions of a book entitled *Conceptions of Giftedness* (Sternberg & Davidson, 1986, 2005). The field of gifted education has progressed very differently from the field of cognitive psychology. The field of gifted education has, in many respects, changed much less over recent years than has the field of cognitive psychology. The theories, paradigms, and methods are not so different from what they were 35 years ago. Of course, things are not totally the same. Howard Gardner's (1983) theory of multiple intelligences did not exist in 1975, but it has been around for almost 30 years with relatively little change (naturalist intelligence was added in the interim). We still hear the same debates about enrichment versus acceleration, single versus multiple indices of intelligence, and pull-out programs versus entirely separate classes for the gifted. IQ is still used by many schools to identify gifted children, as it was in the day of the Terman (1925) studies.

Why has cognitive psychology changed so much and gifted education so little? More generally, what factors lead some fields to become more entrenched and others to transform themselves rapidly? The authors in this volume seek to address this question as it applies to gifted education. Here I summarize and expand on some of their main points.

Some Salient Forces that Can Lead to Stagnation

Real-World Practice

One force that has slowed the progress of gifted education is its relation to real-world practice. Laboratory research can move as fast as findings can emerge from labs. But when a science—and I view education of the gifted as having a strong scientific component—moves forward in the service of some kind of real-world practice, it faces powerful forces that sciences do not face when they (e.g., cognitive psychology) are able to move along at their own laboratory-based pace, relatively uninterrupted by the demands of real-world practice.

Research in gifted education is constrained by the demands of the education marketplace, and this marketplace is not a fast-moving one. Although there have been developments in the way gifted education has been done in schools, they tend to be halting and often to be one step forward, two steps back.

The Accountability Movement

Perhaps the strongest force impeding the development of gifted education has been, I believe, not in the dogmatism of its practitioners, but in a societal force over which they have virtually no control, namely, the accountability movement. Few educators would question the value of accountability; certainly I would not. The problem is not with accountability, per se, but with the way it has been sought.

1. **Emphasis on weak students, not strong ones.** The name of a legislative act behind much of the accountability movement is No Child Left Behind, and that name in itself sends a message. The emphasis in the act is on students who are having difficulty in school, not on those who excel. Because there are legal and financial as well as administrative implications of failing to live up to the mandates of the law, schools are left with little incentive to pay attention to gifted students. On the contrary, resources devoted to gifted students may be viewed as resources that are not being devoted to carrying out the law's mandates.
2. **The nature of accountability as operationalized.** Accountability in many states is taking the form of tests that measure kinds of outcomes that have little to do with the content of many gifted programs. Enrichment activities in gifted programs are a far cry from assessments measuring command of facts, for example. Even accelerated programs may be irrelevant to the assessments because students are often assessed on what they are supposed to know at the grade level they are at, not at some higher grade level. A gifted program may lead to outcomes that are irrelevant or even contrary to those measured by the assessments.
3. **Reluctance of school districts to become involved in research that will not improve test scores.** Because school districts are under the gun, superintendents and principals may be reluctant to get involved in research that will not improve test scores, particularly of low-functioning students. Research on the gifted may seem like an unnecessary frill.

Research in gifted education differs in a fundamental way from research in cognitive psychology and in many other disciplines. The field of cognitive psychology, to some extent, sets its own agenda, and to some extent, follows the agenda mapped out by granting agencies. (That is, researchers go where the money is.) The field of gifted education, in order to stay relevant, finds its agendas largely set by what happens in schools. This need for relevance means that if things regress in the schools, the field of gifted education can regress too.

During the 1980s and 1990s, I believe that many exciting things were happening in gifted education. The field had a sense of moving forward. Joseph Renzulli's (1978, 1986) three-ring model and the Renzulli-Reis revolving-door model were being implemented in more and more school districts. Howard Gardner's (1983, 1993) ideas about multiple intelligences were making their way into more and more classrooms. Then, in 2001, with the passage of the No Child Left Behind Act, these kinds of innovations slowed down or even stopped. First, there was little incentive for schools to have gifted programs, and many dropped them. Second, what the programs emphasized was not on the tests.

Budgets

The accountability movement was not the only force behind the diminished progress of the gifted-education movement. A second force is reduced budgets. When budgets are reduced, historically, gifted programs are among the first things to go because they are viewed as discretionary. It thus becomes harder to get direction from gifted practices in school because of the reductions in force among gifted educators.

Reductions affect not only gifted-education programs, but also, funding for gifted-education research. Funding for research in gifted education has always been small but funding cuts have reduced it to a tiny fraction of the federal education research budget.

Summary of Forces toward Dogmatism that Emerge from the Chapters of this Book

Many of the chapters in this book draw on Rokeach's (1960) concept of dogmatism. According to Rokeach, dogmatism is a closed cognitive organization of beliefs. Dogmatic people tend to believe in absolute authority and to be relatively intolerant of others. The chapters in this book discuss some of the major costs and bases of dogmatism, which are summarized and synthesized here.

What are the costs of dogmatism? According to VanTassel-Baska (Chapter 13), they include cognitive narrowing, authoritarianism, rigidity, unwillingness to compromise, lack of progress in one's thinking, isolation of one's belief system from potentially disconfirming information, and lack of tolerance and even fanaticism. In a word, a dogmatic person is "stuck." He or she is virtually unable to move beyond current beliefs and belief systems because of a great resistance to change in those beliefs. At an intellectual level, the person stops growing.

VanTassel-Baska also suggests remedies for dogmatism, which include multiple approaches to problems, unpacking one's own assumptions, challenging one's own beliefs, synthesizing different models, willingness to engage with new models, understanding sources of agreement and disagreement with others, and use of inquiry techniques.

What are the sources of dogmatism? The authors of the chapters in this book identify a number of them.

Narrow Conceptions of Giftedness

Borland (Chapter 2), Cohen (Chapter 3), Ford (Chapter 7), and Peterson (Chapter 5) identify narrow conceptions of giftedness as one of the major obstacles to progress in the field of gifted education. For many if not most schools, their conception has not changed much since the days of Lewis Terman (1925). For them, IQ still rules the day. Most modern conceptions of giftedness take into account the abilities that constitute IQ (see essays in Sternberg & Davidson, 2005) but go beyond these abilities to include other kinds of abilities as well as motivation and task-oriented aspects of personality.

Bias Toward the Analytic

Ford (Chapter 7), Pierce and Kash (Chapter 14), and Peterson (Chapter 5) all point to a bias toward the analytic as a source of dogmatism in gifted education. What this means is that we identify, teach, and test in ways that emphasize analytical rather than other kinds of skills. Students with other kinds of giftedness will not necessarily fare well as a result. For example, a traditional IQ test, often used to identify the gifted, measures memory and analytical skills, but does not measure the kinds of creative, practical, or wisdom-based skills in Sternberg's augmented theory of successful intelligence (Sternberg, 2003; Sternberg et al., 2011) nor the musical, bodily-kinesthetic, naturalist, interpersonal, and intrapersonal skills posited by Gardner's (2006) theory of multiple intelligences. However, many of the greatest and most gifted contributors to the world were not necessarily the best analytical thinkers or students, but rather excelled in skills not well addressed either on IQ tests or even in traditional school settings.

Traditional Testing

Borland (Chapter 2), Ford (Chapter 7), Ambrose (Chapter 8), Peterson (Chapter 5), Pierce and Kash (Chapter 14), and Subhi-Yamin and Ambrose (Chapter 12) all identify traditional ability testing as a source of entrenchment and dogmatism in the field of gifted education. As mentioned earlier, in some respects, we have not come far since Terman's (1925) studies of the gifted. Many educators see a role for traditional testing. The issue is whether traditional testing covers enough of the skills and attitudes associated with giftedness (Sternberg & Davidson, 1986, 2005).

The question, of course, arises as to whether there are other kinds of tests one can use. Chart, Grigorenko, and Sternberg (2008) have described their Aurora Project, which assesses analytical, creative, and practical skills in the verbal, quantitative, and figural domains for students of roughly 10–12 years of age. It is designed especially for gifted identification. Sternberg and the Rainbow Project Collaborators (2006) and Sternberg (2010) have described assessments usable at the high school and college levels. These assessments measure analytical, creative, practical, and in one case, wisdom-based skills.

Replication of How One was Taught

Ambrose (Chapter 8), Peterson (Chapter 5), and Pierce and Kash (Chapter 14) illustrate the extent to which what we have done in gifted education merely repeats what we have been taught. To some extent, we tend to replicate how we ourselves were taught and, more generally, educated. The result is obviously a very conservative approach to gifted education as we replicate what has been done before.

In earlier work, my colleagues and I spoke of different types of creative innovations (Sternberg, 1999; Sternberg, Kaufman, & Pretz, 2002). The least ambitious of these is what we have called "conceptual replication," which is merely doing what has been done before with minor variations. This is the type of creative innovation that has characterized, or one might say, "haunted," the gifted-education enterprise. The majority of new tests that are introduced are merely cosmetic variations on old tests. They may look different but they measure largely the same thing (namely, the general-intelligence, or g factor).

Falling in Love with Our Own Beliefs, Whatever They Are

Cohen (Chapter 3) and VanTassel-Baska (Chapter 13) have pointed out that the root of dogmatism, at some level, is falling in love with one's own beliefs. One simply refuses seriously to consider others' beliefs. So it becomes hard to move forward because one is so pleased with where things are. The field of gifted education has tended to remain somewhat stuck, according to these authors, because people are smug in their beliefs regarding the value of what they already are doing. In some cases, VanTassel-Baska (Chapter 13) points out, people sometimes have messianic beliefs that leave them thinking that whatever they have is the very best there possibly could be.

We all risk becoming closed to new ideas. As Cross and Cross (Chapter 10), Ford (Chapter 7), Ambrose (Chapter 8), and Peterson (Chapter 5) all recognize, gifted education has been more closed to new ideas than many other fields. In a way, this closure is ironic, because part of giftedness would seem to be openness to new ideas. Yet year after year, schools use roughly the same tests, in updated editions, which have been used for close to a century to identify the gifted. If medicine were using the same tests today as a hundred years ago, think where we would be in terms of treating patients!

Knowledge as the Accumulation of Information Will Move Us Forward, with Technology as the Engine

VanTassel-Baska (Chapter 13) has identified a fairly common belief in schooling, namely, that the goal of education is the transmission of knowledge as accumulated information. A further enhancement to this view is that technology will somehow modernize the communication of this information. The problem with this view, quite simply, is that it fails adequately to appreciate the purpose of schooling, whether of the gifted or of anyone else. Information itself should be accumulated, whether through modern technology or by any other means, in the service of critical, creative, practical, and wise and ethical thinking with this knowledge (Sternberg, 2003; Sternberg et al., 2011). Someone could memorize textbooks in any field—it would not make them creative experts in any of those fields. The people who will move our society forward are those who can utilize their knowledge effectively, not those who are merely walking encyclopedias.

VanTassel-Baska (Chapter 13) has also argued that people who believe that people with an extreme constructivist orientation—those who believe that gifted kids know what they need and how to create it, are also mistaken. Unless gifted children are guided, they are as susceptible as any other children to falling by the wayside. They may be gifted, but they are, above all, children.

Reward System in Higher Education that Gives Credit for the Same Old, Same Old

Cohen (Chapter 3) and VanTassel-Baska (Chapter 13) have both suggested that one of the primary problems in the development of innovative programs for the gifted is a reward system that basically reinforces whatever has been done in the past. One is reminded of the movie *The Dead Poets' Society*, in which an innovative teacher played by Robin Williams was penalized and ultimately fired simply because he wanted to teach in an effective rather than a traditional way.

The No Child Left Behind Act has, if anything, made the situation even worse. Top school-district administrators have become so fixated on test scores measuring traditional forms of learning that they are afraid to try anything new for fear that the risk will end up with a takeover of their school and possibly a loss of their jobs.

Those who stay with the same old, same old often ignore their own experience (Ford, Chapter 7; Gallagher, Chapter 6; Ambrose, Chapter 8). Their experience tells them one thing but their prior conceptions tell them another, and they stick with the prior conceptions.

The same old, same old is supported by conservative, if not reactionary tracts, such as *The Bell Curve* (Herrnstein & Murray, 1994). Essentially, books such as these set up a false meritocracy based on just a single attribute, IQ

(Ambrose, Chapter 8). Conveniently, IQ is highly correlated with socio-economic status, so that it tends to reward (although not exclusively) the haves over the have-nots and to perpetuate the existing class structure. Such tracts are disappointingly insensitive to ethical issues, such as the perpetration of a class structure that benefits the same people and their descendants, over and over again, regardless of their achievements (Ambrose, Chapter 8; see also Ambrose & Cross, 2009; Sternberg, 2009).

View that Intelligence Protects You from Dogmatism

Stanovich (2010) has pointed out that intelligence in the sense of IQ points does not protect one from irrational thinking. Similarly, Van Tassel-Baska (Chapter 13) and Cross and Cross (Chapter 10) have shown that intelligence does not protect one from dogmatism either. Some very intelligent people, in a traditional sense, are quite dogmatic. Sternberg and Lubart (1995) further have suggested that expertise can actually interfere with creative thinking. As people become more expert, they risk becoming entrenched—so comfortable with the way things have been done that they do not wish to try new ways of doing things. As Montgomery (Chapter 11) has put it, they can become "mindless" (Langer, 1990). Montgomery points out that one educational innovation that encourages mindlessness is the existence of packaged programs. It is easy to use these programs without reflecting upon whether they meet the needs of the children for whom they are allegedly designed.

Personality Traits

Several chapter authors—Borland (Chapter 2), Cross and Cross (Chapter 10), Ford (Chapter 7), note that one source of dogmatism is a constellation of personality traits that may be found among some of those who enter the field of gifted education—intolerance of ambiguity, closed-mindedness, certainty orientation, need for rigidity, cognitive closure, low need for cognition, arrogance. A reasonable question to ask is why anyone with these personality traits would go into the field of gifted education. One problem in the field is that identification of the gifted often does not assess these traits. On the contrary, people may be identified as gifted because they have learned how to do what they are told and not to think too much about it. Our risk, therefore, might be that we actually reward students with these characteristics. The fundamental principle of interpersonal attraction is that we are attracted to people like ourselves (Byrne, 1971). If people with dogmatic personality traits enter the gifted field, we risk producing mentees with these same traits in the name of developing gifts. Similarly, if children with gifts come from families that are closed-minded or dogmatic, the children may develop these same characteristics, despite their gifts (Cross & Cross, Chapter 10).

Sometimes this cluster of personality traits expresses itself through the personal epistemology that knowledge is fed to one from an authority (Cross & Cross, Chapter 10). To the extent that teachers encourage students just to believe them rather than to think reflectively on what the teachers say, they risk interfering with the development of the gifts. Repressive societies often have educators who say they want to develop creative thinking in their students— just so long as the students' creativity does not go too far, such as to criticize the government. Students quickly learn the difference between what the educators say and how they act.

Stereotypes About Particular Groups/Ethnocentrism/Racism/Prejudice

As Ford (Chapter 7) points out, we cannot eliminate stereotypes and prejudices as a source of dogmatism in the identification of the gifted. Work on implicit theories of prejudice (Greenwald & Banaji, 1995) shows that, regardless of whether people feel themselves to be prejudiced, they often are, at an implicit level of which they are not aware. The result can be the identification of individuals whose race and ethnicity is the same as one's own, without any intention to show bias in identification. Often, different ethnic groups have different expectations regarding what constitutes good or even gifted behavior, and teachers of the gifted are likely to identify as gifted those students whose behavior conforms to the teachers' own stereotypes about what constitutes gifted behavior (Ford, Chapter 7). Their minds are closed, without their even realizing it. Worse, open-minded people may be unwilling to confront them (Ford, Chapter 7), so little or nothing changes.

Stereotypes About "Good" Behavior

Stereotypes are not limited to racial and ethnic groups. It is easiest to teach children who are well-behaved, and it can be tempting for teachers to identify students as gifted who are, in fact, merely well-behaved (Peterson, Chapter 5). The result is the identification of students who conform as "gifted."

Confusion of a Social Construction with a Natural Reality

Borland (Chapter 2) points out that giftedness is not some God-given state, but rather, a social construction. Different societies may and do have entirely different conceptions of what constitutes giftedness (Phillipson & McCann, 2007; Sternberg, in press). We can construct all the definitions of giftedness we want. We need to remember that, in the end, they are culturally bound. They reflect what we, as a culture, value. One culture may view as gifted a child who is an excellent memorizer of the Koran; another, a child who shows prowess in hunting or gathering; another, a child who scores well on an IQ test. If we are to go beyond dogmatism in gifted education, we have to recognize the limitations in our own thinking, cultural or otherwise. And that, more than anything else, is the theme of the volume you are reading.

References

Ambrose, D., & Cross, T. (Eds.). (2009). *Morality, ethics, and gifted minds.* New York, NY: Springer.

Byrne, D. (1971). *The attraction paradigm.* New York, NY: Academic Press.

Chart, H., Grigorenko, E. L., & Sternberg, R. J. (2008). Identification: The Aurora Battery. In J. A. Plucker & C. M. Callahan (Eds.), *Critical issues and practices in gifted education* (pp. 281–301). Waco, TX: Prufrock.

Gardner, H. (1983). *Frames of mind: The theory of multiple intelligences.* New York, NY: Basic.

Gardner, H. (1993). *Multiple intelligences: The theory in practice.* New York, NY: Basic.

Gardner, H. (2006). *Multiple intelligences: New horizons in theory and practice.* New York, NY: Basic.

Greenwald, A., & Banaji, M. (1995). Implicit social cognition: Attitudes, self-esteem, and stereotypes. *Psychological Review, 102,* 4–27.

Heller, K. A., Mönks, F. J., Sternberg, R. J., & Subotnik, R. F. (Eds.) (2000). *International handbook of giftedness and talent.* Amsterdam, Netherlands: Elsevier.

Herrnstein, R., & Murray, C. (1994). *The bell curve.* New York, NY: Free Press.

Langer, E. (1990). *Mindfulness.* New York, NY: Da Capo Press.

Pfeiffer, S. (Ed.). (2008). *Handbook of giftedness in children: Psycho-educational theory, research, and best practices* (pp. 71–92). New York, NY: Springer.

Phillipson, S. N., & McCann, M. (Eds.). (2007). *Conceptions of giftedness: Socio-cultural perspectives.* Mahwah, NJ: Erlbaum.

Renzulli, J. S. (1978). What makes giftedness? Re-examining a definition. *Phi Delta Kappan, 60,* 180–184.

Renzulli, J. S. (1986). The three ring conception of giftedness: A developmental model for creative productivity. In R. J. Sternberg & J. E. Davidson (Eds.), *Conceptions of giftedness* (pp. 53–92). New York, NY: Cambridge University Press.

Renzulli, J. S., Gubbins, E. J., McMillen, K. S., Eckert, R. D., & Little, C. A. (Eds.). (2009), *Systems & models for developing gifted programs for the gifted & talented* (2nd ed., pp. 477–502). Mansfield Center, CT: Creative Learning Press.

Rokeach, M. (1960). *The open and the closed mind.* New York, NY: Basic Books.

Stanovich, K. E. (2010). *What intelligence tests miss: The psychology of rational thought.* New Haven, CT: Yale University Press.

Sternberg, R. J. (1996). *Cognitive psychology.* Orlando, FL: Harcourt Brace College Publishers.

Sternberg, R. J. (1999). A propulsion model of types of creative contributions. *Review of General Psychology, 3,* 83–100.

Sternberg, R. J. (2003). *Wisdom, intelligence, and creativity, synthesized.* New York, NY: Cambridge University Press.

Sternberg, R. J. (2009). Reflections on ethical leadership. In D. Ambrose & T. Cross (Eds.), *Morality, ethics, and gifted minds* (pp. 19–28). New York, NY: Springer.

Sternberg, R. J. (2010). *College admissions for the 21st century.* Cambridge, MA: Harvard University Press.

Sternberg, R. J. (in press). Intelligence in its cultural context. In M. Gelfand, C.-Y. Chiu, and Y.-Y. Hong (Eds.), *Advances in cultures and psychology* (Vol. 2). New York, NY: Oxford University Press.

Sternberg, R. J., & Davidson, J. E. (Eds.). (1986). *Conceptions of giftedness.* New York, NY: Cambridge University Press.

Sternberg, R. J., & Davidson, J. E. (Eds.). (2005) *Conceptions of giftedness* (2nd ed.). New York, NY: Cambridge University Press.

Sternberg, R. J., Jarvin, L., & Grigorenko, E. L. (2011). *Explorations of giftedness.* New York, NY: Cambridge University Press.

Sternberg, R. J., Kaufman, J. C., & Pretz, J. E. (2002). *The creativity conundrum: A propulsion model of kinds of creative contributions.* New York, NY: Psychology Press.

Sternberg, R. J., & Lubart, T. I. (1995). *Defying the crowd: Cultivating creativity in a culture of conformity.* New York, NY: Free Press.

Sternberg, R. J., & The Rainbow Project Collaborators (2006). The Rainbow Project: enhancing the SAT through assessments of analytical, practical, and creative skills. *Intelligence, 34,* 321–350.

Sternberg, R. J. (Vol. Ed.), & Reis, S. M. (Series Ed.). (2004). *Definitions and conceptions of giftedness.* Thousand Oaks, CA: Corwin.

Sternberg, R. J., & Sternberg, K. (in press). *Cognitive psychology* (6th ed.). Belmont, CA: Cengage.

Terman, L. M. (1925). *Genetic studies of genius: Mental and physical traits of a thousand gifted children* (Vol. 1). Stanford, CA: Stanford University Press.

INDEX